Topodynamics of Arrival

Spatial Practices
An Interdisciplinary Series in Cultural History, Geography and Literature

14

Topodynamics of Arrival

Essays on Self and Pilgrimage

Edited by
Gert Hofmann and Snježana Zorić

Amsterdam - New York, NY 2012

Cover Photo by Snježana Zorić

Cover Design by Inge Baeten

The paper on which this book is printed meets the requirements of "ISO 9706:1994, Information and documentation - Paper for documents - Requirements for permanence".

ISSN: 1871-689X
ISBN: 978-90-420-3538-6
E-book ISBN: 978-94-012-0813-0
©Editions Rodopi B.V., Amsterdam - New York, NY 2012
Printed in the Netherlands

For Our Parents

Ana† and Ante
Werner† and Martha

Acknowledgements

The present book is based on a research seminar organised by the editors in 2008 on the occasion of the Annual Conference of the American Comparative Literature Association on *Arrivals and Departures* in Long Beach, CA. Both the seminar and the publication of this volume were sponsored by Research Funds of the College of Arts, Celtic Studies and Social Sciences of the National University of Ireland, Cork (UCC).

Editors and co-authors thank UCC for its generous support.

A very special thank-you we owe to Michael Shields and William O'Keeffe for their valuable comments and editorial assistance, and to Christoph Behrens for the compilation of the index.

Table of Contents

Introduction: Topo-dynamic of Place and Body

Gert Hofmann and Snježana Zorić

„ [...] das Licht in seinem Wirken, [...] sein Drang im Kommen und Gehen [...] und
das Zusammentreffen in einer Gegend von verschiedenen Karakteren der Natur, daß
alle heiligen Orte der Erde zusammen sind um einen Ort und das philosophische Licht
um mein Fenster ist jezt meine Freude; daß ich behalten möge, wie ich gekommen
bin, bis hierher“
(Hölderlin 1954:433)
(“[...] the effect of the light, […] its thrust in coming and going, [...] the gathering of
different characteristics of Nature in one location, so that all sacred places of the earth
are together around one place, and the philosophical light around my window delights
me now; may I keep, as when I came, hitherto!”)[1]

Where is the place of man? Or *what* is man's place? From the moment
he has arrived in the world of the living, man is looking for his proper
place in life, for a feeling of home and rootedness. However, with
each passing day he approaches death, awaiting final departure from
his ultimate place of arrival and finally deserting a place which may
be filled with the harvest of life's never ending search for meaning
and significance, thus rendering the question of '*Why* have we arrived
at all?' seemingly obsolete. This ultimate clash of arrival and departure, of "coming" and "going", as Hölderlin put it, is the sting of
blindness in the light of human self-awareness.

How can this mortal sting be converted into a stimulus of living
joy, and the locale of this clash be configured as an inviting place for
human dwelling? Hölderlin praises the errant light appearing around
his "window" as delightful, and he calls it "philosophical". Such imagery approves of the "window", the threshold device between inside
and outside, between withdrawal to oneself and exposedness to the
world, as a genuine place of living encounter and delightful enlightenment; but it also invokes the mindfulness – and open-mindedness –

---

[1]   Translated by Michael Shields.

of the philosopher as the indispensible condition to dwell on this
threshold as a confusing place of mutually pervasive intro- and extro-
version – the two incompatible but nevertheless equally defining impulses of the human experience. Living experience engenders the human Self in its very exposedness to the Other, as an ongoing process
of metamorphosis, not as static re-construction of approved identities.
Hölderlin's "philosophical light" does not convey an idea of the philosopher as an expert on cognitive procedures of the human brain, but
as a complete man of art and thought, both sensitive and inspired, who
embodies intellectual courage and creative endeavor and unites both
in an uncompromised affection for human fallibility and relentless
desire for truth.

   This kind of light we would like to shed on the place of human
arrival, light of philosophical and spiritual awareness that includes the
twilight of poetic ambivalence and existential doubt, light that unveils
the ambivalent and perhaps transcending nature of the place itself, its
inspirational dynamic and imaginative motility more than its function-
al position within the coordinates of established socio-cultural systems. What seems necessary is a way of thought that "goes back towards a preorigin which deprives us of this assurance [the assurance
of an 'originative' dichotomy between conceptual principle and experiential case, G.H and S.Z.] and requires at the same time an impure
philosophical discourse, threatened, bastard, hybrid" (Derrida 1995:
126) – in other words: literary, essayistic, suggestive. While human
places normally are defined by the communal and political narratives
of those who belong to them,[2] Derrida suggests that the philosopher's
most genuine place,[3] the one which is dedicated to "[giving] place to
all stories, ontologic or mythic, that can be recounted on the subject"
(Derrida 1995: 117) of truth may rather have the elusive characteristics of an all-pervasive "place without place, a place where everything

---

[2]   Cf. Casey on the meaning of "place" in a phenomenological approach: "Rather than being one definite sort of thing – for example, physical, spiritual,
cultural, social – a given place takes on the qualities of its occupants, reflecting these qualities in its own constitution and description and expressing them
in its occurrence as an event: places not only *are*, they *happen*." (Casey 1996:
26-27)

[3]   Derrida refers to Socrates' reflections on his place as a philosopher within
Athenian society in Plato's dialogue *Politeia*, and to Plato's discourse on
khōra in his late cosmological dialogue *Timaios*.

is marked but which would be 'in itself' unmarked". (Derrida 1995: 108) Such a dynamic of "giving place" to all places is *per se* generic, that is, pervasive in its particularity. It may well be that the only real place of arrival in life's pilgrimages, which is, explicitly or implicitly, the subject of our book, coincides with the pervasive, hybrid and motile place of such a philosophical, fictional or spiritual quest.

In literature as well as in anthropology thinking, experiencing and writing of space and place are connected with aesthetics of perception. Sensual affection towards the 'other' places of a journey and their impact on spiritual experience cannot be realized without performing a corporeal act of leaving and without experiencing physical displacement. Leaving, departing seems to be the condition for higher insights into oneself. Simply to depart, however, does not suffice. Initial intentions and the perceptive horizon of one's vantage point (at the place of departure) remain crucial aspects of the entire undertaking. The place of arrival can only be where our life-histories again 'take place' and acquire further exceptional or singular significance. The place in the event of 'taking place' cannot be found and thought without taking into account time, experience, and embodiment of the individual arriving in it.

This dynamic of crossing time and space dimensions (chronotopia) applies to pilgrimage journeys both in a topological and metaphorical sense. In both cases there are distinctly aesthetic and poetic intentions and impulses which conjure the questions about the place and its meaning in leaving and returning. Places of such exceptional significance, or sacredness, have thus always been converted into texts. Consequently their topographies seem to be absolutely essential, and the conscious and conscientious traveler is required to merge his immediate perceptions of the place with his abilities to imagine and conceptualize. The aim is to raise one's level of awareness, and reflect on a process of metamorphosis of oneself, internally and externally.

Pilgrimage is a primordial example of such experience and process. However, if travelling in general also means to exercise an art of articulate identity transformation, such experience may also apply, in a secularized form, to literary and performative practices, to artistic acts of acknowledged self-disavowal in order to re-create and re-imagine the human self.

Travelling is the art of motion, motion results in moments of human encountering, and such moments manifest themselves in unsettling linguistic repercussions and crises of meaning. Places of arrival also function as inscriptions of such meaningful repercussions, inscriptions of the past crossing the present, of the other crossing the self. The articles in this book explore places, rituals, texts and scriptures as religious or secular inscriptions – "topographies" – of such "arrivals".

Each arrival *happens*, and its very place manifests itself only as momentous component of the process itself. Arrival is an event of conclusion as well as of up-rise and urgency for subsequent explorations of challenging new meanings to be read from the topography of the place, which mirrors thus a signifying dynamic for the metamorphosis of the traveler's self. Embedded in such dynamic every arrival equals another departure, it signifies the re-emergence of the previous one in the "philosophical light" of the new place's unforeseeable discoveries. Therefore, in order to read the topography of an arrival, we need to understand both the generic and particular dynamics of its signifying power – that is what has been envisaged with the entitlement of the present book: *topo-dynamics* of arrival.

Truth and authenticity of meaning are no predicates of the objective place of their occurrence. Truth and authenticity, according to Giorgio Agamben's analysis, *have no place*, they are "revealed only by giving space or giving a place to non-truth – that is, as a taking place of the false, as an exposure of its innermost impropriety". (Agamben 1992: 12,3) The place of true significance can therefore not be thought as a supreme sphere of being "above all things", but as transcendent in the dynamic sense of an all-pervasive particularity, as the actual "taking place of every thing:"

God or the good or the place does not take place, but is the taking place of the entities, their innermost exteriority. [...] that the world is, that something can appear and have a face, that there is exteriority and non-latency as the determination and the limit of every thing: this is the good. [...] the good is not somewhere else; it is simply the point at which [all things, G.H. and S.Z.] grasp the taking-place proper to them, at which they touch their own transcendent matter. (Agamben 1992: 14,5)

If we take Agamben's phenomenological analysis on board, a sense of displacement must be a powerful ingredient in man's motivation to undertake various kinds of journeys, from pilgrimage to tourist travel, looking for a trace of sacredness in the exterior world and exploring their own "innermost exteriority" through exposing it to the real otherness of a place of longing.

And even though such places are usually imagined as transforming, be it blissfully or terrifyingly, not everybody will be affected by them; also for those who do experience them their effect cannot last and proves to be volatile: the counteraction of return (or never-return) and a new departure have always been implied at the moment of arrival.

How to bring about then the writing of the place? If not in letting place 'taking place' ever again through changing and multiplying it, moving to and through it, getting various insights, perspectives, views and discourses, and then again re-writing them in our retrospections and reflections at home? Accordingly the essays of this volume travel through the discourses of place and space, pilgrimage, exile and escape, and through the texts and images incorporating them, using these terms and concepts topically and metaphorically in order to convey something about our initial questions. But travelling through the discourses we also encounter new questions: Which places are forgotten, why do we remember certain others? Why do some places attract us and others not? How do we find ourselves in non- and other-places?[4]

Perception of place carries its own variety of self-enabling horizons: "We continually find ourselves in the midst of perceptual horizons, both the 'internal' horizons of particular things (i.e., their immediate circumambience) and the 'external' horizons that encompass a given scene as a whole." (Casey 1996: 17) There is no knowing or sensing of place except by *being there*, at the very place itself; to *be present* at a place – i.e. the lived experience of being *exposed* to it through mind and senses[5] – determines the actual modality of perceiving it. Knowledge of place is therefore an ingredient in the process of the local perception itself. Such knowledge, genuinely local knowledge, is experiential and eventful in the dynamic manner of a "lived experience" (*Erlebnis*), which neither depends entirely on an archival space of pre-approved cultural memory (*kulturelle Erfahrung*) nor on

---

[4]   Cf. on the concept of "heterotopia" – "Other Spaces" – Foucault 2002; on "non-places", "lieu et non-lieu" see Marc Augé 1992.

[5]   On the phenomenology and experiential-conceptual dynamic of "presence" cf. Jean-Luc Nancy 1993.

any a-priori space of transcendental validity which determines human experience in principle. To live means at first to live locally; to know to be familiar with the places of one's dwelling, or, as Clifford Geertz put it, „no one lives in the world in general". (Geertz 1996: 262)

Perception of place is crucially synesthetic, whole-body experience. Body experience means self-awareness in the most complete but also contestable modus of extendedness and exposedness (cp. Nancy 2000) to the surrounding world and to every thing in it coming forth as an entity in its own right.[6] Such dialectic or rather interference (since there is not always 'synthesis') of perception and place is a never ending process, perception and place are mutually constituted and remain constitutive to each other.

Casey emphasizes therefore the event-character of the place, which is unique, *idiolocal*, and prompts the „imaginative constitution of terms respecting its idiolocality (these range from placenames to whole discourses)". As much as places take on "the qualities of [their] occupants", they also reflect "these qualities in [their] own constitution and description and [express] them in [their] occurrence as an event: places not only *are*, they *happen*". (Casey 1996: 26-27) In the universality of this event-dynamic "place" is "at once concrete, relational, lateral and regional". (Casey 1996: 31)

The place as the event and experience of arrival shatters the static outlet of the geographically, socially, culturally and politically coordinated space, but it also overwhelms the moving subject's predisposed perception of it: an ec-static force in the experience of being-there inevitably affects and transforms the self-awareness of the travelling individual.

Central concepts and ideas dealt with in the essays of this volume include 'self' and 'pilgrimage', their experiential and discursive relatedness in the event of 'arrival' and the modality of a place-related, i.e. 'topo-dynamic' human presence. The formation of self through pilgrimage – be it inter-cultural (Outhwaite, Potter), intra-cultural (Buchanan), or trans-cultural (Zorić, Hofmann) is always topo-dynamic embodiment and liminal experience. Place-induced embodiment of the self and "lived experience" of the place become to-

---

[6]   On the relationship of body and cultural space cf. (i.a.) Claudia Öhlschläger and Birgit Wiens 1997; Markus Hallensleben 2010; Katerina Kitsi-Mitakou and Effie Yiannopoulou 2009.

gether significant as "a location for speaking and acting on the world". (Low and Lawrence-Zúñiga 2006: 2)[7]

If it is true that "in Western culture we perceive the self as 'naturally' placed in the body, as a kind of precultural given" (Scheper-Hughes and Lock 1987 in Low and Lawrence-Zúñiga 2006: 2), then the relation between body and space is characterized through a complex fabric of simultaneously physical, social and meta-physical impulses, through emotions, state of mind, sense of self, sociality of the person. Individual embodiments imply the possibility of 'being self' in a multiple sense, namely in the modality of 'being displaced' (Bucanan, Dzero) and in correlation with the specific topographical characteristics of various 'other places'. *Becoming* oneself is only possible in a situation of homelessness and uprootedness, if one explores one's liminal and transitional capacities in other-, non- and in-between-places and takes advantage of their detached and thus deliberating conditions. Consequently, human "self" or subjectivity has to be thought in a new way, a way that does not depend on "identity" as a categorical presumption. 'Identity' (the intelligible subject) and the identical as such (its formal perception of space) seem to have altered and liquefied; they have themselves become the very event of agency, action and transformation. At this point the topo-dynamic agency of the travelling self is no longer subject to a time-progressive dialectic of self-identification and self-differentiation (as in the modern discourse of enlightenment), but rather to a space-induced metamorphic drift of aleatory alteration, or to an ecstatic split into multiple and parallel narratives of self-realization, which follow a pattern of cartographic contingency rather than of historiographic consistency. When subjectivity is examined in its topo-dynamic characteristics there is no stable 'identity' in the traditional sense; instead, it appears to be replaced by a recitation of various topographically configured assertions of selfhood in their fragmentariness and transience.

The formation of place in space and space in place parallels the creation of 'self' in pilgrimage. As space is not the vessel or "container" wherein the contents of the lived world will be carried and kept (Low and Lawrence-Zúñiga 2006: 5), the contents and meanings of the pilgrim's and traveler's lived experience will not be infused and

---

[7] Body-agency in its performative aspects has long been investigated by Maxine Sheets-Johnstone 2009.

inscribed as signifying complements into an invariably substantial self, either, but absorbed by a sensate living body. Pilgrimage unfolds a "mobile spatial field of interactions between bodily actors and terrestrial spaces" (Munn 1996: 449) which presents itself to interpretation as a culturally significant "corporeal-sensual" sphere "stretching out from the body at a given locale or moving through locales". (Low and Lawrence-Zúñiga 2006: 5)

Therefore we are interested in pilgrimage not in terms of van Gennep's or Turner's "rite of passage" but as a (literary, artistic, religious) phenomenon of complex corporeal, intellectual and imaginary movements which usually peak in the experience of arrival at a signifying and defining place, which may either represent a situation of self-imposed exile, a subversive strategy for self-transformation (e.g. in the Decameron, Heptameron), a randomly chosen city community of globally representative reputation (in the "project 'Año 0'"), self-imposed banishment from human communal life (in Oedipus at Colonus), or in fact "the focus [of] unpredictable encounters between liturgical forms, personal imagination and memory translated into acts of the body" (Coleman and Eade 2004: 17; cf. Snježana Zorić's article on Borobudur).

The place and experience of arrival opens up right in the core of this dynamic as a threshold and in-between space – in one and the same act one is able to come to it and depart from it. In this regard pilgrimage might even be read as metaphor for a modern art of living, which refuses to be anchored in fixed places (Kupatadze); new cultural and particularly artistically framed meanings are thus being created about space, place and identity,[8] and the metamorphosis from pilgrim to tourist mirrors without doubt, in this metaphorical field, certain traits of the altercations about modern and postmodern art.

In all our case studies, pilgrimage is explored as a kind of meta-movement (Coleman and Eade 2004) which includes self-reflection on meaning, form and function of the journey, focusing on the place of arrival as place of unforeseeable encounters, which entice imagination and retro- as well as proto-transforming visions of the previous place

---

[8]   Coleman and Eade (2004: 5-6) agree with Bauman (1996: 19ff.) that "modernity has given the metaphorical figure of the pilgrim new prominence as it comes to signify a restless seeker for identity. Thus, 'destination, the set purpose of life's pilgrimage, gives form to the formless, makes a whole out of the fragmentary, lends continuity to the episodic' (Bauman 1996: 22)".

of departure and the future meaning of return. Crucial for such reflections is often the dialogue with local voices, and other non-discursive forms of expressive communication. Human dialogue is in the most fundamental sense enactment, re-enactment and realisation of the liminal space of encounter which abides in the core of place and event of arrival.

Certain distinguished real and visionary places of arrival such as the Garden of Eden, Santiago de Compostela, and Jerusalem, the "heavenly city", are perceived as 'sacred' places. In the present book's opening essay Snježana Zorić argues that in contrast to them the temple of Borobudur should be more appropriately categorized as 'religious' place, according to the distinction proposed by Park (1994: 252). At the time of the author's anthropological field research in Borobudur (1985) the temple could not be approached and interpreted as the sacred destination, place of arrival and culmination moment of a Buddhist pilgrim's journey; the crucial act of religious performance would, however, be accomplished through one's movements within the architectural site itself, prompting the Buddhist religious search for the annihilation of self in a process of "reading" the teaching inscribed in the walls of the temple. The path to reading Borobudur, its particular topo-dynamic, takes place in the form of circumambulations inside. Whether one succeeds in arriving depends on the interplay of awareness and body experience while ambulating through the galleries of the site, which presents its 'text' in the form of relief images geared to cause the gradual metamorphosis of the self up to the very realization of the void when facing, on the last gallery, the only stūpa of emptiness. The place of arrival, stūpa on stūpa, emptiness harboring emptiness equates with the experience of self absence. The place of arrival is then the realization of absolute placelessness – without rebirth, without arrival, departure and return. The author leaves open further possibilities of re-reading Borobudur, suggesting also the eventual reassignment of the temple as sacred place through newly created inscriptions into it.

Michael Shields analyses aspects of the performance of flagellant dance songs by a group of pilgrims on their arrival at Strassburg in the year of the Black Death, arguing that the locus of arrival is situated not only in the contingent topography of the city but in a delocalised sacral space created through the evocation of Christ's entry to Jerusalem. He suggests that the lack of an external pilgrimage destination is a crucial feature of the flagellant pilgrims' journey, setting them apart from conventional pilgrimages: instead of arriving at a holy place, pilgrims confer 'pilgrimage status' upon each place they visit by virtue of their arrival there. By reconstructing the flagellant *mise en scène* of their arrival from surviving song texts, he shows that the negotiation of arrival at the city involves multiple transactions for the pilgrims both individually and collectively: negotiations with the citizens of Strassburg, with their own bodies and their capacity for experiencing sufferings modelled on those of Christ, with the possibility of identifying with Christ and with a variety of personae made available in the framework of the song texts. Arguing that the performance of arrival involves a destabilisation and refiguration of the texts, he suggests that it offered pilgrims possibilities of self-articulation that can be glimpsed between the lines of the songs and through the criticisms of Fritsche Closener's Strassburg chronicle.

How do the names of sacred places speak to us? How do they contribute to the creation of the place's unique significance? Antonija Zaradija-Kiš explores the relation of place's hagiotoponyms and local pilgrimages in a historical case study on the cult of St. Clement in the region of Croatia's East Adriatic hagiospace. Here it is the cult itself who is the agent of the travel, journeying not only through the Dalmatian coastal area but also through various temporal and cultural contexts. The author differentiates three levels of its spreading, firstly the Roman one in the early centuries of Christianity, then the Slavic traditional level at the time of the Apostles Cyril and Methodius and finally the neo-Clementine level of tradition located in Makarska. Referring to a legend about St. Clement's miraculous ability to detect water, we follow a series of arrivals of the cult in various places connecting events of St. Clement's life-legend to popular beliefs in his transcendental powers invoked through the pilgrimage to these places. In the Neo-Clementine tradition the cult's revival even resulted in the offering of new places to their patron, as in the case of Makarska. Antonija Zaradija-Kiš's paper, varying the approach of other contributions to this volume, deals with space as hagiospace in relation to texts and oral traditions. Reconstructing their journeys through the historical past, she explores the grounds for the revival of the cult, creating places of remembrance in the present.

John Outhwaite examines arrivals and departures in the secular pilgrimage story of Cees Nooteboom's novel *Roads to Santiago*. Here the pilgrimage-view reflects on the modern "challenge of identity" leading to the crucial question of "how is a fragmented self to reconcile multiple and contradictory experiences in order to establish a coherent sense of belonging?" Outhwaite suggests a "layering of identity," or selfhood in the form of an imagining sovereignty which permeates, without claiming authenticity, various established cultural and social communities. Driven by a profound sense of displacement in his home country Holland, Nooteboom questions his individual identity which appears to be caught in a national-transnational interplay of belonging and (self-)exclusion in both the pilgrim's Spanish destination and his Dutch place of departure, engendering a fractured sense of authenticity as "being home in homelessness".

Nooteboom feels a deep spiritual affinity with the traditional pilgrim's Catholic Spain, but to articulate and realize his sense of belonging he relies on modern techniques of travel and literary art. His pilgrimage to Santiago, even though corporeally performed, is a typical journey of the modern mind. Pilgrimage becomes a quest to cultivate the status of being a stranger as a privileged condition; the stranger's and traveler's genuinely eccentric and therefore incommensurable perceptiveness makes him shy away from ultimate meanings of any provenance. His realization of selfhood can never conclude; it remains aporetic. His place of arrival – home – will always remain beyond the pilgrim's reach.

Martin Potter's literary pilgrimage discourse leads us to Jerusalem. On the example of Evelyn Waugh's novel *Helena* and Muriel Spark's *The Mandelbaum Gate* the author gives us his account of two women, both Catholic converts, setting out to find identity in the heavenly city. The narratives resemble each other in the biographical profiles of their protagonists, Helena and Barbara, as members of the Catholic minority on the British Island with other, pagan or Jewish religious roots. Both characters show complex and fragmented personalities which are observed in their interaction with the multilayered identity-fabric of the city of Jerusalem – even though the two novels are set in widely divergent historical periods: *Helena* in a legendary 4th century, *The Mandelbaum Gate* in the second half of the 20th century.

The unresolved fractures in their realization of selfhood are carried along by the protagonists on their pilgrimage to Jerusalem as a hoped-for place of salvation and resolution. At the moment of arrival, however, they both realize that Jerusalem is not just one place but the poly-semantic coexistence of a considerable variety of city-places and the communal narratives creating them; their faces may appear connected or otherwise depending on the various cultural and religious backgrounds of pilgrims encountering them. Helena in her attempt to locate the Cross has to negotiate three historical 'Jerusalems', Jewish, Roman and Catholic, while in her personal life she must relate to pagan, Roman and British elements. In Barbara's Jerusalem of the 1960s, we are confronted with even more layers – of Byzantine, Arab, and Ottoman, British, Israeli and Jordanian origin. The Holy Land and also the earthly-heavenly city of Jerusalem are divided between the states of Israel and Jordan – in between them the threshold of the 'Mandelbaum Gate', passage and check-point for those pilgrims who search for both: Bethlehem and Nazareth.

In spite of their different historical outlets, both novels concur in presenting "the various identities" of the place – Jerusalem – and the character – Helena and Barbara – united "under the umbrella of the spiritual vision" which the city enables.

Gert Hofmann's paper explores *Colonus*, the district of king Theseus' historical city of Athens and infamous mythological site of the Eumenides' holy grove, but also an ultimate place of human arrival in the Sophocles' late play on the ostracized Oedipus. The place of arrival for the *homo sacer* Oedipus proves to be the ultimate destination of a life's journey which, on the threshold between life and death, finally enables a clairvoyant view of the meaning of the human condition.

In juxtaposition to Dionysus's messianic arrival at Athens's Dionysus Theatre during the festival of the Great Dionysia (which resulted in the performances of the tragic *agon*), Oedipus like Dionysus intrudes, as a sacrificial being, upon the heterotopic space of human death, which used to constitute an exclusive sphere of ban reserved for the gods of the underworld. Oedipus' arrival at the Eumenides' garden could be interpreted as the conclusion of an "inverted pilgrimage, originating in a moment not of approved but *failed* faith in the possibility of redemption, [and] terminating not in a state of sublimated life but accomplished death" and approved humanity, while Dionysus' arrival at the theatre realizes not his divine power of redemption, but his affection for both the tragic fatality and comic fallibility of human life. In Sophocles' play on *Oedipus at Colonus*, both arrivals coincide in manifesting on the theatre stage "the fundamental liminality of the human experience: the caesuras of life and death, the threshold experiences and in-between stages of order and chaos, the absences and unconscious states between living and dying – in short all those moments in which the totality of life, literally speaking, is to play for".

Drawing from Mikhail Bakhtin's theory David Buchanan develops the concept of "chronotopos" as of an existential meeting point for Self and Other in applying it to a genealogically selected series of literary case studies. Starting with *The Epic of Gilgamesh* his selection includes the analysis of "chronotopic changes in romance" from Xenophon of Ephesus's *An Ephesian Tale* to Walter Scott's *The Heart of Midlothian* and Anton Chekhov's *Lady with the Dog*. The literary phenomenon of "chronotopos" manifests itself here in a dynamic of historical transformability which mirrors the topo-dynamics of pilgrimage arrival insofar as it synchronizes the experiential impulses of self-metamorphosis and self-excess and results equally in the construction of literary "in-between spaces, that locate the meeting of individuals between finite and infinite, Self and Other".

A non-anticipated coming-together of individuals, which induces the emergence of literature as a communal event, marks the secluded countryside places of arrival in both Boccaccio's *Decameron* and Margret of Navarre's *Heptameron*. Irina Dzero analyses in both texts the analogies in the configuration of such places as venues of a cultivated human self-deliverance from misfortunes inflicted upon them in their home environment. Their means of choice is a ritualized practice of storytelling bringing about a transformative experience that creates a new communal identity and changes the significance of their journey "from exile to escape". Only the violent nature of their departure, caused by "force-majeure" circumstances of catastrophic dimension – plague in the *Decameron*, flood in the *Heptameron* – ensures the emptying of their minds and detachment from their socially restricted roles – processes which eventually foster the corporeal hyper-sensitivity and openness of mind and spirit necessary to meet unknown places and people in that kind of spontaneous manner which is favorable for the telling of stories. Since the storytellers' narrative spirit seems to be drawn from the benign natural characteristics of the new location, not from memories of their desolate home places, it becomes increasingly unlikely that they will ever return. The misfortune of their displacement turns into a privilege and proves to be the condition for the fictional recuperation of their personalities in newly created communal and individual identities. Exile has turned into escape from previous life. Once more the place of arrival proves a place of departure into the (literary and social) adventures of unlimited self-imagination, which, in this historical instance, marks Renaissance as the decisive moment "in the development of literature as a legitimate cultural practice".

With Hubert Fichte and Leonore Mau's novel *Explosion*, pilgrimage becomes the literary endeavor and anthropological quest of a lifetime – "fifteen years of travelling and writing, and researching." Writing and travelling become the expressive form of a genuinely experimental life-style: "My books are no masquerades. They describe experiments: living a life so as to find a form of expression for it."[9] The form of expression, the novel, marks the point of arrival. With Gothóni (1993) and Carrillo Rowe and Licona (2005) Andreas Stuhlmann's essay on "Hubert Fichte's Journeys into the Afro-American Religions in Brazil" describes Fichte's and Mau's endeavor as a pilgrim-like transformative experience of "identity in motion" both at a practical and a discursive level. Here the topo-dynamic of arrival bears "turning points" as signifying markers of selfhood in an artistic "religion of bricolage" and "patchwork mythology." The literary text itself in its fictitiously configured and undefinedly growing multi-perspectivism provides the only true place of arrival. Fichte does not offer "final results" but "engages in what Simo (1991) calls an 'exercise of approximation', in which he blends all of his material into the stream of one radically subjective and fictional *roman fleuve*".

Ketevan Kupatadse analyses the genre of contemporary travel narrative on the example of the project "Año 0 [Year 0]" which was conceived by the Spanish writer Gabi Martinez involving a group of authors who were enticed to travel to selected metropolitan cities and convert their experiences into literature. What starts like a conventional and business-oriented literary enterprise results, however, in an aes-

---

[9]   "Meine Bücher sind keine Maskierungen. Sie beschreiben ein Experiment: zu leben um eine Form der Darstellung zu erreichen." Hubert Fichte in Dieter E. Zimmer 1985: 116.

thetically reflected and subversively critical "meta-text of travel narrative" which on one hand re-enacts the traditional cliché-bound and 'colonizing' perspective of the genre but on the other invests the body of their texts with a layer of critical analysis which exposes the "stereotypical boundaries" of their own traditional and colonial premises. The actual place of arrival emerges for the writers of project "Año 0" only after their return, in the literary in-between layer of their writing between performance and reflection, text and meta-text. In this regard their project appears similar to Hubert Fichte' and Leonore Mau's Brazilian endeavor, but with a poetological rather than anthropological ambition, by (for example) re-inventing the figure of the flâneur, "recuperating the [...] Latin American urban chronicle genre", or experimenting with "ritualistic" form elements.

In the book's final chapter, Adrienne Bernhard takes an "eco-critical" outlook on Sarah Orne Jewett's "preservationist stance towards changes in American life, changes that are reflected in the topographical landscape" of her short story *A White Heron*. "Eco-topic" descriptions of the space of human living oscillate between the real and the fictitious, between the "natural world" and the "magical world of an idealized Nature", assuming a potentially "restorative effect" of nature on the human self. The inspirational power, or the *topo-dynamic* impulse ascribed to the site of nature in the *Decameron* and the *Heptameron* (cp. Irina Dzero's essay) has been turned into an ethical challenge to preserve nature as a biotope from which man finds himself increasingly excluded. Here the *White Heron's* biotope functions as a sphere of aspiration and exclusion, illusion and disillusionment, desire and deferred arrival – place of the nostalgic vision of a naturally-ethically integrated human self.

Be it a "chronotopic" process of selfhood discovery, an act of writing and literary meta-pilgrimage, or even a case of educated tourist travel to urban non-places, in all instances within the present book "place" has been presented, been placed, or has itself taken place in the corporeal awareness of an individual mind. Notwithstanding the different contexts – mythological, Buddhist, Christian or secular, literary, theatrical or religious, historical or current – "to put the place into the proper place" of one's mind, one is urged to travel, to move, to visit, to leap over the threshold of the other place, to be there and sense it. (Feld and Basso 1996)

In tracing divergent paths of pilgrimage and self-transformative journey (in a topological and metaphorical sense) within the spaces opened up by anthropological and literary discourses, the essays of this volume all converge in one fundamental insight: places of arrival are places of eventfulness which affect both physicality and metaphysics as non-separate spheres, spheres of awareness emerging from the same event, act of arrival. The topical locale becomes real; the place of place is encountered in particular moments of the cultural, social and individual life-world on the threshold between embodied spaces of imaginative *selfscapes*, inscribed spaces of discursive *mindscapes* and *landscapes* and *ethnoscapes* related to them.[10]

The "topo-dynamics" of arrival marks a zone of concurring discourses on self and other, pilgrimage and their representation in literature and anthropology, which provides an infinite space for differing and deferring motions of exploration and understanding, facing endless re-constructions and re-creations of the place of arrival and its meaning …

borobudur ist der endlose satz
…
borobudur ist das ende vom anfang
borobudur ist der anfang vom ende
….
borobudur ist nein
borobudur ist   ja
…
borobudur ist tod
borobudur ist leben
….
borobudur ist innen
borobudur ist aussen
borobudur ist der endlose satz
…

(from a poem by Eugen Gomringer)

Cork, Zagreb and Thera in summer 2011

---

[10]   We coined the terms of "mindscape" and "selfscape" in analogy to Arjun Appadurai's concept of "ethnoscape". (Appadurai 2005: 48)

Bibliography

Agamben, Giorgio. 1992. *The Coming Community*, trans. Michael Hardt. Minneapolis, London: University of Minnesota Press.

Appadurai, Arjun. 2005 (1996). *Modernity at Large. Cultural Dimensions of Globalization*. Minneapolis London: University of Minnesota Press.

Augé, Marc. 1992. *Non-lieux: Introduction a une anthropologie de la sur-modernité*. Paris: Editions du Seuil.

Basso, Keith H. and Feld, Steven. 1996. *Senses of Place*. Santa Fe, NM: School of American Research Press.

Bauman, Z. 1996. 'From pilgrim to tourist – or a short history of identity' in: Hall, S. and du Gay, P. (eds.) *Questions of Cultural Identity*. London: Sage.

Carrillo Rowe, Aimee Marie and Adela C. Licona. 2005. 'Moving Locations: The Politics of Identities in Motion' in *NWSA Journal* 17.2.

Casey, Edward S. 1996. 'How to Get from Space to Place in a Fairly Short Stretch of Time: Phenomenological Prolegomena' in Feld Steven and Basso Keith H. (eds.) *Senses of Place*. Santa Fe: School of American Research Press.

Coleman, Simon and Eade, John (eds.) 2004. *Reframing Pilgrimage. Cultures in Motion*. London: Routledge.

Derrida, Jacques. 1995. 'Khōra' in: *On the Name*. Stanford: Stanford University Press.

Geertz, Clifford. 1996. 'Afterwords' in Feld, Steven and Basso, Keith H. (eds.) *Senses of Place*. Santa Fe: School of American Research Press.

Gothóni, René. 1993. 'Pilgrimage = Transformation Journey' in Tore Ahlbäck (ed.) *The Problem of Ritual*. Based on papers read at the Symposium on Religious Rites held at Åbo, Finland, in August 1991. Åbo: The Donner Institute for Research in Religious and Cultural History / Stockholm: Almqvist & Wiksell.

Hallensleben, Markus (ed.) 2010. *Performative Body Spaces. Corporeal Topographies in Literature, Theatre, Dance, and the Visual Arts*. Amsterdam New York: Rodopi.

Hölderlin, Friedrich. 1954. *Sämtliche Werke*, Bd. 6,1 (ed. Adolf Beck). Stuttgart: Kohlhammer.

Jackson, R.H. and R. Henrie. 1983. 'Perception of sacred space' in *Journal of Cultural Geography* 3.

Kitsi-Mitakou, Katerina and Effie Yiannopoulou (eds.) 2009. *The Future of Flesh. A Cultural Survey of the Body*. New York: Palgrave.

Low Setha M. and Lawrence-Zúñiga, Denise. 2006. *The Anthropology of Space and Place. Locating Culture*. Oxford: Blackwell Publishing.

Foucault, Michel. 2002. 'Of Other Spaces' in Mirzoeff, Nicholas (ed.) *The Visual Culture Reader*. London: Routledge.

Munn, Nancy D. 1996. 'Excluded Spaces: The Figure in the Australian Aboriginal Landscape' in *Critical Inquiry* 22.

Nancy, Jean-Luc. 2000. *Corpus*. Paris: Métaillé.

—. 1993. *The Birth to Presence* (trans. Brian Holmes and others). Stanford: Stanford University Press.

Öhlschläger, Claudia and Birgit Wiens (eds.) 1997. *Körper, Gedächtnis, Schrift: Der Körper als Medium kultureller Erinnerung*. Berlin: Erich Schmidt.
Park, Chris C. 1994. *Sacred worlds. An introduction to geography and religion*. London, New York: Routledge.
Scheper-Hughes, Nancy and Margaret Lock. 1987. 'The Mindful Body' in *Medical Anthropological Quarterly* 1 (1).
Simo, David. 1993. *Interkulturalität und ästhetische Erfahrung. Untersuchungen zum Werk Hubert Fichtes*. Stuttgart: Metzler.
Tuan Yi Fu. 1978. 'Sacred space; exploration of an idea' in Butzer, K.W. (ed.) *Dimensions of Human Geography*, University of Chicago. Department of Geography: Research paper 186.
Zimmer, Dieter E. 1985. 'Leben, um einen Stil zu finden, Schreiben, um sich einzuholen. Ein Gespräch mit Hubert Fichte' in Thomas Beckermann (ed.) *Hubert Fichte. Materialien zu Leben und Werk*. Frankfurt a. M.: Fischer.
Zorić, Snježana. 2001. 'The ecotopic thinking and intercultural turn in Korean philosophy' in Pak, Youngsook and Jaehoon Yeon (eds.) *History, Language and Culture in Korea*. London: Saffron.

1. The Stupa of Borobudur – A Place of Inner Pilgrimage

Snježana Zorić

All his sins are left over, annihilated through the act of his journey
Aitareya Brāhmaṇa 7.15

The objective of my paper lies in the attempt to connect the architectural forms of the Javanese temple – *stūpa* Borobudur – with spirituality as exposed in the Buddhist scriptures of *Lalitavistara, Jātakamālā* and *Gaṇḍavyūha,* i.e. to show the correspondences of the semantics of the texts with the symbolism of its material expression in architectural art.

My point of departure is that the analogical differentiation between symbolizing and symbolized is not, in the case of Borobudur, enough to interpret its forms and to understand its meaning in the context of pilgrimage research. The symbolizing, i.e. the *stūpa* forms are neither a mere representation of the textual passages nor is the temple simply a symbol of the "body of the Buddha's law"[1] (*dharmakāya*), as usually interpreted[2]. Further, it is not only a sacred place where people

---

[1] The idea is connected with the *mahāyānic* teaching on three bodies (*trikāya*) attributed to Śākyamuni, according to which he represents the unity with the Absolute of the world and its manifestation in it through the *saṃbhogakāya* ("the body of pleasure" realized in the higher existential level of paradise) and *nirmāṇakāya* ("the body of transformation" of the historical appearances of Buddha and his concrete, physical presence in the world) with the aim of saving all sentient beings. In that sense the *dharmakāya* is this unity with all manifested world and due to it the human beings are able to participate in Buddha's true nature.

[2] "[This] stūpa is called a dharmakāya stūpa. Within it, the guru dwells unchanging. The Buddha said that whoever sees a dharmakāya stūpa will be liberated by the sight of it. Feeling the breeze near the stūpa liberates one by its touch. The sound of the tinkling of the small bells hanging on the stūpa liberates one by their sound. Having thus seen or experienced this stūpa, by thinking of one's experience of it, one is liberated through recollection."

gather together to worship Buddhas and *bodhisattvas,* but also a place where the achievement of the highest Buddhist goal, *nirvāṇa,* should be realized. It implies that for each individual the visiting of the *stūpa* is more of an inner pilgrimage, a process of inner transformation than a performance of their religiosity. The architectural forms of the temple's tripartite construction follow triadic symbolism as it is contained in the hahist texts (e.g. 'three' as a sign of the three existential characteristics – *trilakṣaṇa,* 'four' as the four noble truths – *catvāri āryasatyāni,* 'eight' as the eightfold path – *āryāṣṭāṅgika mārga),* so that proceeding through the temple structures involves proceeding through the teaching itself, in fact transcending it.

The approaching of *stūpa* is conceptualized as an entering of the Buddhist path in general. According to scholastic interpretation of *Abhidharma* texts, the first quadratic level corresponds to the mental analytics of personality (*prajñā*), the hemispheric part corresponds to the realization of moral precepts (*śīla*), while the cupola as a symbol of meditation (*samādhi*) unites the two previous moments – the one of discursive knowledge and the other of ethical predispositions, both as a guiding principle to *nirvāṇa.*

This shows a double nature of the *stūpa* in Borobudur – as an architectural expression of Buddhist spirituality based on texts and as a sacred place of its possible realization through the inner pilgrimage, moving from the differentiating analysis of existential forms in everyday life (*saṃsāra*) to the experience of the void, in *nirvāṇa.*

Pilgrimage

Arrival and departure present an essential part of the dialectical process of pilgrimage. I would even argue that both coincide at the same spatial and temporal point – the point of the border, threshold (i.e. transgression). To start the wandering pilgrimage presupposes that one leave the sphere of everyday life. This is a momentary experience of shortest duration. One enters the Way. To arrive at the pilgrim site is again a momentary experience before readying oneself for new departure. One starts the journey through the sacred site. The difference

---

(H. H. Dilgo Khyentse Rinpoche: http://www.stupa.org.nz/stupa/intro.htm, 28.11.2007: 3)

between journeying *to* it and *through* it is essential. Since the approaching of the site, in the case of some pilgrimages, could still be a kind of collective event in which *communitas* plays an important part, the quality of wandering is transformed in the moment of arrival and simultaneous second departure into a being-alone on the way.

Theory

I want to clarify this preliminary thesis using the example of the temple of Borobudur in Central Java, Indonesia.

Theories themselves require a point of departure too: I am setting out from the field research data I collected in Borobudur twenty years ago. At that time my field research was concentrated on Javanese art, especially dance traditions in the court of Surakarta as it was practiced in ASKI (Akademi Seni Karawitan Indonesia), and visits to Borobudur were an accompanying part of my research. But the really intriguing idea was that Borobudur as a site of pilgrimage has no pilgrims. How was I to deal with that fact? The arrival at conclusions, and at a grasp of the site, will depend on that moment and complement it.

A general theoretical grounding of the research on pilgrimage is connected with names of Edith and Victor Turner. Their idea of pilgrimage as a *liminoid* phenomenon could be traced back to Van Gennep's teaching on *rite de passage* and its triadic structure emphasizing liminality, but it gains an enlarged meaning:

Pilgrimage, then, has some of the attributes of liminality in passage rites: release from mundane structure; homogenization of status; simplicity of dress and behavior; communitas; ordeal; reflection on the meaning of basic religious and cultural values; ritualized enactment of correspondences between religious paradigms and shared human experiences;
[...]
But since it is voluntary, not an obligatory social mechanism to mark the transition of an individual or group from one state or status to another within the mundane sphere, pilgrimage is perhaps best thought as 'liminoid' or 'quasi-liminal', rather than 'liminal' in van Gennep's full sense. (Turner 1978: 34-35)

Observing Borobudur at that time, I couldn't imagine that Turner was right with his thesis that the history of pilgrimage illustrates this "progress from the 'ludergic' liminal to the 'ergic' liminoid." (Turner

1978: 36) It means there were no signs to indicate that "the transformation of the concept of religion [is] becoming less serious, belonging to the leisure sphere or being equated with pastimes, hobby, tourism or entertainment", as Turner put it. (Turner 1978: 35)

Looking today in the Internet for information about events in Borobudur, one would have to pose different kinds of questions about the changes which would complement Turner's insights, but I will not attempt to deal with them in this paper. Nor am I going to follow the analysis of pilgrimage as "metasocial commentary", as "critique of the life-style of our epoch of wars and revolutions with its increasing signs of industrial damage to the natural environment". (Geertz 1972: 26, Turner 1978: 38) Social categories as analytical tools will be absent in the production of knowledge aimed at in my study. I agree with Morinis that

pilgrimage suggests unlimited possibilities for anthropological analysis, drawing on the ideas, symbols, behavior, social forces, and experiences woven into the practice. (Morinis 1992: 1)

Sacred places are connected with sacred journeys, they are connected with religious experiences and they are responsible for the main religious task – that of metamorphosis, be it metamorphosis of inner being or of social environment. According to Morinis, the anthropological interest in pilgrimage is slowly increasing because of the 'dangers' of its spiritual effects: "nothing is less amenable to investigation by social science." (Morinis 1992: 2) Our text is precisely committed to this 'dangerous' journey. Understanding pilgrimage as multilayered phenomenon, Morinis outlines several levels of its investigation: from the 'ego plane' via the cultural, social and physical to the 'meta plane'. I will describe each of them briefly. The *Ego plane* relates to the pilgrimage as a personal act emphasizing personal experiences and psychological mechanisms operating in them (Bowman, Thayer, Turnbull in Morinis 1992), whereas the *cultural plane* gives all of them a more consistent general patterning. It would be interesting to observe the development of narratives connected with a pilgrimage center and the creation of meaning. In the case of Borobudur it generates a double cultural matrix, i.e. the Buddhist one of the site itself and the Islamic one of Indonesian/Javanese culture in general. It can be assumed that its cultural Otherness will be responsible for the creation of contemporary cultural meanings of Borobudur, since the Buddhists from abroad are visiting the place and not Javanese Muslims. The creation of meaning wouldn't be situated in the Indonesian/Javanese culture itself but instead allow Borobudur to emerge as a kind of transcultural locale of a single Buddhist culture. The *social plane,* according to Morinis, is a kind of aporetic construct, being a part of the pilgrimage process yet sensitive to, and reflective of, forces at work in society. The *Physical plane* is connected with the spatiality of the site, the architectural and physical arrangements of the shrine, representation of symbols and religious practice. (Morinis 1992: 21-25) At the end a synoptic interpermeation of all the planes feeds into the *meta plane* as a matrix of all previous relationships.

Valuable research contributions on the transformation of profane place into the sacred can be found in religious geography. (Park 1994: 245) They can be created through hierophantic and theophanic events, and for most religious beliefs are conceived of as "being real places on the ground". The Buddhist tradition recognized eight such places, the place of birth in Lumbinī, the place of enlightenment with the *stūpa* built on the banks of the river Nairañjanā, the place of "turning the wheel" in Benares, of miracles in Śrāvastī, of "descent from Tuṣita" in Sāṃkāśya, of "reconciliation with monks" in Rājagṛha, of "complete victory" in Vaiśālī and of "parinirvāṇa" in Kuśināgara.

Isaac argues further that "sacred places are not transferable (they are valued because of their associated holiness) and they do not need to be re-established with each new generation (there is an inherited appreciation of the holiness of the site)". (Isaac 1964: 28 in Park 1994: 250) Looking from the perspective of the Tibetan community in exile this statement is not tenable, as they are re-producing and duplicating on Indian soil the main temples and shrines which they left behind in Tibet after the Chinese occupation. A smaller copy of the Borobudur architecture can be found in the Tibetan Kumbum.

Even though there are many critics of Turner's theory (Bowman, Rotondo, McKewitt, Dahlberg, Stirrat in Eade and Sallnow, 1991), no systematic attempt was made to show its inconsistencies until Gothoni's study Pilgrimage = Transformational Journey (1993: 101), where he listed the main errors of Turner's argumentation and concluded with seven suggestions for their correction:

a) the quality of a pilgrimage is the pilgrim's experience of spiritual transformation, i.e. a shift from worldliness towards spirituality;
b) a pilgrimage should be conceived of and defined as a transformational journey;

c) although the pilgrim is usually in company, [...] he nevertheless considers his own endeavor as a private undertaking; the choice to go on a pilgrimage is individual, spontaneous and voluntary; he often travels incognito;
d) a pilgrimage route forms an ellipse with the sequence structure departure-journey-return;
e) the ellipse metaphor of pilgrimage epitomizes the binary character of the pilgrimage route, i.e. departure:return, deficiency:deficiency made good, old man:new man and so forth;
f) the journey – the transformative phase between departure and return – provides a period of reflection during which the pilgrim mirrors and reviews his life, perceives the discrepancy between precept and practice and begins to long to bridge the gap;
g) regardless of whether the pilgrim experiences an ecstatic or a moderate spiritual transformation when encountering the divine, the result nevertheless usually leads to some change of attitude and life-style. (Gothoni 1993: 113)

The first two of them are axiomatic and I could agree with their assumptions, the third one introduces a social moment which immediately appears as non-essential, and the fourth needs to be corrected. In the sequence structure of departure-journey-return and in the binary opposition departure:return, Gothoni misses the notion of arrival not only as an analytical category, but as the existential highlight of the whole pilgrimage undertaking. I want to emphasize the theoretical importance of the notion of arrival with its character of event: the coincidence of upheaval and coming, the metamorphosis of knowledge into intense and vivid experience, and as a place of threshold and transgression. In understanding the journey as a transformative phase between departure and return (f), Gothoni overlooks the fact that the transformation doesn't take place on the journey but at the place of arrival and at the time of arrival. Indeed, place and time do not always coincide.

Together with this inner process of metamorphosis, the physical place of arrival could turn into the image and gain a metaphysical status or, to express it in a more buddhistic fashion, if the process is completed it turns into the Void and the place can be forgotten. The imagination caught in the memory is the reason for possible returns to the sacred place; in the Void there is no place. In the case-study of Borobudur, where the meaning of place/image and text, memory/amnesia and realization are closely connected within human psyche, I recommend the notion of inner pilgrimage as the main hermeneutic tool.

Borobudur

Borobudur was probably built between the 8th and the 9th century, and represents the biggest monument known in the Buddhist world. As already mentioned, at the time of my research it was a lonely site, visited only rarely by a few pious Buddhists from Java or abroad. Its displacement in the Islamic cultural context cannot be overlooked, as Coomaraswamy's description illustrates:

Borobudur is wonderfully situated in the Kedu plain, an eminence commanding an extensive view of green rice fields and more distant towering conical volcanoes, comparable in grandeur with Fujisan. [...] A rounded hill has been terraced and clothed with stone; the result is a truncated terraced pyramid supporting a relatively small central *stūpa* surrounded by seventy two much smaller perforated *stūpas* arranged in three concentric circles; a stairway in the middle of each side of the pyramid leads directly to the upper platforms with the *stūpas*. The ground plan of the six lower terraces is square with reentrant corners, that of the three upper terraces is circular; [...] Each of the lower terraces is a perambulation gallery whose walls are occupied by long series of reliefs illustrating the life of Buddha according to the *Lalita Vistara,* and stories from the *Divyāvadāna, Jātakamālā* of Śūra, and the *Gaṇḍavyūha* and other sources. The rich and gracious forms of these reliefs, which if placed end to end would extend for over five kilometers, bespeak an infinitely luxurious rather than a profoundly spiritual or energized experience. There is here no nervous tension, no concentration of force to be compared with that which so impresses the observer at Ankor Vat. Borobudur is like a ripe fruit matured in breathless air; the fullness of its forms is an expression of static wealth, rather than the volume that denotes the outward radiation of power. (Coomaraswamy 1965: 204)

For Coomaraswamy Borobudur doesn't appear as a contemporary place of living spiritual experience. As a matter of fact Borobudur was unknown in Java for a long period of time. Excavated in the late 19th century and restored in the 20th, it cannot serve as proof of a long continuity of Buddhist tradition. It is obvious that the intensity of today's pilgrimage to Borobudur is part of a renewed but not invented tradition.[3]

Let us depart from the topography itself, from "writing a place, locale, site". Borobudur is, indeed, a visually "rewritten text" of Buddha's teaching in various architectural forms, statues and reliefs which tell the story about different levels of human existence and human beings wandering through them. Prescriptive rather than descriptive, it

---

[3]   Internet: http://www.vanamaliashram.org/Borobudur.html, 03.03.2008.

advocates a path of ritual circumambulations (*pradakṣiṇa*) through the temple and a way of observing it in order to generate a special kind of Buddhist experience transgressing the *saṃsāric* life conditions and shifting towards *nirvāṇic* conditionlessness or voidness. The phenomenon of the Borobudur inner pilgrimage contradicts usual theoretical interpretations of pilgrimage, which mainly originate from Christian-rooted research traditions. It is not a place of manifestation of the divine, or of theophanies and miracles. Our approach shares the skepticism, communicated in a recent study on pilgrimage (Eade and Sallnow 1991), regarding the validity of classical pilgrimage and ritual theories for non-Christian traditions.

My exposition examines the study of pilgrimage and pilgrimage places in Asia, grounding it mainly on the textual tradition which already in itself represents a kind of hermeneutics and self-reflection of religious theoreticians and practitioners including their oral communications on the relation between inner religious experience and any external form of expression. Consequently, even though I apply a kind of interdisciplinary approach in this paper, the prevalent orientation shall remain anthropo-/buddhological, using the scriptures on Buddha's *dharma* and its expression in the artistic forms of Borobudur on the one hand, and dealing with the ways of their internalization in each pilgrim individually (without informants, but based on the text) on the other.

Borobudur's historical encounters with Hinduism as well as various other intercultural permeations with India certainly merit future research, but they won't be included within the frame of this paper, which cannot include all of the transformations which the place has undergone in recent times. Anthropologists would possibly consider my recommended paradigm as belonging rather to the science of religion. I would argue, on the contrary, that the exclusion of textual understanding cannot result in proper anthropological understanding of the phenomenon concerned.

I found Borobudur a place of peace and remembering in which inherent religious meaning was not to be annihilated through secular, social moments which are essentially foreign to these pilgrimage events. It was a place of contemplation and of memory placed in the stones.

Exposition

In the Buddhist world view the world itself is a journey (*saṃsāra*), life is repeated travelling from one body to the other (*punarbhāva*). Being-in-the-world means being separated from the real nature of *tathātā*, being other to the self. Each birth is a dislocated and decentred state of being. From this existential fact of being apart from one's own nature (*buddhatā*), the first noble truth derives an evidence of suffering (*duḥkha*). Arrival to the world thus presupposes then a departure, absence from the world of the real nature of being. From the moment of his birth a man is wandering through life in search of his true nature.

Travelling expatriates, passers-through in *saṃsāra* are homeless but at the same time guided back to the originating point of their *saṃsāric* departure. Within *saṃsāra* the wheel of life (*dharmacakra*) is directing us mainly into something unpredictable. Collecting new karmic seeds (*karmaphala*) the only thing we know is that our return is secured. The pilgrimage to Borobudur can affect us and then encourage us to a new departure, or put an end to all these re-arrivals.

Once at the Borobudur site, the pilgrim departs on a new journey. Even though the site and the monument are deeply rooted in the *saṃsāric* world, its function is to transcend it (*saṃvṛtisatya*). In the sense of the highest truth indeed (*paramārthasatya*) there is no place to arrive and no place from which one should depart. The monument itself is just a skilful means (*upāya kauśalya*) for those who are ignorant of the immanency of the true nature within their own being and in the world. As a medium, Borobudur emphasizes the importance of aesthetic moments and their decisive significance for the quality of the existential experience of transfiguration.

Borobudur is an enlarged *stūpa*[4]. The main elements brought into play to elaborate its symbolism are clearly defined geometrical el-

---

[4]   *Stūpa* means a "knot of the hair" and relates to the traditional Buddhist monument which contains relics of Buddha and represents a place of devotion. In the *hīnayānic* text of *Mahāparinirvāṇasūtra* the Buddha explained that *stūpa* should be built in order to remember that one should intend to reach *nirvāṇa*. It is also highly recommended to build a *stūpa* and to reach merits for future existence, as is explained in *Saddharmapuṇḍarīkasūtra*. Originally a very simple grave-site, the *stūpa* develops various forms, among others the famous enlightenment *stūpas* which represent the path to Buddhahood. Its most elaborated form finds its expression in Borobudur as a cosmographic representation (*maṇḍala*) of different levels of human existence and of Buddha's teaching.

ements – a quadratic foundation, circular forms in the middle and a hemisphere with a cube, as well as conic upper parts called *harmikā* and a tree of life. The monument as a whole has the form of a terraced pyramid. As such it represents the stone *maṇḍala*,[5] oriented like a diagram towards the four world directions to which it opens itself through the four gates, *toraṇas*. These forms are applied to create the architectural entity of the monument which is divided in four quadratic terraces, three circular terraces and the last level comprising a new *stūpa*, a kind of *stūpa* on *stūpa*.

Following the instructions of the Buddhist texts, the world as represented in Borobudur is divided in three spheres – the sphere of craving, *kāmadhātu,* the sphere of form, *rūpadhātu* and the sphere of formlessness, *arūpadhātu. Kāmadhātu* is restricted to the first quadratic terrace and originally was not exposed to the pilgrims, in order to save them from observing the images of the world of passion. Another reason for the quadratic base could have been to make the whole foundation structure more stable. The relief-scenes are taken from the *Mahākarmavibhaṅga-sūtra* (Lévi 1932 in Gonda 1975), one text describing the consequences of good and bad deeds, through which heavens and hells are supposed to be reached. The scenes also tell the story of social life in the time of Buddha and illustrate how different occupations practiced in life cause the next incarnation. The world of the lower terraces, representing its *saṃsāric* aspects, is gradually left behind as one ascends to the higher levels. On the second terrace the world of form begins, *rūpadhātu,* followed by three further terraces.

As the place of memory, the *stūpa* commemorates decisive events of Buddha's life, the place of his birth in Lumbinī, the place of his enlightenment in Bodhgaya, the place of the first sermon in Sārnāth and finally the place of his death, *parinirvāṇa*, in Kuśināgara (compare the symbolic description of *stūpa* in Newbery and Spens 2000).

[5] *Maṇḍala* means circle and is an imaginative representation of the universe. It could be two- or three-dimensional depending whether it is drawn on sacred images, *thanka* or as a temporary formation in sand or as small three-dimensional offerings to the house altar which in that case take the form of the *stūpa*. The temple in its architectonic form could be built *maṇḍalic* as well, what shows the case of Borobudur. (more in Mus [1935] 1978)

Even though the land of its origin was India, the *stūpa* developed its sophisticated forms first in Tibetan Buddhism and Tantric ritualistics. The meanings of forms applied to create a maṇḍala are strictly prescribed in the texts.

Three circular terraces with a hemisphere relate to the formless world, *arūpadhātu.*

On the first gallery on the main upper wall are depictions of the *Lalitavistara*[6] while the *Jātaka/Avadāna*[7] stories are visually narrated on the balustrades. On the second, third and fourth gallery we see pictures of the stories from *Gaṇḍavyūha*[8] on the main walls, and, *Jātakas*

---

6   *Lalitavistara* or "unfolding of Buddha's play" is a prose text (written in Sanskrit) including verses, gāthā (written in Hybrid), describing Buddha's life as a play of the supernatural being. It is preserved in a Nepalese manuscript and is used as a powerful protection. The text was translated into Tibetan in the 9th century, the period in which Borobudur was built. The text belonged probably to the Sarvāstivāda school of Buddhism and was expanded by Mahāyāna teachers, and is regarded as belonging among the earliest Mahāyāna sutras. (see Lefman 1874, Winternitz [1920] 1968: 199, Katičić 1973)

7   *Jātaka* or "Birth-stories" contain also descriptions on Buddha's former existences and emphasize his virtues of selflessness during the time of his *bodhisattva* career. They are collected in the *Kṣudraka-Nikāya* of *Tripiṭaka*, and they describe how his behavior in former existences conditioned the circumstances of the following rebirth. The *Vessantarajātaka* describes Buddha's life as a prince Vessantara who was so generous that he gave away all his possessions, including his wife and two sons, gaining great merit. From *Jātakas* was developed highly sophisticated iconography in India, which spread with Buddhism all over South and South-East Asia.

Jātakamālā ("Garland of *Jātakas*") is ascribed to Āryaśūra. I-Tsing mentions it as a very popular text in the India of his time. The scenes from the text, besides in Borobudur, are also found in Indian fresco-paintings of Ajanta.

Avadāna or "Magnificent deed" is a literary genre of Buddhist texts comprising popular moral stories told by monks to inspire a common people to practice love, compassion and a feeling of surrender which is believed to lead them to a better rebirth. *Divyāvadāna* ("Heavenly *avadāna*"), depicted in Borobudur, probably originated in the 3rd century. (Winternitz 1968: 221)

8   *Gaṇḍavyūha-sūtra* ("The Showing of the Protuberance" [on the Head of Buddha]) is a part of the much larger text of *Buddhāvataṃsakasūtra* meaning a "Flower Garland of Buddha" containing the preaching of Buddha after his enlightenment and his discourses with *bodhisattvas* Mañjuśrī and Samantabhadra. The descriptions emphasize the *bodhisattva* path differentiated in ten levels, his vows and entering into the primordial unity with Buddha. This teaching later became an independent text, *Daśabhūmika-sūtra,* and the remaining part of *Avataṃsaka* became the already mentioned *Gaṇḍavyūha.* Throughout the text, the personality of Buddha figures as a centre of spiritual energy and all-encompassing love *(karuṇā)* which is to lead all beings; in the enlightened state of unified mind worldly differentiations will be transcended.

The relief at Borobudur portrays a young man called Sudhana in search of wisdom. On the way he encounters fifty-five spiritual teachers, "good friends"

again on the balustrades, with the exception of the balustrades of the
third and fourth gallery, which once more illustrate the stories of the
Gaṇḍavyūha.

In *rūpadhātu,* on the four terraces we observe various Buddha
statues which differ from each other in their hand-gestures, *mudrā.*
They are five in number corresponding to the *mahāyānic* concept of
dhyāni-buddhas[9]. According to their position in the *maṇḍalic* diagram
we find Buddha Akṣobhya on the eastern wall with the hand-gesture
of *bhūmisparśa-mudrā,* the sign of invoking the earth to witness his
victory over the bad spirits and to show his inner strength. On the
South wall, Buddha Ratnasambhava is giving a blessing with his
varada-mudrā. On the northern side, Buddha Amoghasiddhi invokes
the feeling of security and protection in the soul of the pilgrim with
the gesture of *abhaya-mudrā.* On the west side, Buddha Amitābha
with his hands in the gesture of meditation, *dhyāna-mudrā,* is welcom-
ing the human beings in his paradise *Sukhāvatī.*[10] On the fifth terrace
reigns Buddha Vairocana, the Primordial One, with his hands in the

---

who help him to realize supreme enlightenment. Each of them demonstrates a
single aspect of his own spirituality; travelling from one teacher to the other,
Sudhana contemplates what he has just learned from each of them. Sudharna
is enlightened not only by gods and *bodhisattvas* but by common people.

"From a fisherman he learned sea-lore. From a doctor he learned compassion
toward sick people in suffering. From a meditating monk he learned that the
pure and peaceful mind had a miraculous power to purify and tranquilize other
minds. He learned patience from a poor, cripple woman, he learned a lesson of
simple happiness from watching children playing in the street." (Bukkyo
1966).

[9]   *Dhyāni buddha* or transcendental Buddha is the name for five beings existing
in the sphere of meditation and containing the world within their meditating
processes. In the *maṇḍala* they are representations of human psyche and its
corresponding aspects in the world. Their names are also *jīnas* or *tathāgatas,*
because they are not depending on time or space and are always present and
aware, in opposition to Buddhas who have already come or are going to come
to fulfill their mission of exposing the teaching and enter *parinirvāṇa* afterwards. *Dhyānibuddhas* however are connected with four heavenly directions:
Akṣobhya (East), Amoghasiddhi (North), Ratnasambhava (South), Amitābha
(West), with Vairocana in the centre. According to Lama Anagarika Govinda
it is important to notice this juxtaposition and "read the stūpa in the cosmic as
well as in the psychic sense." (Govinda 1976: 84)

[10]   This is the text describing the life of Buddha Amitābha and the superabundant
place of Bliss belonging to him (for more see *Sukhāvatīvyūhasūtra,* Cowell
and others [1894] 1969).

bodhyagri-mudrā, a gesture of the final extinction and highest truth. The index finger of the right masculine hand is embraced by the fingers of the left female hand representing the Oneness of the Absolute and its relation to the multifarious phenomena of the *samsāric* world. Altogether there are 432 Buddha statues on the terraces of *rūpadhātu.* These terraces have to be circumambulated in order to practice the four forms of *dhyāna*-meditation resulting in the state of mind shared with the gods in the *dhyāna*-heaven.

The three circular terraces are not representations of the texts: rather, they relate the Visible to the Invisible, mediating between the spiritual and physical world. Here is a new departing point for the pilgrim. Free from all earthly cravings and contemplating further on *dhyāni-buddhas,* which are now enshrined in the geometrically arranged perforated *stūpas,* he enters a sphere of formlessness, *arūpadhātu.* The number of *stūpas* on each terrace follows the arithmetic symbolism of Buddhist scholastics. (Govinda 1976) On the first terrace there are 32 *stūpas,* with eight less on each following one: 24 on the second and 18 on the third. It implies a reduction of the eightfold path. Art historians cannot explain the meaning of the *stūpa*-perforations, but, looked at it *emically,* they could signify the still existing possibility of communication between the spheres of *rūpa-* and *arūpadhātu.* It is interesting to mention that each pilgrim who succeeds in touching the statue inside the *stūpa* with rhombic perforations[11] will have good fortune.

The proper practice for venerating the *stūpa* is circumambulation, *pradakṣiṇāpātha,* following the course of the sun leaving the object of veneration on the right side. Leaving the circular terraces the pilgrim arrives at the highest point, the central *stūpa.* This arrival point is that at which the pilgrim is ready to depart completely from the *samsāric* bonds and can enter *nirvāṇa.* There is nothing more. The *stūpa* is empty; it is imagery of some/no-thing, nameable only as the Void. Here the *akmé* of all discursivity is reached, language can no longer cope. It is pure experience, final arrival at empty space where time stands still. It is freedom, nothing. There will be no more rebirths. The *topos* overcomes itself. Transfigured, the pilgrim can enter the world again and wait for his final departure (*parinirvāṇa*).

---

[11]   The perforations on the first two terraces are rhombic, the ones on the third are quadratic.

                                    Snježana Zorić

So far we have dealt briefly with the visible architectural forms of Borobudur. Let us return now to see how the inner pilgrimage proceeds in accordance with these forms.

Body and awareness

The preparatory steps of the spiritual procedure were performed on the quadratic base. According to the teaching, in the preparatory phase for the Buddha's path one should carry out the mental analysis of nature as far as it is accessible in the psycho-physical constitution of man. The second preparatory step requires the pilgrim prepare for insight into the nature of life morally. The third step of preparation intensifies the mental and moral achievements which are the precondition for enlightenment. Because these moments are essential for the final liberation, they are visualized in the *pradakṣiṇā* contemplation on the first terrace of Borobudur. More exactly, following the Buddhist taxonomy, on the first terrace one should contemplate four kinds of mindfulness,[12] on the second the pilgrim is supposed to cultivate four efforts,[13] and on the third four psychic powers.[14] The fourth level is the introduction to the practice of five faculties[15] in their latent, pas-

---

[12]   I.e. *kāyānupassanā satipaṭṭhānam* – contemplating the body, *vedanānupassanā s.* – contemplating the feelings, *cittānupassanā s.* – contemplating the mind and *dhammānupassanā s.* – contemplating the phenomena. (Satipaṭṭhāna sutta: http://www.palikanon.com/diverses/satipatthana/satipatt_10.html, (12/07/2011); also Majjhimanikāya, 10. (Mehlig 1987: 180-192)

[13]   That is, the effort to destroy the evil which has arisen, the effort to prevent the evil which has not yet arisen, the effort to produce the good which has not yet arisen and the effort to cultivate the good that has arisen.

[14]   I.e. *Ṛddhi* are "the steps toward transgression" and according to translation of the term they should lead to the realization of magical power in the practitioner. (Dayal [1932], 1975: 104)

     Lama Anagarika Govinda mentions them as psychic powers corresponding to the third level of the Borobudur's architectonic foundation as *chandiddhipādo* – the desire to act, *viriyiddhipādo* – energy, *cittiddhipādo* – thought and *vīmaṃsiddhipādo* – investigation. (Govinda 1976: 56)

[15]   They are the faculty of faith, *saddhindriyaṃ*, the faculty of energy – *viriyindriyaṃ*, the faculty of mindfulness – *satindriyaṃ*, the faculty of concentration – *samādhindriyaṃ* and the faculty of reason – *paññindriyaṃ* (Govinda 1976: 57). Detailed analysis of Abhidharma is also to be found in Dayal (1932, 1970, 1975).

sive aspect. The quadratic form of the four foundation terraces also indicates the connection of the practices cultivated on them with the earthly, *saṃsāric* element.

The pilgrim arrives on the circular base, and his cognitive process taking place on these hemispheric levels is intended to set in motion the psychic elements of enlightenment. It starts with the cultivation of five forces (*pañca balāni*). They are same as the preceding ones, representing now their active aspect. The world of form is behind us. We arrive and depart again simultaneously. The border is crossed again. The moments of *saṃsāra* inscribed in rich decorations on the walls of the lower quadratic terraces are absent and the whole concentration should be directed to the seven elements of enlightenment[16] (*satta bojjhaṅga*), leading to voidness/emptiness, the only appropriate expression for the aim of the pilgrim's whole undertaking.

The *harmikā*, starting on the second terrace, synthesizes a quadratic and a circular conceptualization of space. It is a way to practice the eightfold path. Right views (*samyagdṛṣṭi*)[17] and a right intention (*samyaksaṃkalpa*)[18] are the outcome of the analytic knowledge prepared in the first step. Right speech (*samyagvāc*)[19], action (*samyak-karmānta*)[20] and a right way of life (*samyagājīva*)[21] are the consequence of right insight and proof of the morality *(śīla)* developed upon it.

The eightfold path culminates in the last triad of right endeavor (*samyakvyāyāma*),[22] concentration (*samyaksmṛti*)[23] and meditation

---

[16] I.e. *satisambojjhaṅgo* – mindfulness, *dhammavicaya s.* – discerning the truth, *viriya s.* – energy, *pīti s.* – rapture, *passaddhi s.*- serenity, *samādhi s.* – concentration and *upekkhā s.*- equanimity. (Govinda 1976: 57)

[17] It implies the recognition of Four Noble Truths and their dependence on the absence of *ātman* in the foundation of the world (*anātman*).

[18] *Samyaksaṃkalpa* means the disappearance of craving.

[19] That is, talk without lies, hate and stupidity.

[20] These are actions prescribed for the laymen and monks. Five prescriptions for laymen are as follows: not to hurt other living beings, not to take what is not given, not to enjoy sensual pleasures or engage in wrong speech, avoid taking alcohol and drugs. For the monks there are five more precepts to observe: not to eat after midday, not to entertain others with senseless talk, not to enjoy jewelry and fine perfumes, not to sleep on high beds and not to take money or valuable presents.

[21] Not to hurt others.

[22] To produce a good *karma*.

(*samyaksamādhi*),[24] on which the five elements of existence (*pañca skandha*) are supposed to reach the highest level of their potentiality and actualize it in the form of its own extinction.

The stem of the tree of life is connected with an area of the big central *stūpa* and represents the teaching of tenfold knowledge (*daśa-jñānam*) as follows: knowledge of the law *(dharma),* knowledge of

---

[23]   To practice prescriptions contained in the *Satipaṭṭhāna*.

[24]   The practice of *dhyāna* is clearly elaborated in eight steps. The first four steps are connected with a meditation on form (*rūpa-dhyāna*) and the second four steps on the meditation on formlessness (*arūpa-dhyāna*). The goal of such practice is to direct the mind upon one point (*ekagrata*) in order to attain peace (*śamatha*) which supports the development of understanding (*vipaśyanā*). It is possible only through the strict neglect of sensuality and sensual perception. Because the experience which follows has an enstatic nature it is easy to confuse it with *nirvāṇa*.

The meditation continues with a choice of one object (*kṛtsna*) on which the observation should be fixed. The image should be contemplated until the capacity to recall it in memory is established. Further contemplation of the memorized image follows*),* which transforms itself into its ideal form, being purified of sensual elements. In this condition the meditating can enter the first *dhyāna*. The condition obtained through the first step is the absence of *nivāraṇa*, which are the usual impediments/obstacles to the meditating practice. Instead of *nivāraṇa*, the five elements of concentration are established: the ability to direct his mindfulness on the object of reflection – *vicāra*, the ability to keep the attention on the reflected object – *vitarka,* the apparition of the excited joy – *prīti,* the transformation of excitement into the peaceful joy – *sukha,* and continuous onepointedness – *ekagrata*. In the process of deepening in the idealized image, the meditating one rejects the *vicāra* and *vitarka* as disturbing factors and puts them aside. Then he enters a second *dhyāna*. The third *dhyāna* will be realized when he get rid of *prīti*. He reaches the highest level of corporeal joy, which is characterized as tranquility (*upekṣā*) and consists of mindfulness (*sati*) and consciousness (*samprajanya*). The fourth *dhyāna* is realized when all forms are canceled and only *upekṣā* and *smṛti* remain. It is on this level that full concentration (*samādhi*) is reached and the man is free from all sensual impurities.

Now meditations are prepared to cultivate the so called intermediary meditating forms *brahma-vihāras* and *abhijñās* and enter the realm of formlessness. This passage is a shift to the level of bodylessness and absence of differentiating thinking. One enters the fifth *dhyāna* and concentrates on the void or endless space without image. The transfer from endless space to endless consciousness leads to the sixth *dhyāna*. On the seventh *dhyāna* the meditating one removes even consciousness and nothing more remains. On the eighth *dhyāna* the imagination disappears in nothingness and the consciousness is no more present. (Cf. Veljačić 1978: 241-256)

other persons' thoughts, knowledge of relations, empirical knowledge, knowledge of suffering, of cause and effect, of annihilation of suffering, of the way leading to the annihilation of suffering, of the things connected with despair and finally the knowledge of the non-production of things.

The central *stūpa* is a culminating form of Borobudur's architecture and a culmination of the experience that is supposed to be generated and reached through the pilgrimage and meditating process.

According to *Aṅguttara Nikāya* this experience could be characterized in terms of the ten powers of Buddha (*daśa-tathāgata balāni*). The first one is to perceive the reality as it is (*yathābhūtam*), "possible as possible and impossible as impossible", the second is to recognize the *karmic* actions of the past, the consequences of it in the present and the causality for the future, the third is the perception of all that could result from doing a deed, fourth is seeing the world with its different elements, fifth the perception of the intentions of all beings, sixth the insight into the nature of all beings either inferior or superior, seventh the differentiation of the meditative states in terms of their purity or impurity, of concentrations and their achievements; the eighth power gives the ability to remember all one's former existences, the ninth includes the realization of the celestial eye which enables an all-encompassing view, and the tenth power is that which conquers all passions and eliminates hate, craving and ignorance in order to be definitively able to get rid of *karma* and to enter a void *nirvāṇic* state. Some interpreters consider the *stūpa* on *stūpa* empty; others regard it as containing a statue of Ādi-Buddha, the symbol of the Void.[25]

Conclusion and prospects

Pointing out the coincidence of several arrival and departure points expressed in the architectonic forms of Borobudur and its psychic counterparts, I wanted to show how pilgrimage could become an experiential process of inner metamorphosis. The aesthetics of the site not only supports and guides this process but also combines several

---

[25] *Śūnyata*, voidness or emptiness is the most difficult concept of Buddhism and it does not describe the spatial characteristic but to the unsubstantiality of the world and human being. Buddhists differentiate about 20 various kinds of *śūnyatā*, even the emptiness of emptiness.

discourses – textual, devotional and reflexive – which supplement each other if the pilgrim is progressing on his way. Once realized, the way leaves no further possibility of textualizing the experience.

Assuming at the beginning the validity of the general theory on pilgrimage and its tripartite structure of separation, liminality and reintegration, I showed that this doesn't apply to the case of Borobudur. Nevertheless a ritual pilgrimage to Borobudur is a transfigurational, liminal phenomenon that doesn't focus on the anti-structural subversion of social structure. If there is something to be subverted at all, it is the pilgrim himself in his craving for existence. The recurrent critique of Turner's view that pilgrimage reinforces a social structure rather than dissolves it has no relevance in the case of Borobudur either. The journey is not embedded in a social context and the fact that it is neither supporting nor subverting it, makes a pilgrimage to Borobudur *a-social.* The individual on the journey is not in contest with social orders but with his own nature. This had to be shown in the description of the architectonic forms of the temple and the corresponding forms of contemplation and mindfulness. Furthermore, the site gives the opportunity of relocating the *axis mundi* from the external place into the human body, thus realizing the shift from place-centered to person-centered pilgrimage. Both based on the knowledge, cognition, representation and practice of several texts of Buddhist teaching, they make the pilgrimage to Borobudur into a complex architectonic, textual and existential process. The pilgrim will verify the scriptures and test the efficacy of the sacred place, his intention being not only to make them real but to make himself real while reducing himself to the Void. The ritualized relation between the site, text and person which takes place in the pilgrimage process, doesn't grant the possibility of excluding even one of them from the exegesis of Borobudur.

They could be regarded as mirroring the three major pillars of Buddhist practice, i.e. *prajñā* – knowledge, *śīla* – morality and *samādhi* – concentration. They are interrelated; none of them has value in itself but only in conditioned origination, *pratītya samutpāda,* the main heuristic concept of Buddha's explanation of the world. Morality cannot emerge without knowledge and concentration can only build upon morality. (Govinda 1976)

The body (*kāya*) as *axis mundi* is considered as related to speech (*vāc*) and mind (*citta*) in the person-centered pilgrimage.

Speech and mind are strictly part of sensual and bodily experience according to Buddhists, and each change in consciousness and awareness is simultaneously a change of the condition of the body. Entering the foot terraces, the body (*kāya*) is visualized; on the round terraces the pilgrim visualizes speech (*vāc*) while on the main *stūpa* it is contemplation upon mind (*citta*)[26] that realizes the awareness of *śūnyatā*, the Void itself.

In opposition to common theoretical and experiential representations of the body in pilgrimage rituals, which are related to physical sickness and dramatic healings due to the thaumaturgic powers of the site, I cannot prove such as intrinsic to the Borobudur case. As far as Buddhism is concerned, we can say that the dialectic between bodily suffering and bodily restoration does not confirm the parallelism to Christianity upon which most theories are built.

My elaborations on pilgrimage as an interpermeation of site, text and person are necessarily limited because of the considerable time gap between today and the time of research, and because of the character of the place at that particular moment. As the site of Borobudur has undergone various historical and cultural "displacements", it offers impulses for new theories leading in a chrono-topographical direction, but also opens horizons for further theoretical orientations.

Bibliography

Bays, Gwendolyn. 1983. *The Voice of Buddha*, 2 vol. Boulder: University of Colorado Press.

Bukkyo Dendo Kyokai. 1980 [1962]. *The Teaching of Buddha*. Tokyo: Bukkyo Dendo Kyokai.

Brown L. Robert. 2003. 'Place in the Sacred Biography at Borobudur' in Granoff, Phyllis and Shinohara, Koichi (eds.) *Pilgrims, Patrons, and Place: Localizing Sanctity in Asian Religions*. Vancouver, Toronto: UBC Press.

Buddhist Suttas (trans. from Pali Rhys Davids T.W.) 1969 [1881]. New York: Dover Publications, Inc.

Cleary, Thomas. 1993. *The Flower Ornament Scripture, A Translation of the Avatamsaka Sutra*. Boston&London: Shambhala.

---

[26] Here we can observe the Tantric elements which offer material for further comparison with the Tibetan temple of the same *maṇḍalic* structure in Gyantse Kumbum.

Coomaraswamy, A. K. 1965. *History of Indian and Indonesian Art*. New York: Dover
        Publ. Inc.
Cowell E.B. and others (eds.) 1969 [1894]. *Buddhist Mahayana Texts*. New York:
        Dover Publ.Inc.
Dayal, Har. 1975 [1970, 1932]. *The Bodhisattva Doctrine in Buddhist Sanscrit Litera-
        ture*. Delhi, Patna Varanasi: Motilal Banarsidass.
Eade, John and Michael J. Sallnow (eds.) 1991. *Contesting the Sacred: The Anthro-
        pology of Christian Pilgrimage*. London and New York: Routledge.
Gothóni, René. 1993. 'Pilgrimage = Transformation Journey' in Ahlbäck, Tore (ed.)
        The Problem of Ritual (based on Papers at the Symposium on Religious Rites
        Held at Åbo, Finland on the 13th – 16th August 1991). Åbo: The Donner Insti-
        tute for Research in Religious and Cultural History.
Govinda, Lama Anagarika. 1976. *Psycho-cosmic Symbolism of the Buddhist Stupa*.
        Emeryville: Dharma Publishing.
Groslier, Bernard P. 1968. 'Borobudur. The colossal Javanese sanctuary, the world's
        largest ensemble of Buddhist reliefs threatened by imminent destruction' in
        The UNESCO Courier.
Isaac, E. 'God's acre-property in land; a sacred origin?' in *Landscape* 14.
Jatakamala or Garland of Birth-Stories by Aryasura (trans. J. S. Speyer). 1985. [Lon-
        don]: Electronic edition 2010:
        http://www.ancient-buddhist-texts.net/English-Texts/Garland-of-Birth-
        Stories/Garland-of-Birth-Stories.pdf
Katičić, Radoslav. 1973. *Stara indijska književnost*. Zagreb: Nakladni zavod MH.
Lefmann, Salomon. 1874. *Lalita Vistara* (aus dem Original des Sanskrit und des Gâ-
        thâdialects zuerst ins Deutsche übers. und mit sachlichen Erklärungen verseh-
        en von Salomon Lefmann). Berlin: Dümmler.
Lévi, Sylvain. 1975. 'Mahākarmavibhaṅga et Karmavibhaṅgopadeśa' in: Gonda, Jan.
        Selected Studies, Vol.IV: History of Ancient Indian Religion. Leiden: E.J.
        Brill.
Mehlig, Johannes, ed. 1987. *Weisheit des alten Indien*. Band 2 [Buddhistische Texte].
        München: Verlag C.H.Beck.
Morinis, Alan (ed.) 1992. *Sacred Journeys. The Anthropology of Pilgrimage*. West-
        port, Connecticut, London: Greenwood Press.
Mus, Paul. 1978 [1935]. *Barabudur* (Esquisse d'une histoire du Bouddhisme fondee
        sur la critique archéologique des texts, vol. I, II). New York, Hanoi: Arno
        Press (Imprimerie d'Extreme-Orient).
Newbery B. and Spens. I. 2000. 'Der Stupa, Symbol des erleuchteten Geistes' in *Tibet
        und Buddhismus* 55 (Vierteljahresheft des Tibetischen Zentrums e. V. Ham-
        burg).
Nyanaponika, Thera and Bhikkhu Bodhi. 1999. *Anguttara Nikaya: numerical dis-
        courses of the Buddha. An anthology of Sutta from the Anguttara Nikaya*.
        Lanham: AltaMira.
Park, C. Chris. 1994. *Sacred Worlds, An introduction to geography and religion*.
        London, New York: Routledge.
Robert, A. Paul. 1976. 'The Sherpa Temple as a Model of the Psyche' in *American
        Ethnologist* vol.3, no.1.
Sansone, Vito. 1978. *Pietre di salvare*. Torino: Societé Editrice Internazionale.

Schuman, H. Wolfgang. 1997 [1986]. *Buddhistische Bilderwelt. Ein ikonographisches Handbuch des Mahayana- und Tantrayana-Buddhismus*. Darmstadt: Wissenschaftliche Buchgesellschaft.

Sharma, Sharmistha. 1985. *Buddhist Avadanas. Socio-political Economic and Cultural Study*. Delhi: Eastern Books Linkers.

Takeuchi, Yoshinori (ed.) 1995. *Buddhist Spirituality*. New York: Crossroad.

Turner, Victor and Edith. 1978. *Image and Pilgrimage in Christian Culture. Anthropological Perspective*. New York: Columbia Univ. Press.

Veljačić, Čedomil, 1978. *Razmeđa azijskih filozofija. Knjiga prva*. Zagreb: Sveučilišna naklada Liber.

Winternitz, Moritz. 1968 [1920]. *Geschichte der indischen Literatur*, Band 2. Stuttgart: K.F.Koehler Verlag.

Zimmer, Heinrich. 1987. *Kunstform und Yoga im indischen Kultbild*. Frankfurt a. M.: Suhrkamp.

Zorić, Snježana. 1985. 'Buddhistička stūpa kao zrcalo kozmosa. Prilozi semiotici arhitekture – Borobudur' in *Kulture Istoka* 4.

Internet

http://www.stupa.org.nz/stupa/intro.htm (on 28.11.2007).
http://home.pages.at/jung/indonesien/borobudur.html (on 06.09.2007).
http://www.vanamaliashram.org/Borobudur.html (on 03.03.2008).

2. Coming to Oneself: Structures of Arrival in Songs Sung by Flagellant Pilgrims in Strassburg in 1349

Michael Shields

Probably it is never possible fully to chart the significance of arrival, of any arrival, if it is a transformative one: the arriving self encounters the foreign place, makes it part of itself, is itself encountered by the unknown, encircling uncertainties of arrival within patterns of the known while orienting itself upon an unknown center. Arrival exists in terms of a kind of topical homecoming some features of which (however different from one's own) one recognizes and appropriates; an exchange process transforms both the person arriving and the place arrived at. Though he does not say any of these things Fritsche Closener seems to have been in some way aware of them while writing his carefully orchestrated account of the arrival, itself highly orchestrated, of a group of 200 or so flagellant pilgrim dancers at the city of Strassburg, about two weeks after Midsummer in the year 1349. An unusual feature of the flagellant pilgrimages was that they were not oriented upon arrival at a particular place but rather upon arrival at any place. Each place they came to was the hallowed place of arrival; or rather, the normal journeying phase between a pilgrim's place of departure and arrival at the holy place was replaced by an open-ended succession of arrivals. Looked at in a general cultural sense, the direction of the pilgrimages was from South to North, starting in Italy, moving through Germany and the Low Countries and spreading virally outwards before terminating with one brief visit to England by seafaring flagellants who disembarked, performed their flagellant 'liturgy' and sailed off once more (Horrocks 1994: 153-4); they do not appear to have reached Ireland. Unlike other pilgrimages such as those to Santiago da Compostela, their songs were not moral-raising songs performing pilgrims' departure (*In gotes namen fara wir*) or concerned with the difficulties of travel (the late medieval *Jakobslied* (Moser and Müller-Blattau 1968: 196-8, 338-9) charts stations along the route from Germany to Santiago in a 'song-line' that records places through memorable or humorous anecdotes), but songs of arrival at the land of Our Lady (*in unserre lieben Frowen lant*), a notional liminal space which prefigures a future arrival in the kingdom of Christ's father, "*in sines vatters rich*". (Hegel 1870: 105) Given that the news of the impending Black Death was a catalyst for the 1349 pilgrimage, that future place might not be far distant. Each pilgrim followed the unending chain for 33½ days and experienced these as a succession of arrivals: the study by Beat Koelliker demonstrates that arrival is configured as an *imitatio* of Christ's entry into Jerusalem followed by a collective enactment of His scourging at the temple, just as the number 33½ symbolized the years spent by Christ on earth.

My attempt to elucidate some of the processes of the flagellants' arrival at Strassburg is based on a belief that the replacement of a fixed geographical, 'official' place of arrival by a free-moving and, to a degree, arbitrary and infinite series of destinations represents an important reversal in the way the hierarchical relationship between pilgrims and place is perceived. A traditional pilgrimage defines pilgrims in terms of their having visited a particular sacred space, but here it is the pilgrims (collectively or individually) who define spaces by virtue of the fact of their arrival at them. Moreover, one potential effect of this power to define place is that it gives the pilgrims a certain power to define themselves (rather than be defined by the place they visit), even if this power is circumscribed by texts and rituals they bring with them as well as by the unpredictable reality of the places they arrive at. In fact, given the aleatory nature of place in the pilgrimage, it could be argued that its only stable constituent is text (insofar as this was inherently stable). I will engage in close reading of the texts in order to ask whether the pilgrims had possibilities of self-definition within the pilgrimage, either as a community of pilgrims or as individuals within that community, and whether traces of this are to be found in the text.

The Flagellants' Letter

Textually the ritual at Strassburg is virtually identical with that performed across Germany at many different towns. It consists 1) of a compilation of popular processional songs (*leise*) used during an impressive entry procession that evoked Christ's entry into Jerusalem, 2) a flagellant round dance which Closener refers to both as a *leich* (dance song) and as a *leis* and which formed the core of the ritual, and 3) the "Flagellants' sermon" (*der geischeler bredie*), which was read publicly after the dance. This is related to a 13th-century text, the "*vrone botschaft ze der Christenheit*" ("The Lord's Message to Christendom"). Both texts appear to derive from the same version of the Latin "Heavenly Letter", a copy of which survives in a later Erfurt manuscript dated to 1347. Far older versions of the Heavenly Letter also survive, the chief preoccupation of which was the enforcement of Friday fasting. (Ladisch-Grube: 1156-7; Hegel 1870: 116-7) I will consider the letter briefly, before examining the songs which are the main object of investigation.

Versions of the Heavenly Letter circulated in Europe into the early 20th century, when it appears to have been replaced by a secular successor, the chain letter, with which it shares many features. For example, it engages in self-referential description of the route it has travelled in the past before arriving at the addressee. Closener transcribes the text of the *geischeler bredie* in his chronicle: its itinerary takes the listener from Jerusalem (by supernatural agency?) to the king of Sicily, then on to Krakau, Hungary, Meissen, Brandenburg, Eisenach, Würzburg, Halle, Esslingen, Kalw, Weil, Bulach, Herrenberg, Tübingen, Rottenburg, Lichtenau in Baden. The pilgrims at Strassburg identify themselves as being from this last village: "now we, the people of Lichtenau, are leading this pilgrimage." The letter's main functions for the 1349 pilgrimage (apart from the obvious function of self-legitimation) are to initiate listeners, in this case the burghers of Strassburg, into the idea of the pilgrimage, and to perpetuate its own dissemination by issuing (as modern chain letters still do) dire warnings of the consequences if the listeners do not obey the injunction to maintain the chain of penance, by themselves joining in the flagellant pilgrimage. Significantly, the list of towns visited by the pilgrims is mirrored by a parallel list of the places visited by the Black Death. (The multi-layered reduplication of lists is also a feature of 20th-century chain letters before their disappearance, or transformation, with the advent of email.) The geographical sequence is comparable but less predictable here:

All those who see this letter or hear it read out should know that from Apulia to Sicily and in Cyprus, and from Cyprus as far as Tuscany and in Catania, at Genoa [and] as

far as Avignon, and down from Avignon to Lyon, from Lyon to Rome and down-
wards in all their regions, and in Padua and its environs there is not one person in
three alive. Now death has come to Verona and Carinthia, the Eastern kingdom
[Northern Austria] and to us in Alsace. (Hegel 1870: 117)

The purpose of the parallelism between the two lists was probably to
clarify the role of the pilgrimage as anticipatory antidote and to
heighten the sense of urgency, but it also has the effect of conveying a
sense of mistrust in places and an awareness of their arbitrariness. No
place is safe from the plague. When the letter was read aloud at the
conclusion of each flagellant performance, it contained a warning:
*"Ich schaffe, welich mensche nüt geloubet an die botschaft, der würt
in die ahte verbannen meines vaters vom himel. Aber wer es geloubet,
deme kumet min segen in sin hüs."* ("I will see to it that whoever does
not believe in this message will be outlawed by the ban of my father
from heaven. But whosoever believes it, my blessing will enter his
house.") The implication is that only those who perpetuate the pilgrimage will remain unpunished. This warning is clearer in the Latin
version of Erfurt: *"Et si fuerit homo, qui non tradiderit epistolam is-
tam, anathema erit."* ("And if there should be a man who does not
pass on this letter, he shall be anathema.") (Hegel 1870: 114) The only
thing that gives safety (of a kind) in the face of universal death is
membership of the flagellant brotherhood. According to what Closener refers to as the flagellants' rule,[1] pilgrims were to make full confession to a priest and were to free themselves from material constraints
by first paying all outstanding debts, righting all outstanding wrongs
and providing themselves with 11 shillings and fourpence maintenance money (that is, a daily stipend of fourpence for each of the 34
days) before entering the pilgrimage, which they appear to have done
by taking a performative step forward into the community of pilgrims
(*in die bruderschaft treten*). In conception at least, there is something
quite unworldly about this pilgrimage. As Georg Steer puts it, the pen-
itential theology and practice of the flagellants are derived from the
formulation of the Heavenly Letter in *Der geischeler bredie*. (Steer
1980: 1155) One could argue that the entire pilgrimage has the structure and fleeting materiality of a chain letter, and that it finds its cor-

---

[1]   He provides a paraphrase but not a transcription of the rule (*regel*), which
        survives in a version from Bruges. A German translation of the *regel* is given
        in Brandt (1922: 120-121).

poreal realisation through the songs, in which the texts give scope for expression of a collective pilgrim identity while the musical and choreographical performance, if that is the right word for an act of flagellation with sharp iron points, allow expression at an individual, physical level.

The Songs

Closener prefaces his account of the 1349 pilgrimage by noting that there had been previous pilgrimages at Strassburg in 1261 and 1296, and distinguishes the 1349 pilgrimage from the earlier ones by calling it the "great" pilgrimage (*die große geischelfart*). He reports that the 1296 pilgrimage only had 28 flagellants. Clearly the 1349 pilgrimage, with its 200 participants, made a completely different impression from those preceding it, and not just because of its scale and sumptuousness. The difference is also borne out by the unprecedentedly dense and detailed coverage given it in chronicles from all over Germany. One reason for its exceptional significance was that it was preceded and followed by a particularly unfortunate series of natural and man-made disasters: not just the plague but a huge earthquake whose epicenter was at Villach (Carinthia), in 1348, and a countrywide massacre of Jews earlier in 1349; in Strassburg this had taken place on St. Valentine's Day, about five months before the flagellants arrived. The massacre gave grounds for collective trauma and repression: at least this is how Closener appears to have regarded the matter, as he says that after the massacre the burghers of Strassburg agreed that no Jew had lived there for a hundred years (Hegel 1870: 104). Such repressed trauma might find catharsis in pilgrimage without necessarily clarifying the question of right and wrong in relation to the massacre of Jews: the Heavenly Letter calls them a "hellish people" (Hegel 1870: 113) and criticizes practices (engaged in by Christians) that could be regarded as Jewish, both the non-observance of Friday and Sunday as holy days and the charging of interest on money loans (*wuchern*). The burghers of Strassburg are accused of these and other vices both in the letter and in the text of the flagellant dance, during the performance of which various participants enact symbolically the roles of individual categories of sinners: usurers, murderers, adulterers.

Though it is impossible to say whether the texts of the 1349 songs are the same as those sung in 1261, as only two lines of the 1261 song text are preserved, the general outlines of the earlier pilgrimage are close to that of 1349.

In the year 1261 an order of flagellants arose, which was called "lay penance" and whose origins were ascribed entirely to God and his mother. The rich, the noble, those of low birth and the poor, the old, those who were approaching adulthood and those who were boys, all praised her [Mary] in song, walking naked in public processions around the churches, enunciating the passion of Christ [...] and they sang this song: "You whip yourselves cruelly in Christ's honour. For the sake of God, forbear in future from sin. (Wattenbach 1851: 728)

The closing lines *Ir slaht euch sere / in Christes ere* are still used at the emotional conclusion of the 1349 dance, and in 1349 they are sung to a melody that is used only in this stanza. This is important because it supports the statement of one chronicler, Tilemann Elhen von Wolfshagen,[2] that the songs used in 1349 were new. (Wyss 1883: 33) It looks as if the two lines are a quotation taken from the earlier pilgrimage, and are being used here for authoritative emphasis because listeners will be familiar with them. That would support the consensus of more recent scholars (Koelliker, Steer) that the 1349 texts are the premeditated, carefully shaped product of a focused act of composition,[3] and is relevant to my assumption that pilgrims were defining a new identity through the songs, insofar as pilgrim groups are more likely to have perceived their activities as innovative if the texts were newly adapted for their use. While the generally conservative, fixed character of the texts and their widespread uniformity could be seen as hindering the possibilities of self-definition by pilgrims, I will suggest that the physical performance may allow room for participants to articulate personal and distinct identities within the framework of their collective pilgrim role. I will concentrate on the two main song texts,

---

2   *"Item du salt wißen, daz dise vurgeschriben leisen alle worden ghemachet unde gedicht in der geiselnfart, unde enwas der leisen keine vur gehort"* ("And you should know that the aforementioned songs were all made and texted during the flagellant crusade and none of the songs had been heard before").

3   Cf. Steer, for whom the song "has a simple and clearly structured form that suggests the author was following a strategic plan" (Steer 1980: 1155). Earlier scholarship had believed the songs were less co-ordinated, older and traditional, transmitted orally rather than composed.

the *leis* sung as the pilgrims entered the city and the dance text known as the "penance," which on the first day was performed outside the city walls, before the processional entry into Strassburg.

The Introit (*Einzugsleis*)

Nu ist die bettevart so her.
Crist reit selber gen Jherusalem.
Er fuort ein krütze an siner hant.
Nu helfe uns der heilant.

Nu ist die bettevart so gut.
Hilf uns herre durch din heiliges blut
Daz du an dem crutze vergoßen hast
und uns in dem ellende geloßen hast

Nu ist die stroße also breit
Die uns zu unserre lieben frowen treit
In unserre lieben vrowen lant.
Nu helfe uns der heilant.

Wir sullent die buße an uns nemen,
Daz wir gote deste baz gezemen
Aldort in sines vatter rich.
Des bitten wir sünder dich alle gelich.
So bitten wir den heiligen Crist
Der alle der welte gewaltig ist

> A journey of pilgrimage is noble:
> *Christ himself rode to Jerusalem.*
> He held a cross in his hand.
> *May the Saviour help us.*
>
> A journey of pilgrimage is good:
> *help us, Lord, by your holy blood*
> which you shed on the cross,
> *leaving us as exiles here.*
>
> See how wide the road is
> *that leads to our Dear Lady,*
> into our Dear Lady's land.
> *May the Saviour help us.*
>
> We should undertake penance
> *in order to be more pleasing to God*

> beyond, in his father's kingdom.
> *We, sinners, ask this of you.*
> Let us pray to the most holy Christ
> *who has power over all the world.*

Koelliker has demonstrated convincingly to what extent the compilation of processional songs and flagellant dances is a coherently planned cycle conceived in terms of the *imitatio Christi*; for him, it is a "valid artistic expression of what holds the flagellants' performance together at its innermost centre" ("*einen gültigen Ausdruck dessen,* [...] *was den Geißlerauftritt* [...] *im Innersten zusammenhält*", Koelliker 1977: 104), though he refrains from defining what that is. I would suggest that much of what it expresses must remain undefined because the ritualized act of arrival itself explores open significations that only become clearer as the arrivers engage with the arrived-at; Closener is chiefly concerned with its meanings for the latter, the inhabitants of Strassburg, for whom the flagellant ritual appears to offer a possibility of venting traumatized emotions within the city: the pilgrims entering the city may not have realized the full complexity of these meanings, though they certainly knew about (and helped to exacerbate as well as alleviate) fears of earthquakes and of the impending plague that was to decimate the population of Europe.

Closener tells us that two or four lead singers sang ("*sungent* [...] *vor*") the first part of the strophic melody while the other pilgrims sang the response. His vagueness as to exact numbers indicates that he is not just describing the performance of 8th July, but a model for performance that was repeated every time pilgrims came to Strassburg (he tells us that groups of them came and went for more than three months). Closener is conflating many memories here. In the following translation of the song texts preserved by Closener I have italicized the (conjectural) refrain sections. Responsorial performance was the normal structure of a *leis*; melody notations of the genre survive as far back as the 9th century.[4] What is clearest about this *leis* is the social firmness of its collective processional "*Wir*". The 200 pilgrims, many of them apparently from the last port of call, Lichtenau (near Rastatt),

---

[4]   The "Petruslied" of Freising, *Unsar trothin hat farsalt* (Munich, clm 6260) is notated with neumes that confirm the same performance practice; see Lipphardt (1976) for a survey of the genre.

present a unified front. However, when one examines the speech situation within the *leis* more closely, it becomes apparent not only that the lead singers (who were not priests) adopt a priestlike role in relation to the other pilgrims, but that the pilgrims as a group occupy an intercessionary role between Christ and the people of the place arrived at. Christ is first mentioned in the third person (lines 4-5), in a description that is addressed to the people of Strassburg and feeds straight into the traditional collective refrain melody of the *leis*, here a translation of the *Christe eleison*.

This was sung by the main body of pilgrims, but it is likely that those witnessing the procession would have joined in singing it too, thereby accepting that their native town was being transformed into a place of pilgrimage by outsiders. Already in the second strophe, the pilgrims are assuming the role of intercessioners for themselves and on behalf of the people of Strassburg. By addressing Christ directly they are acting on behalf of all "exiles" from His kingdom. This speech act is important since it indirectly gives the pilgrims power over the people of Strassburg.

The *Hauptleis* (flagellant dance)

Closener describes (again, somewhat imprecisely) how after the processional entry, accompanied by the vigorous ringing of church bells, singing the *Einzugsleis* and carrying "richest banners of velvet cloth, both smooth and deep-piled, and the best baldachins that were available, perhaps 10 or 8 or 6 of them, and perhaps as many coiled candles" (Hegel 1870: 105), the pilgrims entered the church and knelt down. Three times, apparently to mark a transition to the universal timeframe of ritual, they fell down and rose up, singing a couplet: "Jesus' thirst was quenched with bitter gall / So we should fall down in the form of a cross." ("*Jhesus wart gelabet mit gallen / Des sullen wir an ein krütze vallen.*") At this point the pilgrims fell violently to the ground with their arms outstretched, making a great rattle ("*daz ez klaperte*"). After lying silent for "a while" on the ground they rose when the songleader sang the words "Now lift up your hands [in pleading], / that God may turn away this Great Death!" ("*Nu hebent uf die üwern hende, / daz got dis große sterben wende*"). Closener's account of the ritual is interrupted at this point by his description of the flagellant Rule. He tells us later on that actual flagellation did not take place in the church but outside, after a procession to a designated *geischelstat* (whipping place), and that the first ever flagellation performed by the 1349 pilgrims was held in the morning, at Metzgerau (outside Strassburg to the South), in fact before they made their processional entrance to the church. It appears, however, that the usual sequence involved the initiation of the ritual inside the church, followed by flagellation outside. Closener's version of the text differs slightly from that of other good versions found in the chronicles of Hugo von Reutlingen and Tilemann Elhen von Wolfshagen, in that it is somewhat shorter and positions the 'privately' cathartic lines 91-96 "Weep with your eyes in secret, keep Christ's sufferings in your heart" (i.e. the quotation from the 1261 pilgrimage) earlier in the performance than in either Hugo's or Tilemann's versions. Problematically, the *Hauptleis* is the only sung text of a medieval German round dance which has been preserved; because it is unique, there are difficulties about evaluating its status in the context of 14th-century performance practices. For instance, we don't know for certain whether the textual discrepancies between Closener's and other versions of the text represent a normal level of variation for this kind of text. Its tripartite structure (three parts separated by two refrain sections) does not appear to have been unusual and could be compared with structures in the surviving examples of the 13th-century leich, which was a courtly art form.

The Hauptleis

(The flagellants strip to their underclothing, covering their lower bodies with white garments, and lie down in a circle. They use hand signs to denote the sins of which they are guilty: perjurers lie on one side with three fingers held over their head, adulterers lie prone, etc. One man, the leader, (*meister*) goes round the circle stepping over those lying on the ground, touching them with his whip and repeating the formula: *Stant uf durch der reinen martel ere/ Und hüt dich vor der sünde mere* – "Arise in the name of chaste penance and avoid sin from henceforth."

As they stand up one by one, the penitents follow the *meister* around the circle, also stepping over those still lying on the ground. Once the circle has been com-

pleted and all have risen, they perform the *Leiß oder leich*: one or two lead the singing
and the others respond. Walking or dancing in pairs, the participants form a large
circle and flagellate themselves as they move forward.)

I
Whoever wants to do penance should come and join us!
Let us flee from the heat of Hell.
Lucifer is a bad companion,
his desire is to make us fall
for he brings [burning] pitch as a reward .   5
So we should forsake our sins.

Whoever wants to do our penance
will repay debts and make amends.
Let him make proper confession and turn away from sin,
and God will have pity on him.   10
Let him make proper confession and repent,
And God will show Himself to him afresh.

Jesus Christ was caught
and hung on a cross.
The cross became red with blood.   15
We are lamenting God's pangs and his death,
For God's sake we shed our blood;
let this be our remedy against sins.
Help us in this, dear Lord God!
We ask you this for your death's sake.   20

Sinner, what will you pay me with?
Three nails and a crown of thorns,
The noble cross, a spear's thrust –
O Sinner, I suffered all that for you.
What will you undergo now for my sake?   25

Let us call in a loud voice as follows:
„We give you our service in payment.
We shed our blood for your sake;
this is our remedy against sins.
Therefore help us, dear Lord God!   30
We ask you this for your death's sake."

You liars and takers of false oaths,
God on high has no love of you.
You do not repent any of your sins fully,
and will go to Hell.   35
Save us from this, Lord God!
We ask you this for your death's sake.

Refrain section (l.38-47)
(The flagellants kneel, raising their arms, and sing.)

Jesus was comforted with gall;
therefore let us fall down in the shape of a cross.

(They fall to the ground in the shape of a cross and remain there until the singers re-sume singing, then they rise to their knees, raise their arms in prayer and sing the re-sponses.)

Now lift up your hands	*that God may turn away the Great Death.*	
		40-41
Now hold up your arms	*that God may have pity upon us.*	
Jesus, by the threeness of your names	*Free us, Lord, from sin.*	44-45
Jesus, by your red wounds	*protect us from sudden death.*	

Part II
(The pilgrims stand up and resume the round dance, scourging themselves as they move forward.)

Mary suffered greatly
when she saw her dear child being killed.
A sword cut through her soul.   50
Sinner, let this be cause of pain to you.
Help us in this, dear Lord God,
we ask you this for your death's sake.

Jesus called all his angels
in heaven together.   55
He spoke sadly to them:
"Christendom is trying to escape me,
So I will make the world come to an end
Know this for a certainty."
Save us from this, Lord God!   60
We ask you this for your death's sake.

Mary asked her sweet child.
"My darling child, allow them to do penance for you,
  and I will make sure that they
repent. I ask this of you.   65
Dear son, grant me this."
We sinners all ask likewise.

Whichever women or men break their [marriage] vows,
God himself will take vengeance on them for it.
Sulphur, pitch and gall –   70
the devil will pour it into them.
They are truly the devil's messengers.

Save us from this, Lord God!
We ask you this for your death's sake.

You murderers, you street robbers,   75
The case against you is too heavy on one side;
you refuse to have pity on anybody
and so must go to hell.
Save us from this, Lord God!
We ask you this for your death's sake.   80

Refrain section (l.38-47 are repeated)

Part III
(The pilgrims stand up and resume the round dance, scourging themselves as they
move forward.)

Woe to you, usurers of the poor:
God has no love of you.
You lend a half pound for a pound;
this will drag you down to the bottom of Hell,
so that you are be lost eternally.   85
God's anger will bring you to this.
Save us from this, Lord God!
We ask you this for your death's sake.

The earth shakes, the rocks split –
Weep, O you hard hearts!   90
Weep with your eyes   **in secret,**
keep Christ's sufferings   **in your heart.**
Strike yourselves cruelly   **in Christ's honour!**   95-6
This is our remedy against sins.
Therefore help us, dear Lord God!
We ask you this for your death's sake.

Whoever does not fast on Friday   100
or rest on Sunday,
Truly he will be lost eternally
in the pains of Hell.
Save us from this, Lord God!
We ask you this for your death's sake.   105

This law is a pure life
which God himself has given us.
I advise you, women and men alike,
to lose your arrogant pride.
For God's sake – lose your pride,   110
and then God will have mercy on us.

Help us in this, dear Lord God,
we ask you this for your death's sake.

Concluding refrain section (repeated as in l.37-46)

After singing the refrain section, the participants lie down and repeat the introductory absolution ceremony before once more putting on their clothes and collecting money for candles and banners. Finally, the Flagellants' Sermon (*Der geischeler bredie*) is read out by a lay pilgrim.

As they perform their penitent dance, circling in patterns of death and revivification while flagellating themselves, the pilgrims are in a delocalized space. Though at first the citizens of Strassburg, who are invited to become recruits, are still perceptibly present, they fade quickly into the background or are transported into the textual spatiality of the leich with its movements and speech acts. The *Hauptleis* is structured around changes in person, alternating between '*wir* (we)', '*du* (you singular)', '*ir* (you plural)', and an '*ich* (I)' which is that of Christ; performers and listeners have already encountered role-switches in the *Einzugsleis*, and are receptive to such possibilities. Somebody who 'wants to do penance' is invited to join a collective 'us'. There follows a passage narrating Christ's passion, a reversion to the communal *wir* (l.16) and a challenge (l.21) to an unspecified sinner who may be one of the pilgrims or a spectator; the challenge comes not from the flagellants but from Christ or a lead singer. 'We' reappears in line 26 and seems here to include not just the flagellants, but all the sinners to whom Christ has appealed. Further challenges (l.32, 75, 81) follow in parallel to that of line 21, but here it is no longer clear whether it is Christ or the flagellants that make the accusation; the 'we' that answers seems to include everybody present. A clearer pattern emerges from these switches when text, music and the pilgrims' movements (which have not been notated but can be reconstructed) are examined together. The *Hauptleis* uses just five melodies A, B, C, D, E. Except for the refrain sections (using melodies C and D, 38-47)

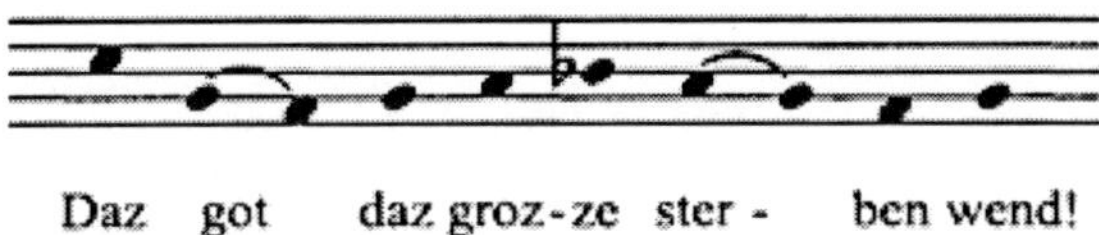

and the distinctly trochaic stanza *"Weep in secret"* (melody E, 91-96),

everything is sung to just two alternating melodies, 'A

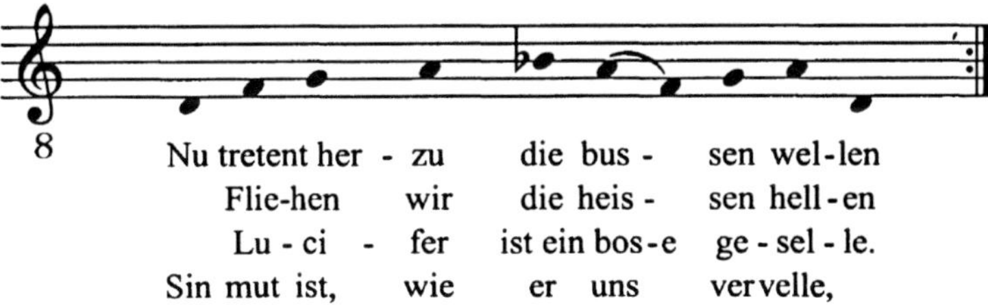

and 'B'

Melody 'A' ("*Nu tretent* [...]") is declamatory and pitched at the up-per end of the melodic range, while melody 'B' ("*Wande er hette* [...]") seems better suited to dancing, with melismata on the stress of the first and third metric feet of the melody. In my translation the sec-tions sung to melody 'B' have been italicized because I believe that these passages were the responses sung by the entire community of flagellants: comparing the alternation between 'A' and 'B' melodies with syntactic breaks in the text structure (my translation is accurate enough to reflect these), it becomes apparent that there is a strong tendency for a change in person, tense or theme to occur where the 'A' melody returns. The 'A' melody serves to mark new strophic sections, and these are characterized by changes in perspective. There is no corresponding break where the 'B' melody returns, rather a tendency to continue the theme initiated by the 'A' melody, as in lines 57-8, 64-65. The first person singular pronoun only occurs three times in an 'A'-section (24, 58, 65-66), the second person being the norm, while the 'B' sections favor the first person plural.

Since the text generally makes a fresh start every time the 'A'-melody is sung, and we know that the singing alternated between lead singers and the group, it seems virtually certain that the declamatory 'A' melody was that sung by the leader or leaders. The function of the 'B' sections is to corroborate themes developed in the 'A' text; they do not introduce new material. It is thus possible to draw some conclusions about the performance of the dance. If the 'A' sections were sung by lead singers and contained the textually important passages, we can assume that the dancers paused to listen while these were sung, resuming the round dance while singing the 'B' section. This would make it possible to follow the song even if the communal singing was incomprehensible or drowned out by background noise. Parallels for this stanza-ripresa format exist in other medieval dances such as the ballata. (Coincidentally, the characters in Boccaccio's *Decameron*, also fleeing the same socially destructive plague, sing a ballata at the end of each day's storytelling.)

But the flagellants weren't just dancing to the 'B' melody, they were scourging themselves. Bearing this in mind, texts sung to the 'B' sections acquire a physical immediacy. The greater the number of times the 'B' melody is repeated, the more intense the self-chastisement. When the text mentions Christ's passion there is a systematic intensification in the frequency with which the 'B' melody is sung, lines 15-20. In the phrase "Let this be our remedy for sins" ("*daz ist uns für die sünde guot*", l. 18 and 29) the pronoun *daz* refers both to the shedding of blood in the text and to the application of the whip to the pilgrim's naked back: the journey to Jerusalem progresses through the city, the text and now through the body to the pilgrim's self, which is expressed here not only in terms of the encounter with Strassburg through the 'we' of collective pilgrimage but in terms of an encounter between the repentant self and the limitations of its own tolerance for physical pain. The refrain section (l. 38-47) gives some respite before the performance of the second part, which mainly deals with Mary's suffering at the crucifixion and her subsequent intercession for sinners; in the third part (l.80-113) comes the most intense use of the 'B' melody, culminating in tears when it is combined with the 'E' melody: "Weep with your eyes in secret, keep Christ's sufferings in your heart; strike yourselves cruelly in Christ's honour!" (*"wainent tougen / mit den ougen / habt in hertzen / Christes smerzen / schlahent üch sere durch Christus ere."* l. 91-6).

Situated at this distance from the event, it is difficult to know whether one is overestimating the exceptionality of the texts simply because comparable texts happen not to have survived. I have deliberately refrained from commenting on one striking element in the *Hauptleis*, the catalogue of sins which sub-groups among the pilgrims enacted using hand-signs and prescribed body positions (for example fornicators lay on their stomachs, murderers on their backs). Such role-playing may have been a common feature of German dance or not (special hand movements are recorded often enough in descriptions and iconographic representations of dance to make it seem probable). It would be tempting to argue that the opportunity to act out the part of repentant usurers, perjurers etc. added a further dimension to the possibilities of self-realization available to the pilgrims, especially if they led blameless lives at home. If one supposed that they had the opportunity of finding not only Christ's pain in themselves, but also discovering the criminal (or criminals) within themselves, it could offer a way for them to integrate additional aspects of themselves in the ritual, and this might be experienced as liberating if it offered scope for something resembling what we would now call individuation.[5] A comment in Tilemann Elhen von Wolfshagen's Limburg chronicle could be interpreted as pointing in this direction. Immediately after describing the hand and body positions adopted by different categories

---

[5] Such possibilities may have found continued (if ambivalent) expression through parody, even after the flagellants had been discredited. The Bern chronicle reports that in 1350 upwards of one thousand armed men danced in mockery of the flagellants, singing the words: "The man who wants to do our penance / should take horses and cattle / geese and fatted pigs! / That's how we pay for the wine." (*"Der unser Buß well pflegen / Der soll Ross und Rinder nehmen, / Gäns und feiste Swin! / Damit so gelten wir den Win."* Müller-Blattau 1935: 13).

of sinners, he observes that "even though knights, soldiers, burghers and farmers all went with the flagellants in simplicity of heart, yet they all lost their spiritual intent by administering absolution themselves without the permission of the holy church, and made themselves into rogues and ruffians. For, a man who had been regarded as an honourable and good man within his station and in the place where he was known (*"in sime contract unde in siner kuntschaft"*) now made himself into a rogue (*"der machte sich selber zu eime schalke"*) so that his honour and good fortune never recovered in this world." (Wyss 1883: 33). Not that such catalogues of sinners were new – a similar list, together with the evocation of an angry Christ, is found almost 500 years earlier in the *Ludwigslied* (881 AD): *"Sum was luginâri, sum skâchâri, sum fol loses, Ind er gibuozta sih thes."* ("One was a liar, one a thief, one full of falsehood, and he did penance for it." Braune 1907: 150). Here the limitations of close reading without sufficient context become acute. Was the classification of sinners an ancient textual element that was being put to creative or changing new uses as the singers danced at Strassburg?

We know from Closener's account that he felt something new was happening:

It should be known that when the flagellants whipped themselves, the gatherings of crowds running together, and devout weepings, were the greatest that any man would ever see. And when they read the letter, great lamenting broke out among the people, because they all believed it was true. (Hegel 1870: 118)

The newness of the event was not just a matter of the scale of social disruption – the planned dynamic structuring of the *Hauptleis* as an inward journey shows it is more than that. It still remains unclear to what extent one should locate such newness in a release of pent-up trauma, guilt or fear on the part of the citizens of Strassburg, or in the collective and personal possibilities that were opening up to the pilgrims as they made their entrance, or in a belief (one that was mistrusted by Closener and the other chroniclers) in the transformative power of arrival itself. After all, with each arrival the texts too were changing, if only slightly. The pilgrims' arrival brought various forces together in performance on 8th July 1349, but would also convert them back into various types of altered text: that written on the increasingly scarred backs of individual pilgrims, the word 'Strassburg' which could now be added to the list of places visited by the Flagellants'

Letter, and, ten or more years later, the containing and reflective text written by Closener himself.

Bibliography

Brandt, Otto H. 1922. *Die Limburger Chronik*. Jena: Eugen Diederichs.

Braune, Wilhelm (ed.) 1907. *Althochdeutsches Lesebuch*. Halle: Niemeyer.

Closener, Fritsche. 1870. 'Strassburg I' in: Hegel, Carl (ed.) *Die Chroniken der oberrheinischen Städte* (Die Chroniken der deutschen Städte, vol.8). Leipzig: Hirzel.

Elhen, Tilemann (Tilemann Elhen von Wolfshagen). 1883. In: Wyss, Arthur (ed.) *Die Limburger Chronik* (Monumenta Germaniae Historica, deutsche Chroniken, 4,1). Munich: Weidmann.

Horrocks, Rosemary (ed. a. trans.) 1994. *The Black Death*. Manchester: Manchester University Press.

Hübner, Arthur. 1931. *Die Deutschen Geißlerlieder. Studien zum geistlichen Volksliede des Mittelalters*. Berlin Leipzig: De Gruyter.

Koelliker, Beat. 1977. 'Das Geißlerlied 'nu tret her zu der boessen welle' und das Geißlerritual' in Rupp, Heinz. *Philologie und Geschichtswissenschaft*. Heidelberg: Quelle u. Meyer.

Lipphardt, Walther. 1976. 'Leisen und Rufe' in Friedrich Blume (ed.) *Die Musik in Geschichte und Gegenwart*, vol. 16. Kassel: Bärenreiter.

Moser, Hugo and Müller-Blattau, Joseph (eds.) 1968. *Deutsche Lieder des Mittelalters von Walther von der Vogelweide bis zum Lochamer Liederbuch. Texte und Melodien*. Stuttgart: Klett.

Müller-Blattau, Joseph. 1935. 'Die deutschen Geißlerlieder' in *Zeitschrift für Musikwissenschaft* 17.

Runge, Paul. 1900. *Die Lieder und Melodien der Geißler des Jahres 1349 nach der Aufzeichnung Hugos von Reutlingen*. Leipzig: Breitkopf u. Härtel.

Schnell, Bernhard. 1983. 'Himmelsbrief' in Kurt Ruh (ed.) *Verfasserlexikon* (2nd ed.), vol. 4. Berlin: De Gruyter.

Spechtshart, Hugo (Hugo von Reutlingen). 1881. Gillert, Karl (ed.) *Die Chronik des Hugo von Reutlingen* (Forschungen zur Deutschen Geschichte 21). Göttingen: Dieterichsche Buchhandlung.

Steer, Georg. 1980. 'Geißlerlieder' in Kurt Ruh (ed.) *Verfasserlexikon* (2nd ed.), vol. 2. Berlin: De Gruyter.

Wattenbach, Wilhelm (ed.) 1851. 'Continuatio praedicatorum Vindobonensium' in Pertz, Georg Heinrich (ed.) *Monumenta Germaniae Historica* (Scriptores), vol. IX. Hannover: Hahn.

3. St Clement of Rome:
The Romanic-Slavic Symbiosis of the Cult and its Tradition in the Croatian Lands

Antonija Zaradija Kiš

The territory of Croatia is marked by a host of hagiotoponyms that are often characterized by a rich folk Christian tradition and local pilgrimages, sometimes almost unknown to the broad public. They bear a thousand years of reverence of Christian saints through which one can read off many important historical events and cultural shifts that have sunk into oblivion today. Their evocation uncovers a treasure chest of testimonies whose powerful faith, narratives and legends strengthen the expression of distinctness and autochthony – the sacrosanct work of folk philosophy that has been transmitted through the generations, despite technological development and the dynamics of the life of which we are a part.

It was in that sense that the Institute of Art History in Zagreb compiled a computer program of hagiotopography by which one is able in a speedy and effective manner to identify all the hagiotoponyms with the basic geographical, ecclesiastical, temporal, stylistic and patronage characteristics of localities that bear the name of particular Christian saints. Based on that program and studies to date on veneration of Pope (Bishop) Clement of Rome, we shall endeavor to cast more light on the importance of this Early Christian saint's cult, its dissemination throughout Croatian territory and the significance of his tradition today.

Three levels of tradition

During research into the Croatian hagiotoponymic tradition of St Clement of Rome, 17 localities have been confirmed that are linked directly or indirectly with veneration of the fourth Roman pope, a pupil of St Peter. The attached map displays the distribution of known saints, clearly showing that the majority of the remembrances of St Clement are found in Dalmatia (12), then in Istria[1] and the Quarnero Bay area (3), while they can also be found in continental Croatia (2). Three of these shrines from the 13th/14th century have disappeared and knowledge of their existence comes solely from existing literature. They are: St Clement on the Hill near Ljubač not far from Zadar; at Dračevo Polje on the island of Vis, and at Vrh in Pula.

The oldest information on the Early Christian shines of St Clement in continental Croatia is that of the Gora locality, west of today's Petrinje, lying on what was once the main road coming from Hungary and leading south through Sisak, playing an active part in the regional and cultural connection of the area.[2] More definite data on the shrine emerges in the 13th and 14th century, when the Church of St Clement was mentioned as the parish church up until the disbanding of the Order of Templars. It is found in 16th and 17th century documents, but all traces of it disappear from then on (Dobronić 1984: 72, 76). Along with the toponym *Klimen* in Croatian Zagorje, 5 km north of Konščine, there is also the toponym *Kelemen* not far from Jalžabet in the Varaždin area, where the 12th century chapel of St Clement is found, this having been renovated in the Baroque style during the 18th century.

---

[1]   There is the settlement of Klimni in Istria, 6 km south-east of Žminj and the church of St Clement on Kras in central Istria, 13 km south-east of Buzet. The church dates from the 15th century, and was rebuilt in 1899 (Cul 1999: 80).

[2]   Hence the piece of information about the St Clement shrine dates from the 4th/5th century at the Gora locality (as is noted in the hagiotopographical list of the Institute of Art History in Zagreb).

Map

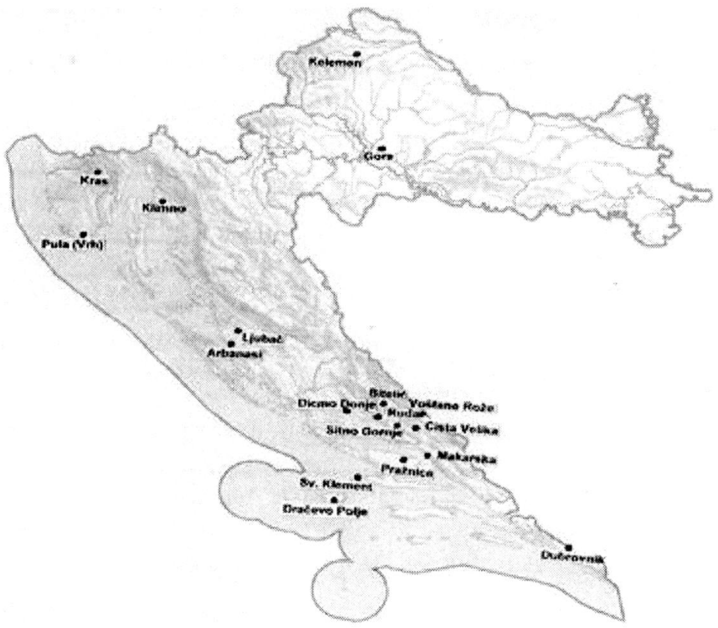

We shall be concentrating our research in this paper on evocation of the tradition and cult of St Clement along the Croatian coast, observing its survival through hagiotoponyms and preserved shrines and customs along three traditional levels:

- The first is the Roman and refers to the first centuries of Christianity and the time in which the earliest Christian saintly cults spread, prior to the arrival of the Slavs on the Adriatic coast. The very popular cult of St Clement of Rome spread in that historical context along the eastern coast of the Adriatic from the powerful Roman centers, among which that of Salona[3] was particularly important. A diocese was established there in the mid-3rd century and it encompassed all the existing Dalmatian Christian communities, through which the

---

[3]   Bishop Hezihius of Salona (405-426) is cited (with some doubt) as the author of the *Life* of St Clement of Rome (legacy of the Glagolist, Šimun Kožičić Benje) (Katičić 1998: 101-277).

cults of the Christian saints became more quickly rooted in the broader region.

- The second is the Slavic traditional level, linked with the 9th century and closely connected with the cultural and enlightenment mission in Great Moravia conducted by the Slavic Apostles, Constantine Cyril and Methodius, during which the discovered relics of St Clement of Rome were carried to Chersoneson (Heson in today's Crimea) on the Holy Brothers' journey to Rome, confirming the already existing cult of St Clement and establishing it in places in which it had not previously existed. Here a special role was played by the Glagolists, devoted promoters of the Cyril and Methodius heritage, which gained full impetus over the 13th to 16th century period.

- The third level is of more recent date and we have called it the *neo-Clementine* level, since the St Clement of Rome tradition was introduced and popularized by priests in analogy with the Clementine tradition in the areas from which they had come. This cultic and traditional specificity relates to the broader region of Dalmatian Zagora within which the cult spread from Poljice, a Glagolitic cultural hothouse. A particular place in the neo-Clementine tradition belongs to the town of Makarska.

Through the typified culturological and religious motif of movement and/or pilgrimage, one should concentrate on the motif of arrival and departure, that is, the movement of the cult through time intervals and space with the specificity of its denotation and evaluation. This is how the tradition of a particular area is shaped and strengthened, whose nature along with religious color contributes to the targeted return of inhabitants who have moved away, looking for more favorable conditions of life. However, for the feast day of St Clement of Rome, drawn by the power of the tradition of their forefathers and their inherited pious stance towards their implanted heritage, the emigrant inhabitants regularly make a pilgrimage back to their native place.

The first traditional level

We monitor the spread of the cult of St Clement from the 4th century, the time from which the first traces of the basilica of St Clement in

Rome[4] date. In that connection, it is important to bear in mind the legend of Clement's exile to distant Herson in what is now The Ukraine (Gk. Χερσόνησος, Lat. *Chersonesus*), after he had refused to bow down to pagan idols. His miracle in discovering water defines Clement's sojourn in Herson. The shortage of water and the search for a spring brought down a death penalty on prisoners, and their entreaty for water puts on trial Life, awareness, reason and belief and/or Christianity. Clement's miraculous discovery of the spring promotes the force and will of a human being for Life. It is for that reason that we hear an ode to Life through the source of water.

So it was the imperial administrator Mamertin, convinced of Clement's holiness, bade farewell to him in tears as he left for exile with the words: "May the God whom you serve help you!" He gave him a boat supplied with everything necessary for the voyage; on his way to exile he was seen off by a large number of priests and laymen.

Arriving in Herson, Clement encountered more than two thousand Christians sentenced to quarrying marble to be used in the sculpting of statues of the pagan gods. The convicts met him with tears, and he comforted them, saying: "I do not at all deserve the honour given to me by the Lord in selecting me as the leader of martyrs such as you!" After they had told him that they were being forced to search for water six miles away, Clement said: "Let us pray to our Lord Jesus Christ that in the same way that He caused water to spurt from a stone in the desert of Sinai, He will also make a gift of a spring of fresh water to his followers in this place." And after he had prayed, Clement caught sight of a lamb that seemed to be pointing to something with its raised foot. Immediately recognising Christ's presence, Clement went towards the indicated spot and said: "In the name of the Father, the Son and the Holy Ghost, strike the ground at that spot!" However, since no-one else had seen the lamb, no-one could strike at the place in which it was. Only Clement took up a staff and gently struck at the ground below the lamb's foot; and a spring immediately appeared and quickly transformed into a torrent.

News of the miracle spread throughout the region so quickly that more than five hundred people took baptism in one day, and throughout one year seventy-five churches were built there. Three years later, learning of Clement's miracle, the Emperor Trajan sent his officer to Herson. But he, seeing that the entire nation was prepared to die, drew back from such a huge number of executions and satisfied himself with ordering that only Clement be cast into the sea with an anchor around his neck, saying: "From today, at least these people will not be able to worship you like a God!" However, since a mass of people was standing on the shore, two of Clement's pupils, Cornelius and Febus, begged God to show them the body of their martyr. At that, the

---

4   Pope St Siricius (384-399) had the Basilica of St Clement built. Today it is an important Slavic Christian pilgrimage destination since it guards the grave of both Clement, whose bones were brought to Rome by Constantine the Philosopher, but also of St Constantine Cyril himself, who became ill after arriving in Rome and died on February 14, 869 (Bratulić 1985: 129).

sea ebbed three miles away from the shore; walking on the dry sea-bed, the people arrived at a marble grotto in which they saw the body of St Clement with an anchor beside it. And a voice from heaven forbad them to take the body from that place. And since then, on the day each year of the martyred death of St Clement, the sea ebbs away for a week in the same way so that the faithful can cross the dry sea-bed and visit the saint's tomb.[5]

Water has a twofold meaning in this legend: on the one hand, it is a necessity, it gives Life; on the other, it takes Life away from Clement, that is, as he drowns.[6] Through the aforementioned opposite motifs – arrival and departure, the twofold role of water, Life and Death – the constant nature of the motif and the eternal repetition of its components is underscored.

Everything that this legend tells us, along with the one that relates to the discovery of the marble grotto with Clement's mortal remains – and parts of his body several centuries later – explains the saint's patronage over those people whose activities are bound up with the sea, with the watery expanse that means life to so many. It is in that context that the sea and seafarers, and ships and ship-owners are connected with St Clement, who became the patron saint of ship-owners. For that reason, the rare Clementine hagiotoponyms on the Adriatic coast in what were once strategically important places should also be interpreted in relation to the 'ship-owner motif' of the martyrdom of St Clement. Through it, the already-mentioned motif of arrival and departure – leaving a place by ship and returning again to the same place, that is, by sea – becomes recognizable. The seaworthiness of the ship is primary for the departure so as to ensure physical arrival at Herson, where Clement is to serve his punishment. It is essential for the return so as spiritually to achieve the objective, and that is Rome, where the saint's relics will be placed. Both cases are connected by the strength of existence in the building up of the cult of St Clement: firstly the physical and secondly the spiritual, which mean Life in all its fullness.

---

[5]   Jacopus de Voragine. 1998. *La Légende dorée*. Paris.

[6]   The indispensability of water in maintaining life and its capacity for destroying life were shown by Vladimir Nazor in his tale *Voda* [water], which elaborates this *Clementine* motif in a subtle way (Nazor 1965: 154-183).

St Clement of Hvar

The island of St Clement (*Kliment*)[7] in the Hvar Paklini Islands[8] group obtained its name from the patron saint of ship-owners and shipping activities, which have been carried out on that island from ancient times. The settlement of the islands, too, was linked with Hvar's maritime tradition (Mihovilović 1995: 120-136) and ship maintenance activities. The church consecrated to St Clement of Rome dating from the 11th/12th century was built for that purpose; it was first mentioned in 1331 and, unlike many other old Hvar churches, which have fallen into ruin and disappeared with time, it has been restored and is still preserved today. The underlying reason for this can be sought in the powerful nature of the patronage that was handed down by legend through the generations. Although the small church has unpleasant memories from the time of the French authorities, it did not fall into complete disrepair but was fully renovated in 1870, not only with funding from the people of Hvar but also from the Emperors Franz Joseph and Ferdinand.[9] This shrine and the efforts made that it survives confirm the power of the cult of St Clement as the patron saint of ship-owners, which has deep roots on the island and has persisted to contemporary times.

Two current celebrations are connected with the church of St Clement on the island of Hvar. The first takes place on the last Sunday in July and evokes remembrance of the victims of the Battle of Vis (July 20, 1866); the second is held on St Clement's feast day, November 23. The Church of St Clement of Rome is a special one for the people of Hvar (although the walls are cracked and a large fissure has appeared near the altar) and it is not unusual for baptisms to be con-

---

[7] St *Kliment* or Veli Otok is the largest island in the Hvar archipelago, which numbers some twenty islands and crags.

[8] The islands received their name from the pine pitch or resin, *paklin*, whose name derives from the lexeme *pakao* [hell] and is connected with "the concept in folklore of burning pitch in hell" (Skok 1972: 588). Pitch is otherwise used by shipwrights as a protective and impregnational layer for smearing on boats.

[9] The small church was renovated in memory of the Austrian victory in the sea battle near to the island of Vis, which took place on July 20, 1866, and the loss of the frigate Radenzky, with the intention of preserving remembrance of the dead mariners. There is a commemorative text above the main doors to the church and at the base of the altar painting (cf. Suić 1995: 104).

ducted there, that is, celebrations of new life that commence with the arrival of the boats at St Clement.

St Clement of Krk

The hagiotoponym *Klimno* (San Clemente) is found on the island of Krk; it is a settlement located in a deep bay, originally called Soline, that belonged to Dobrinje, and is mentioned in sources as early as in 1381 along with a chapel that belonged to the Malatestinić family, and then again later in the 15th century (Bolonić, Žic Rokov 2002: 396, 413). Although the customary opinion today is that the name is connected with the church of St Clement from the 14th century,[10] the existence of the chapel is only the result of the much older presence of the cult of St Clement that developed on the basis of the ancient shipping tradition in the western part of the island, and particularly in the Soline Bay, where the original exploitation of salt was superseded by ship-building, by which the emphasized strategic importance of the locality came to the fore particularly in the 19th century, when Austria took possession of Klimni meaning the taking of the entire island.[11] The existence of the St Clement confraternity that is mentioned from the 16th century is linked to the chapel (Bolonić 1975: 32).

The importance of shipping for the eastern part of the island is also confirmed by the frescoes uncovered in the Romanesque church in the bay of St Juraj [George] not far from Vrbnik (Prister 2008: 211-217). The depiction of a three-masted sailing ship and its crew, dating from the 12th/13th century (Fučić 1997: 257-261), speaks for the developed seafaring occupation on this part of the island during the Middle Ages. This had been inherited from the time of Antiquity, with which the manifestation of the maritime saint cults (Sts Clement,

---

[10]   A confraternity mentioned in 1576 was active at the church and it assisted, no doubt, in the maintenance and appearance of the church, which had a bell and a bell-tower in 1609. It lost its importance at the time of the Napoleonic invasion, but managed to survive and was repaired during 1823 and again in 1926 (Bolonić, Žic Rokov 2002: 413, 420).

[11]   Klimno was mentioned in the hostilities between Austria and Napoleon; on May 6, 1809 the Austrian army under the leadership of Baron Peharnik arrived in Klimno and established definite authority over the entire island (Bolonić, Žic Rokov 2002: 72).

George, Nicholas and St Martin) is also linked. The fact that shipping was developed on the island of Krk from times long past is supported by data in the Krk Statute dating from the 13th century, and also by notations from the 15th and 16th centuries and onwards through the centuries, during which Klimno played a leading role in shipping because of its strategic and naturally protected position. The importance of maritime activities on into the 20th century is supported by information from 1937 that Klimno was second on the island of Krk in its number of boats, while the Svetozar Jurić shipyard that had been established in 1883 as the third in size on the island (Bolonić, Žic Rokov 2002: 235-238, 403) was still active at the beginning of World War II.

Although shipping in Klimno today is a story from the past, modest celebration of the feast of St Clement of Rome continues in the church on the very sea-shore that is graced by the recently restored polyptych depicting on the right side the saint holding a lamb (one of his attributes)[12] – "the animal of conciliatory victims" (Chevalier, Gheerbrant 1994: 217). The lamb is a symbol of gentleness, purity, submissiveness and inoffensiveness. Its light-giving aspect expresses the peak of cognition at which one arrives by seeking and sacrifice, the source of the sacrificial characteristics of the lamb (Chevalier, Gheerbrant 1994: 216). For that reason, the lamb in Clement's arms symbolizes the saint's intersession for the preservation of peace, unity and faith as is reflected in his epistle *Prima Clementis*, which the historian Batiffol calls "the Epiphany of the Roman primate" (Zaradija 1986: 148).

St Clement of Zadar

The preserved remnants of the small church of St Clement of Rome stand right beside the shore. It is small in dimensions (7.70m x 4.0m), and is located in the southern part of the island of the same name in the Arbanasi Bay (Zaradija 1986: 152). The oldest preserved but very stark data dates from 1288 (Strgačić 1956: 245-252) in the context of a will and a vineyard that mentions *ad sanctum Clemente*. The church

---

[12]   Apart from the lamb, which underscores the meaning of the word *clementia* (goodness, gentleness, love – the virtues of the most elevated of souls) with its symbolic attributes, an anchor (most frequently) and a well are also depicted with St Clement.

and the island are then mentioned in similar documents from the end of the 13th and from the 14th century (Praga 1935: 214-215), and particularly in the report of a Zadar sea-captain, Vincenzo Moresini, where there is mention of a *lazaret* [quarantine hospital] that operated actively throughout the 14th and 15th centuries (Stipčević 1977: 17-18).

The folk legend from Zadar that speaks of reaching the island by walking on the sea-floor after the sea had ebbed (Stipčević 1977: 19)[13] is an interpretation of the Early Christian legend and its later Slavic variant, according to which the sea in Herson ebbed on the same day each year so that the faithful (who included Constantine and Methodius at one juncture) could walk to Clement's grave.

A possible identification, even today, of the belief in the grave on the sea-bed, is perhaps spoken for by the frequent leaving of posies of flowers on the remains of the small Zadar church of St Clement.

The second traditional level
St Clement of Poljice

The most expansive monograph about Poljice to date is that by Fran Ivanišević [1906], 1987), which offers a host of material demonstrating life through the centuries in that Dalmatian area, continuing to be a source of many research projects, particularly those that relate to old customs that time obliterates further with each passing year. Their sinking into oblivion does not mean their disappearance for all time but merely a strictly defined spatial limitation leading to certain events being less widely known and thus less interesting to the broad public, particularly among people not connected any way with Poljice. It is in that context that the Poljice Clementine heritage,[14] a mere pebble in the rich Poljice culturological mosaic – which we could classify at the second, Slavic, level, in keeping with the above-mentioned traditional

---

[13] It is also possible to do this today, as the water is only half a metre deep during ebb-tide.

[14] Two more recent preserved manuscripts about the life of St Clement, classified as being located in the time in which they were written, speak of the importance of St Clement to the Poljice region. One is from the 18th century and is kept at the parish office in Sitno Donja, while the second is from the 19th century and in housed at the Archaeological Museum in Split (Alaupović-Gjeldum 1997: 149-150).

level – continues still to live today to the extent that people with ties to this area return from wherever they may be to celebrate the feast day of this saint.

The imprints of the Poljice Clementine tradition should be sought in the Cyril and Methodius legacy of the Slavic Mission that lasted from 663 to 885. According to the *Life* (ŽK), Constantine found Clement's relics in Herson on January 30, 861 (the feast day commemorating the transfer of the relics in the Slavic Church[15]) in a desecrated grave on the sea-bed which, according to the *Legendae aureae* was of marble and/or located in a marble grotto. Some time later, on their journey to Great Moravia and/or Rome, the Thessalonica brothers carried with them the uncovered relics of St Clement of Rome. The vital Western European force of the cult of this saint was a spiritual accompaniment to the entire Cyril and Methodius Mission to the Slavs, becoming its trademark and giving it an ecumenical character, deeply entrenched in the territory through which it passed. And that is the territory of the Adriatic, particularly if one bears in mind the assumption about the journey of the Holy Brothers to Great Moravia by the Adriatic maritime route from Constantinople, Thessalonica and Dures, the *Via Egnatio*, and by way of the eastern Adriatic coast to Venice, and then taking the Amber Road towards Great Moravia (Petrović 1988: 41).[16] Through this enlightenment mission, the significance of the cult of St Clement became re-enforced in places in which it already existed (the Byzantine areas: Pharos, Issa, Curicum, Iadera), and more widely accepted along that part of the coast where there had been echoes for centuries of the Slavic Mission (whether that of the Holy Brothers in 863 or the later one of their disciples after 885) (Petrović 1988: 41-47).[17] The cult of St Clement of Rome, whose famous

---

[15] This is confirmed by the calendar of the canonical Assemanianus Evangelistary (the *Codex Assemanianus*) dating from the 10th century (Ivanova-Mavrodinova, Džurova 1981; Bratulić 1985: 49).

[16] In texts that express this view, data and interpretations about the baptism of the people living around the Neretva River that is attributed the Holy Brothers are important mainstays (Ravlić 2000: 49).

[17] Relying on this theory about the journey of the Holy Brothers along the Adriatic, the Clementine Poljice cult could be directly linked with them. For its part, if one inclines towards the mainland theory about the Holy Brothers' journey, then the cult of St Clement would have been brought to the Adriatic coast by the disciples of Cyril and Methodius, after Cyril's and/or Methodius' death.

epistle *Prima Clementis* gained wide repute (Jedin 2001: 151, 175), was thus instilled by the Cyril and Methodius mission among the Slavs, reviving the personality and work of the bishop seven centuries after his life had ended, the same bishop whose meticulously organized baptismal "mission of the seven" in Gaul (Zaradija 1989: 261-265) must have been the model and mainstay of the Slavic Mission, which achieved credibility in that way. The Slavic conveyance of the discovered relics by whole-hearted advocate of the Christian Church who *utvrdi s petromъ i pavlomъ vъ mirê d(u)h(o)vnuju cr(ь)kvь* [founded with Peter and Paul a more spiritual church in the world], as was written in the *Laudation* by Clement of Ohrid (Angelov 1970: 301), elevated the authority of the Holy Brothers and the credibility of their work, as well as being a guarantee of the success of the Slavic culturo-enlightenment mission based on the theology of St Paul, just as the Clement's earlier mission to Gaul had been. The full significance of the cult of St Clement of Rome both on Byzantine soil and among the Slavs is shown by the oldest translations of the Mass Canon in honor of St Clement of Rome. Standing out particularly among them is the translation by St Joseph the Hymn-writer, a contemporary of the Holy Brothers, whose translation was also included in the Russian *Book of Ilin* from the 11th century (Hristova-Šomova 2008: 72-73).

The multi-layered thousand-year-old heritage of legends gives an indication of the multitude of culturological shifts but, because of rare, fragmentary confirmations that are often of doubtful authenticity, it is difficult to establish the Slavic path of the cult's dissemination. It is possible to seek the sole authentic Clementine relics of the 'dark' beginning of the Slavic past among the rare Clementine hagiotoponyms and small Clementine churches that continue even today, on the saint's feast day, November 23, to evoke and revive inscrutable history by the gathering of the faithful and the domestic population and the procession, church service and benediction. The latter is specific to the Poljice area where the blessing of livestock takes place, and this requires additional explanation.

Due to the location of Gornje Poljice that is some distance from the sea with its inhabitants' lives linked with the mountain, the patronage of St Clement was connected with the exploitation of stone, which is still obvious today through the existence of the quarry with its origins back in the time of Antiquity. "There is a lot of lovely stone in

Poljice for all uses. It is extracted from the mountain, in the fields, around the houses, it's everywhere, but you have to come across a healthy stone (*petrada*)." (Ivanišević 1987: 12) In Sitno Gornje, where the Clementine tradition comes from, the exploitation of yellow marble (at the Zagrađe locality) has been known since ancient times. In that connection, it is interesting to recall the legend that tells of the Emperor Diocletian extracting gold at Sitno (at the Zlataruša locality). According to Ivanišević's notation, it was based on that legend that "people came on several occasions from abroad, from Greece and some Jewish people from Palestine, bringing old charts and maps, accompanied by some of our own domestic people from Split and Omiš, and they collected and dug around, setting up three matches to play and look for gold – but there you have it, trouble, all in vain, they didn't even find a grain!" (Ivanišević 1987: 14). Later research showed that gold had never been found in the area, but that rare yellow marble, the color of gold, had been quarried at the Sitno location. So it is through that yellow marble that one can explain the preserved legend about gold at the time of Diocletian. Seeking for an explanation of the emergence and survival of the cult of St Clement in Sitno, we return to the legend of Clement's expulsion to the Crimea during the reign of Emperor Trajan and his slave-labor with Christian convicts in the Crimean quarries. It was thus that St Clement became the patron saint of marble – and stone-masons in Sitno (Réau 1958: 321-322).

However, in Poljice the saint appears as a patron of animals, particularly horses and mules. The question arises as to why St Clement is the protector today of those animals, as is confirmed by the following notation: "It is difficult to cure a horse of ailments like parasites, asthma, lung infection, convulsions, rabies; let it suffer, until it dies or kill it beforehand. For more serious illnesses, they go to the priest for a prayer, pay for a mass to purify the soul, or make a pledge to St Clement in Sitno." (Ivanišević 1987: 246) St Clement cares "for the health of animals, horses, and mules" (Ivanišević 1987: 457),[18] that is, draught animals, which have always co-existed in this region with the human inhabitants, the Slavs,[19] Croatians, and Dalmatians.

---

[18] The conditions in the Poljice mountains and hills did not suit oxen, and that is why they are not mentioned in Clement's Poljice patronage.

[19] The Slavic, Glagolitic character of central Mediaeval Istria should also be included here. Istria has preserved the Cyril and Methodius Clementine herit-

The horse and the mule were used for hauling various loads, and the stone from the quarries as well. Work in the quarries relied largely on the strength and health of the animals, just as work in the Crimean quarries once relied on the health and fitness of the imprisoned Christians.

Today, too, the location of the blessing of the animals is the old church of St Clement [*Klement* or *Kliment*] dating from the 11th/12th century, whose saint's day observance that takes place on November 23 is one of the nine most significant ones held at this church.[20] It is held on the Sunday following the saint's feast day, if this falls on a working day, to make it possible for as large a number of people as possible to attend, particularly those from distant places and even from abroad (Zaradija 1988: 39). It is lively around the church from early in the morning, with the prospect of a folk celebration to be preceded by the solemn mass for St Clement, and then the blessing of the animals that have been led around the church three times by their owners behind the simple fenced *cimitero*, or graveyard, intoning three Lord's Prayers while doing so. After that, the parish priest gives the blessing with water and the cross.

There is a solemn mass in Sitno on St Clement's day (23. XI.). Many people come together from all sides and they all lead their animals around the church in a procession, and they pray to God with a certain number of Lord's Prayers in honour of St Clement for the health of the animals; oil, wax and alms are presented as votive offerings. (Ivanišević 1987: 457)

Just how important the cult was to the people of Poljice and how deeply it was thus entrenched in Poljice everyday life is clearly shown by the statement of a young couple employed in Germany, noted down in 1987 around the feast day of St Clement: "Some come to Sitno for Christmas and some don't, it's the same at Easter, but there is

---

age right up until the present day, at Kras, a village between Ročko Polje and Hum. The small church of St Clement dates from the 15th century, that is, "the Golden Age of Croatian Glagolism" and we could thus, due to the time of its being built and the rural clime to which it belongs, also connect it to the animal patronage of Pope St Clement, a subject that should be researched further.

[20] The Romanesque church of St Clement of Rome with a semi-circular apse (Fisković 1952: 181-195) is one of the oldest in Poljice, once the parish church, located between Gornje and Donje Sitno. It was there that the famous Poljice Statute was drawn up in the 14th century (Junković 1968).

no job and no employer that would stop us from going to Sitno for St Clement." (Zaradija 1988: 39)

St Clement of Brač

The Poljice cult of St Clement should be observed in parallel with the similar one on the island of Brač, since the Clementine tradition in both localities relates to the hinterland stock-raising part of the region, and not to the coastal area. When speaking of the exploitation of stone from ancient times, one must inevitably mention the production of white Brač stone on the island in relation to the Clementine tradition. This white stone is the Brač marble known from Antiquity. One finds particular evidence of this in the traces of quarries near Split and Škrip on the island of Brač, known as Diocletian's quarries[21] and the stone sculptures found in them, and elsewhere (Dunda 2006: 16-21). The Clementine tradition on the island of Brač and the existence of the church of St Clement of Rome in the Pražnice area[22] has to be included in the Dalmatian stone-masonry concept already dealt with. The small church is located at the Klinja Glava locality,[23] the name being derived from the name of the church's titulary (Klinje glave < *Klimnje* < *Kliment, Klement*).[24] There is a preserved relief dated 1535 in the church depicting the young Pope Clement in a shallow niche. The rustic stylization of that relief, particularly the robe drapery, heralds the time of the more mature Brač Renaissance (Pelc 2007: 300). A strik-

---

[21] The stone from those quarries is still known today as Diocles stone.

[22] "Selo na Pražnicah" [the village at Pražnice] is mentioned in the Povalje Papers from 1184.

[23] This was once the graveyard of the Mediaeval settlement of Straževnik that developed as the early, prehistoric settlement located in the island's hinterland because of improved security on the ruins of the former fortress, or *gračišće*, meaning the ruins of a former fortified town, from which one could keep watch and defend the inhabitants. That was the source of the former settlement's name, *Straževnik*, a place from which one could keep watch and guard. Straževnik is mentioned in a document dating from the 12th century; the inhabitants moved out and settled in Pražnice and Pučišće and it died away in the 16th century.

[24] The Pražnice surname *Klinčić* derives from the same root, as do *Kelement, Kelemente, Kliman* and the Dalmatian hypocoristics *Kleme* and *Klime* (Šimunović 1972: 222; Šimunović 1995: 274; Šimunović 1997: 123).

ing detail is Clement's huge laborer hands. The anonymous author seemed to have wanted to emphasize the onerous labor of the stone-masons whom Clement had once joined in Herson, otherwise a feature of all quarry laborers.

The second Brač Clementine hagiotoponym is the name of the cove between Postira and Pučišća – *Klinica, Klimnica, Klivnica* – which is a derivative from the shortened and diminutive form of *St Klime > St Kleme*, from St Clement (Šimunović 1972: 222). It is diffi-cult to establish today whether the name of the cove is a reflection of the Clementine tradition in the hinterland, or if the cove of that name existed before the shrine as a refuge for ships and their repairs with pitch (as on the island of Hvar). Since the Slavs at the earliest phase of their settlement of the coastal area accepted the existing Romanic hag-iotoponyms that were later submitted linguistically to Slavic phono-logical changes, it is reasonable to conclude that St Clement's cove on Brač existed much earlier, for the very reason of the existence of an early stratum of the cult connected exclusively with the coastal area and boats. If that is indeed the case, then Klinica Cove belongs to the first, Roman stratum of the Clementine cult, making the Brač tradition of St Clement even more interesting.

The third traditional level

Several localities in Dalmatia have venerated St Clement of Rome for only one or two hundred years. By analogy, the imported neo-Clementine tradition revives the saint's cult according to what is al-ready existing and known. The reason for their manifestation could be twofold:

1.   The phenomenon of selecting a local patron saint came about in the 18th century since diverse political conditions, such as Turk-ish rule, had prevented this being done earlier (Lupis 2006: 124). So it was that St Clement became the patron saint of the town of Makarska.

2.   During the 19th century, the phenomenon of transfer of the cult to the villages of Dalmatian Zagora appeared. Was the need for new Clementine shrines the result of the cult's exceptionally positive effect on horses and mules that was passed on by leg-end and the wish to achieve that effect? Or was this a reflection

of inborn tradition and the Poljice parish priest's ability at that time (if so desired) to transfer the cult of St Clement from his native place to another in which he was serving as priest?

St Clement of Makarska

Makarska has been venerating St Clement of Rome as its patron saint since 1725 when the Makarska noblemen Antun Ivanišević and Jakov Kačić successfully entreated Pope Benedict XII to give them the relics of St Clement, and then brought them from Rome to Makarska. The sailing ship with the saint's relics was greeted in the town harbor by the bishop of the time, Nikola Bjanković.[25] The relics of the new patron saint of the town were laid on Clement's altar in a marble tomb when building of the cathedral was completed in 1770, and they are still there now.

Through the custom of veneration of the Makarska St Clement, the legend was evoked of the exiled Clement finding a spring of drinking water in the desert, water for which the Christian convicts were pleading. Bearing in mind the importance of sources of drinking water in Dalmatia, it is not surprising that the faithful of Makarska carried to the church a glass vessel holding water to be blessed along with their rosary beads, being able only on that occasion to touch the displayed bones of the saint.[26] According to that old custom, the saint's bones still pass in procession today across the main Kačić Square, and the solemn concelebration of the mass in St Mark's Cathedral concludes with the displaying of the relics of St Clement, and the singing of a hymn in honor of Makarska's patron saint.

---

[25]   The Makarska bishop wanted symbolically to recall the martyrdom of St Clement the Pope, so he awaited the ship in his feet bare and with a rope around his neck, leading the townsfolk and shouting "We welcome you Clement the Holy: be gentle to us and merciful" (Kaer 1996: 19).

[26]   It is somewhat unclear which bones are actually in question here and the opinion exists that these were the bones of the Roman martyr of the same name through which Pope St Clement the Martyr is venerated (Zaradija 1986: 154).

The neo-Clementine shrines in Dalmatian Zagora

The strength of the Poljice cult of St Clement and particularly the custom of blessing the draught animals, the horses and mules, was so penetrating through the centuries that the cult of the saint, and the blessing of the animals together with him, was transferred to other villages, so that small churches were built and processions were held around the shrines on the feast day of St Clement of Rome. Perhaps the intention was in this way to alleviate the journey of the horses and mules on the way to their patron saint. Perhaps it was simply the nostalgia for his domestic saint that led a priest, who was originally from Poljice, to bring the cult to his parish and to have built a chapel dedicated to St Clement of Rome. Such an example is found in the small church in Dicma Donja at the Osoje locality, where the parish priest, Brother Lovro Milović, had a Clementine shrine built in 1882. The churches of St Clement in Bitelić (1870) in Cista Velika (1874), at Voštane and the chapel by the parish church in the village of Ruda all came about through similar motivation.

Concluding thoughts

All the above details that relate to the distribution of the cult and tradition of St Clement of Rome in the Croatian lands, particularly the Dalmatian Clementine tradition, confirm the continuity of veneration of the fourth Pope that threaded through changes in civilization and the times, sinking slowly into oblivion just as his shrines also disappeared. However, the inherited spirituality of the Clementine Croatian heritage, no matter how much it may seem to us at first glance to have been superseded, has found its ways of survival and entrenched itself through evocation of the past, saving it from oblivion, whilst also confirming itself in the present.

Hence, where the Slavic nomadic populations settled in the early Middle Ages the cult of St Clement settled with them, as the saint took patronage over the key factor of life in the Poljice area, their draught animals: the horse, the mule and the donkey – animals that had always been closest to Humankind, sharing living space with it, be it the sea or the land.

Bibliography

Alaupović-Gjeldum, Dinka. 1997. 'Sveti Klement u pučkoj pobožnosti Poljica' in *Ethnologica Dalmatica* 6.

Angelov, B. St. 1970. 'Pohvalno slovo za Kliment Rimski' in B. St. Angelov, K. M. Kuev, Hr. Kodov (eds.) *Kliment Ohridski. Sъbrani sъčinenija. Tom pъrvi.* Sofija: Izdatelstvo na Bъlgrskata akademija na naukite.

Bolonić, Mihovil. 1975. *Bratovština sv. Ivana Krstitelja u Vrbniku, Kapari (1323-1973) i druge bratovštine na otoku Krku.* Zagreb: Kršćanska sadašnjost.

Bolonić, Mihovil i Žic Rokov. Ivan. 2002. *Otok Krk kroz vjekove.* Zagreb: Kršćanska sadašnjost.

Bratulić, Josip. 1985. *Žitja Konstantina Ćirila i Metodija i druga vrela.* Zagreb: Kršćanska sadašnjost.

Chevalier, Jean i Gheerbrant, Alain. 1994. *Rječnik simbola.* Zagreb: Nakladni zavod Matice hrvatske, Mladost.

CuI. 1999. *Crkva i u Istri: osobe, mjesta i drugi podaci porečke i pulske biskupije* (eds. Marijan Bartolić, Ivan Grah). Pazin: IKD 'Juraj Dobrila'.

Dobronić, Lelja. 1984. *Posledi i sjedišta templara, ivanovaca i sepulkralaca u Hrvatskoj* (RAD Jugoslavenske akademije znanaosti i umjetnosti. Knjiga 406). Zagreb: Jugoslavenska akademija znanosti i umjetnosti.

Dunda, Siniša. 2006. 'Hrvatski kamen – Veselje' in *Graditelj* 13.

Fučić, Branko. 1997. *Terra incognita.* Zagreb: Kršćanska sadašnjost.

Hristova-Šomova, Iskra. 2008. 'Rannite slavjanski prevodi na kanona za sv. Kliment Rimski ot Josif Himnopisec' in *Preslavska kniževna škola* 10.

Ivanišević, Frano. 1987. [1906.]. *Poljica: narodni život i običaji.* Split: Književni krug.

Ivanova-Mavrodinova, Vera and Džurova, Aksinija. 1981. *Assemanievoto evangelie. Starobъlgarski glagoličesti pametnik ot X vek.* Sofija: Nauka i izkustvo.

Jedin, Hubert. 2001. *Velika povijest crkve I.* Zagreb: Kršćanska sadašnjost.

Kaer, pop Petar. 1996. [1914.]. *Makarska i Primorje.* Makarska: Matica hrvatska, ogranak Makarska.

Katičić, Radoslav. 1998. *Litterarum studia. Književnost i naobrazba ranoga hrvatskog srednjovjekovlja.* Zagreb: Matica hrvatska.

Mihovilović, Miro. 1995. 'Pomorstvo otoka Hvara' in Miro A. Mihovilović i suradnici (ed.) *Otok Hvar.* Zagreb: Matica hrvatska.

Mardešić, Andrija Vojko. 1995. 'Crkva na Hvaru' in Miro A. Mihovilović i suradnici (ed.) *Otok Hvar.* Zagreb: Matica hrvatska.

Nazor, Vladimir. 1965. 'Voda' in Marin Franičević (ed.) *Pet stoljeća hrvatske književnosti: Vladimir Nazor II.* Zagreb: Zora, Matica hrvatska.

Pelc, Milan. 2007. *Renesansa.* Zagreb: Naklada Ljevak.

Petrović, Ivanka. 1988. 'Prvi susreti Hrvata s ćirilometodskim izvorištem svoje srednjovjekovne kulture' in *Slovo* 38.

Praga, Giuseppe. 1935. 'L'itinerario dalmata di Amadeo VI di Savoia, il Conte Verde (1366-1367)' in *Archivio storico per la Dalmazia.* X/19 (facs. 113).

Prister, Lada. 2008. 'Kult sv. Jurja na frankopanskim posjedima Hrvatskog primorja' in Ana Marinković i Trpimir Vedriš (eds.) *Hagiologija. Kultovi u kontekstu.* Zagreb: Leykam International.

Ravlić, Jakša. 2000. [1934.]. *Makarska i njezino Primorje.* Makarska. Matica hrvetska Makarska.

Réau, Louis. 1958. *Iconographie de l'art chrétien.* Tome III. Paris: Presses Universitaires de France.

Skok, Petar. 1972. *Etimologijski rječnik hrvatskoga ili srpskoga jezika.* Knjiga druga. Zagreb: Jugoslavenska akademija znanosti i umjetnosti.

Stipčević, Aleksandar. 1977. *Kulturno povijesni spomenici u Arbanasima (Zadar) povodom 250-godišnjice doseljenja zadarskih Arbanasa.* Zadar: Centar JAZU.

Strgačić, Ante Marija. 1956. 'Otočić sv. Klementa južne zadarske luke u prošlosti' in *Zadarska revija* 5/4.

Šimunović, Petar. 1972. *Toponimija otoka Brača.* Zagreb: Grafički zavod Hrvatske.

—. 1995. *Hrvatska prezimena: podrijetlo, značenje, rasprostranjenost.* Zagreb: Golden marketing.

—. 1997. *Brač. Vodić po otoku.* Zagreb: Golden marketing.

Zaradija, Antonija. 1986. 'Kult svetoga Klementa Rimskog na hrvatskoglagoljaškom tlu' in *Slovo* 36.

—. 1988. 'Svetkovina sv. Klementa Rimskog – ćirilometodska baština Poljica". *Poljica* 13:35-39.

—. 1989. 'Sedam učenika sv. Klementa Rimskog i Sedmočislenici' in Mateja Matevski, Blaže Koneski, Dimče Koco (eds.) *Kliment Ohridski i ulogata na Ohridskata kniževna škola vo razvitokot na slovenskata prosveta.* Skopje: Makedonska akademija na naukite i umetnostite.

4. The Literature of Pilgrimage and the Search for Community:
Cees Nooteboom's Roads to Santiago and the Imagining of National and Pan-European Identities

John Outhwaite

This paper wants to examine the contemporary Dutch poet and novelist Cees Nooteboom's account of an essentially secular pilgrimage in Spain, entitled Roads to Santiago. Nooteboom's narrative, as an account of a search for self understanding and cultural roots in a foreign country, opens up the question of how self-knowledge is imagined to arise from the act of departure from the familiar. Nooteboom's admission of an infatuation with Spain as a polar opposite culture to that of his homeland poses the challenge as to whether the narrative could ever be an exploration of that which is other on its own terms. Is the pilgrimage ever really a journey of exploration, a radical departure, or is it as much a journey of affirmation, an act of fixing oneself more securely to a given identity?

In addressing this question I want to examine how the Christian pilgrimage as an allegory of the journey might be sustained in the contemporary European context. Is the sacredness that is attached to the sites of Nooteboom's journey confined to a Christian heritage or is it the transgressions of the journey itself which effects to sanctify places encountered on route? I will examine how the sacred connects with the tensions of a pilgrimage journey: of the disruption of the linear time of the play of past and present; and of the confusion of identity between the strange and familiar. I argue for the importance of Nooteboom's text as exposing essential structures of pilgrimage that are integral to, yet transcendent of, its European Christian heritage.

Introduction

This paper wants to explore issue of identity as it is seen to be informed by the dichotomy of the exile and the nation state. Its aim is in response to such writers as Edward Said and Homi Bhahba whose work puts into question received wisdoms with regard to how the status of the exile has been conditioned by specific notions of the individual and of the condition of belonging. In his essay, *Reflections On Exile*, Edward Said asks how, of the contemporary discourse, "if true exile is of terminal loss, why has it been transformed so easily into a potent, even enriching motif of modern culture?" (Said 2001: 137) Said initially insists that the typical elevation of the exile in literature as a figure of enlightenment and insight effects to diminish the pain of loss the true exile experiences such that he asserts that "exile cannot be made to serve notions of humanism" (Said 2001: 138). However, as the essay progresses he admits of a creative and positive process at work when he states that "all nationalisms in their early stages develop from a condition of estrangement" (Said 2001: 140). Said in effect returns to the original thematic he initially disparaged by opening up the question of how the condition of exile, of departure and estrangement, invigorates an authentic sense of the meaning of community. If we are then to continue to pursue the thought that the exile's endeavour to return to the fold leads us to the path of authentic community, how can this be accomplished whilst insisting that the anguish of loss itself affirms the original ideal of community?

Homi Bhabha's work also attempts to engage with the question of identity formation. In *Nation and Narration* (Bhabha 1990) Bhabha questions traditional ideas concerning the nation and representation and the imagined process by which homogenous communities are located through identifiable historical continuities. He reflects upon how communities in actuality are identified through the interaction of difference; through collaboration and dialogue but also through conflict and antagonism. It is this notion of the creativity of difference that undermines the ideal of a historically given and intrinsically coherent identity. In the context of post-colonial thought Bhabha has developed the notion of "hybridity" and that of the "third Space" (Bhabha 1994; Bhabha 1996) which effect to deny the authority of hegemonic narratives and essentialist identities. It is not simply a dialectics of difference from which an authentic constitutive identity emerges but that "hybridity" is a state of intrinsic impurity. The position of "in-betweenness" of the "third space" which stands apart from essentialist concepts does not simply negate but also contributes positively to ideas of cultural identity. Whilst it is a space that does not allow for a "primordial unity or fixity" of identity (Bhabha 1994) it is also a space that Bhabha describes as "interruptive, interrogative, and enunciative". (Bhabha 1994)

It is clear that with both Said and Bhabha simplistic notions of antagonistic oppositions, which come to the fore in the context of the post-colonial tensions that is their principle area of concern, hinder productive explanations for the condition of identity. If the contemporary discourse on identity, so intrinsically linked to conflict, is thus dissolved the question arises as to what alternative explanation can we turn to and to what extant structure of thought that can still claim recognized historical presence could authenticate such an explanation? This paper wants to examine a discourse linked to exile and the affirmation of identity that may represent such a structure, that of the pilgrim, a kind of 'third space' through which the essential elements of belonging – selfhood, community, culture, earth and spirit – are primordially exposed.

Roads to Santiago is a collection of essays by the Dutch poet, novelist and travel writer Cees Nooteboom covering forty years of periodic journeys throughout Spain. Nooteboom was born a catholic in The Hague in 1933 and was educated at convent schools run by Franciscan and Augustinian monks, although he no longer professes a belief in God. He left Holland at an early age and has spent much of his adult life travelling around the world. He has used these experiences in his profession both as a travel writer and a novelist. Many of his novels have centered upon the experiences of dislocation or of an event that has broken a characters habitual existence within the familiar cycle of life, exposing the self to the question of the meaning of their identity and existence. One of the most important recurrent themes of his works is that of the ultimate occasion of estrangement from the world – death – and how the self can attempt to make sense of life incorporating this event that is both intensely familiar and radically alien.[1] In *Roads to Santiago* the exploration of these themes re-

---

[1]   See for example Nooteboom's novels *All Souls Day* (2001), *The Following Story* (1991), *Rituals* (1980).

turn from being shifted into the realm of the imagination of the novel to the person of Nooteboom himself in the genre of the very personal reminiscences of the travel writer. Richard L. Kagan in his review of *Roads to Santiago* for the New York Times considered that "although difficult to categorize it resembles a classic pilgrim's tale written for purposes of spiritual edification, a kind of Michelin for the soul" (*The New York Times*, April 6, 1997). And whilst each essay based upon his own experiences travelling throughout the country becomes the basis for an examination of the art, history and culture of Spain and includes many digressions into reflections upon such interests as literature, philosophy, and politics it is the concept of pilgrimage that holds the book together into a coherent whole. Despite the essays being essentially self-contained and their composition extending over a prolonged period of time, there is a narrative tension to the whole given by the sense of a purposeful progression to the goal of the realization of the self's place in the world, a prospective outcome that draws many towards the pilgrimage road.

But like many pilgrimage roads the route is marked by images and symbols that serve to remind the pilgrim of the context of their journey and its purpose. For Nooteboom these are the canonical images and symbols of a European high culture that draws deeply upon a classical and Christian heritage. Notions of identity are embedded in history and in *Roads to Santiago* Nooteboom meanders through the history of Spain like a Renaissance collector of curiosities intent upon stocking a cabinet from which to build a picture of an authentically European world. But, like the characters in many of his novels, Nooteboom is exposed to the question of the (im)possibility of locating the self coherently in time and space. How can such diachronic notions of identity be activated in a modern world where the essential transience of existence is concealed by the allure of a present of a plurality of choices of ways of being? If the self is invited to make of itself what it will from the menu of lifestyle possibilities on offer in modernity, then why should it be concerned with an attachment to a past than can only represent a limitation of the vision of its possibilities? In modernity, the individual has to negotiate historically partitioned identity claims against experiences that draw them towards a sense of belonging to an aggregate globalized world. Nooteboom as an independent traveller epitomizes this existential condition of freedom that characterizes modernity, and it is his insistent identification with this radical individuality, not allowing him to fully let go of the modernity he despises as culturally vapid, that introduces irresolvable tensions in his attempts to associate himself with a profound European heritage. Nooteboom has left his catholic upbringing in Holland behind him. He no longer believes in God, yet he is intoxicated by the idea of a spiritual identity with a traditional, deeply Catholic Spain. He also utilizes all the technological trappings of modernity to travel around the globe, conspicuously driving by car to Santiago even though the Camino de Santiago pilgrimage is unique in Western Europe for maintaining a working infrastructure, extending over eight hundred kilometers of marked paths and an extensive network of dedicated hostels, encouraging travellers by foot.[2] Yet, he expresses criticism of the culture and standards of modernity and part of the allure of Spain for Nooteboom is that in his eyes the country retains a uniquely intimate relationship with its past.[3] As he observes, "in Spain, history need not repeat itself, it can simply stay the same" (Nooteboom 1992: 20). *Roads to Santiago* is a search for connections and continuities. Underlying Nooteboom's particular pilgrimage is the challenge of identity in modernity; how is a fragmented self to reconcile multiple and contradictory experiences in order to establish a coherent sense of belonging?

On one level the book is of interest as an exploration of the interplay between conceptualizations of individual, national and transnational identities. Illustrative of the layering of identity, Nooteboom attempts to unravel the significance of his affinity to Spain for his own sense of identity through the examination of Spain's relationship to a wider European cultural heritage. As indicated by the title of the book, Nooteboom's destination is the traditional pilgrimage site of Santiago de Compostela, yet it is not the traditional way of the pilgrim along the route of the Camino that he follows. His account is of a plurality

---

[2]   As Nooteboom admits: "I am making two journeys, one in my rented car and another through the past as evoked by fortresses, castles, monasteries and by the documents and legends I find there." (Nooteboom 1992: 40)

[3]   According to Said, this antipathy towards modernity profoundly informs the prevailing ideas of exile: "We have become accustomed to thinking of the modern period itself as spiritually orphaned and alienated, the age of anxiety and estrangement." (Said: 137) In the essay Said quotes George Steiner who describes the modern phenomenon of the writer as exile as characterized as "Eccentric, aloof, nostalgic, deliberately untimely" (cited in Said: 137).

of *Roads* travelled along both in space and time, given that he writes of it as also a pilgrimage "to an earlier, shadowy self, the recapture of a past passage" (Nooteboom 1992: 5). Nor, as the title suggests, is he travelling on foot along paths but by that modern symbol of mobility, the car. And he navigates his way through Spain using the symbols, architecture and artifacts of Christianity not specifically for their religious significance but for their place in a European high culture. It is not scripture, nor the accounts of previous pilgrims he is guided by, but canonical figures of Western literature and philosophy, and, connectedly, his own past experiences.

Nooteboom's approach to the question of identity evolves from an initial assumption of a correlation between personality and place. The self is to be made sense of through an exploration of the place where the self is imagined to belong. As he states at the beginning of the book: "The Spanish character and the Spanish landscape correspond to what in essence I am, to conscious and unconscious things in my being, to what I am about" (Nooteboom 1992: 5). Yet, as Nooteboom is not constrained to equate this place of belonging to the land where he was born and lived, it becomes, paradoxically, a journey of discovery. And, locating the answer to what he is about within a country other than his own, sets Nooteboom up to present his quest as a pilgrimage.

What is to be explored is the interplay between these two discourses concerned with investigating the Spanish national identity and with the motifs of pilgrimage running parallel to each other within the text. The pilgrimage journey is often represented as a journey of self-discovery: a process of spiritual exploration by which an individual human being becomes aware of the true purpose of their existence, which leads to the question as to how the act of displacement that is the departure from a homeland becomes the search for a true self? In a world wherein the individual is fundamentally identified by their national identity what meaning can be ascribed to the notion of finding ones 'authentic' self through becoming an outsider?

In *Roads to Santiago* Nooteboom conjoins the separate journeys together into a singular pilgrimage narrative. And it *is* a pilgrimage narrative in that it goes beyond the genre of simple travel writing. There is a reflective, meditative, tone to the book; Nooteboom is not simply describing events, painting a visual picture for the readers' eyes, but he is trying to extract meaning, not only from the building, city or artwork he encounters, but also the experience of the encounter itself. And there is a necessary interconnectedness between the two; what Nooteboom understands about himself through his journeying through Spain cannot be separated from what he understands about Spanish culture, history and thought. The travel writer may describe their experiences as enlightening in terms of a culture clash; two given ways of being meeting each other and learning of differences and similarities. But the travel writer already knows who he or she is; the encounter with the Other does not effect to deprive the travel writer of their identity, but rather serves merely to set it in its global context. The pilgrim, on the other hand, brings the truth of their being with them but then exposes this truth to its groundlessness. The experience of the Other for the true pilgrim is not simply as difference, as an alternative manifestation of what it is to be, when what it is to be retains its essential given attributes. Rather the pilgrim experiences the Other as the annulment of the foundational framework of a given existence; the pilgrim turns away from the physical to the metaphysical realm in search of the truths by which they could hope to obtain an existential security. Pilgrimages are quests; they have a goal, which is predetermined when the journey is embarked upon. But that goal originates from the framework of meaning of the fixed society from which the pilgrim departs. Upon the journey this framework is vulnerable to the dissolving of its power. The original mandate for the pilgrimage no longer necessarily holds sway and the goal shifts from being the affirmation of a belief to the question of the meaning of belief in all its existential significance.

Nooteboom's search for a foundation for his being draws initially upon conventional elements of contemporary discourses upon identity. It is such concepts as nationality, culture and religion which provide the framework by which the individual is able to locate him/herself in space and time in such a way as to be recognized as who they supposedly really are. Yet what is disclosed through the text is that, viewed through the optics of the pilgrimage, the basic precepts of identity and community upon which contemporary society is constructed are radically tenuous. The sense of the radical separation of the event of pilgrimage from the normative structures of society can be found expressed in the anthropological interpretation of pilgrimage of Victor and Edith Turner. In their seminal work theorizing the Christian pilgrimage, *Image and Pilgrimage in Christian Culture* (Turner

1973) they argue that on pilgrimage the pilgrim enters a state of detachment from convention, or 'liminality'. Having thus stepped beyond the confines of society to where social norms and hierarchies have been discarded the pilgrim experiences what they term 'communitas', a radically open and unstructured community of equals. To be a pilgrim is to put on the cloak of an outsider. To dress in pilgrimage attire is to lose ones association to a national identity. Nevertheless, the totality of the experience is still ultimately to be understood in terms of the extant society the pilgrimage is associated to. The Christian pilgrim does not escape from the images and symbols of the Church, in fact, on the pilgrimage route this metaphysical truth of existence becomes foregrounded *in extremis*. Within this reading there is an evident connectedness between the destination and the locale of departure which maintains itself as a frame of reference for the experience of pilgrimage as a state of exception. Thus, within the context of the pilgrimage journey the distinction between departure and destination loses its clarity. Is the destination ever the site of a new beginning or is its meaning always essentially informed by the act of departure?

What is also brought to the fore is the importance of the journey as a mode of engaging with essential questions of existence. The journey becomes more than simply a necessary process to be undertaken in order to reach a destination. It represents an important experience in itself integral to the meaning of the pilgrimage as a whole. It is this essential merging of the three constituents of the structure of pilgrimage – departure, journey and destination – which gives to pilgrimage its unique importance as a form of transnational movement bearing upon the question of identity.

Although the focus of this paper will be through a reading of the text as a contemporary application of a pilgrimage narrative, it is notable that Nooteboom is initially hesitant in claiming for himself the status of a pilgrim. At the beginning of the book, when he describes his enacting of the pilgrimage rituals within the Cathedral at Santiago, he disassociates himself from the authentic pilgrims of the Camino. And he remains ambivalent about the genre of his own narrative: "call it a pilgrimage or a meditation if you wish." (Nooteboom 1992: 40) This reflects the uncertainty of his status that pervades the book. It becomes impossible for ultimate meanings to be extracted from his experiences.

The Individual in Exile

The real traveller finds sustenance in equivocation, he is torn between embracing and letting go, and the wrench of disengagement is the essence of his existence, he belongs nowhere. The anywhere he finds himself is always lacking in some particular, he is the eternal pilgrim of absence, of loss, and like the real pilgrims in this city he is looking for something beyond the grave of an apostle or the coast of Finisterre, something that beckons and remains invisible, the impossible. (Nooteboom 1992: 337)

The word pilgrim is derived from the Latin *peregrinatio* meaning a stranger, a traveller in a foreign land. A pilgrim is also a seeker, a devotee; they are meant to suffer hardship and to embrace poverty. Yet it is the attribute of a stranger that gives the word that is used to designate the act. Perhaps it signifies that above all it is this condition of estrangement, of exile, that is the key to understanding what pilgrimage means. The act of departing from a homeland to travel through unfamiliar lands is not unique to the pilgrim, but only for the pilgrim does it become the essence of his or her experience. Thus it is through the concept of pilgrimage that the European tradition of thought engages most profoundly with the question of what it means to be a stranger and how, through the insight this condition gives, the individual relates most self-consciously to the Other, the world, and ultimately their own selfhood.

Throughout the narrative of his travels, despite his belief in a personal identification with Spain, Nooteboom consistently calls attention to his being a stranger, a status he appears to actively cultivate. He travels almost entirely without a companion, stays in Hotels out of season, visits towns in the heat of midday when all is closed, and frequently expresses an antipathy towards the crowd: of experiences shared with others. He maintains that it is only in solitude that one can properly experience the meaning of the cathedrals, museums, and royal palaces he visits:

But the days of the lone tourist are over in places such as these. The straggler from one guided tour is swallowed by the next shoal of visitors. His glance lingers on a tapestry on the wall, a royal throne, a tomb, a tabernacle, all the things everyone else seems capable of taking in with a single, vacuum-cleaner-like glance to the drone of rudimentary explanations offered by those who have made this their business. What a dream to have, to be let into the Escorial at night by an accomplice and to roam those deathly silent, ghostly rooms on one's own, with only a candle and a ground plan for company. (Nooteboom 1992: 122)

For the stranger the senses are heightened. The stranger is perspicacious; the world does not really show itself for those for whom the sights and sounds present themselves in a collective context. It is of the intimacy of a personal contemplation of a physical object, unmediated by the trite explanations of the guide, that such experiences are rendered meaningful. To be in the position of an outsider, not simply of an outsider group but of an incommensurable individuality, is to possess a privileged vision. One of the few times he gives a voice to the Spanish people in the text is to cite common yet perverse explanations for Spain's relative economic and political backwardness. Being of the nation of which they are expressing their opinion deprives them of the capacity to see the truth of its condition.

Nooteboom does not apologize for the inconsistencies and contradictions of his quest. He recognizes that as a Dutchmen of the twenty-first century he will never be accepted as belonging to the abstract, historical Spain that is his obsession. Rather, he is insistent about his status as an outsider. Finding himself alone again in a church gazing at the tombs of Aragonese Kings he reflects that if they should come back to life, "when they slide the stone lids off their resting places they will recognise everything around them, except me" (Nooteboom 1992: 312). And similarly, a familiar theme within the narrative is an awareness, real or imagined, of a dismissive attitude towards him of the locals in Spain; when he knocks upon the door of the monastery of Beatus in Cantabria, only to be ignored again, he betrays his sensibility to being an outsider when he complains that "I continue to be excluded" (Nooteboom 1992: 202). This raises questions as to what the journey is meant to achieve. The pervading sense of isolation – he wanders alone, and there are few conversations recorded – seems to be at odds with the idea that he feels that he belongs in Spain. Whatever it is of Spain that Nooteboom identifies with – the culture, the landscape, the obsession with death – it does not seem to be the people.

Countering this essential element of social detachment is a physical intimacy with things that allows for the bringing forth to presence that European culture that Nooteboom identifies so closely with.[4] An important early medieval Christian text is preserved in the Cantabrian monastery, Beatus' illuminated *Commentary* upon Saint John's Apocalypse, but, refused entry Nooteboom is left merely with reproductions from the book on display. With reproductions though, something essential is lacking: "I want the shock of the real, I want to run my finger over the parchment when no one is looking. Nothing can beat that sensation, a thousand years melting away under the tip of your finger to reveal the monk in his scriptorium hunched over his cabinet of horrors." (Nooteboom 1992: 202) Communing with the past is a physical act. It is through the body, signifying the condition of absolute individuality, that the connections are made through which the world is brought to presence. Even in relation to discourse, Nooteboom is drawn to the very physical presence of words, "I am almost physically in love with the Greek alphabet, I delight in mouthing the Greek syllables even when the precise meaning of the words escapes me" (Nooteboom 1992: 210). It seems that he is drawn to language not principally because it provides him with access to discourses but because of its relation to his own bodily experiences. It is through escaping from the community of people, disparaged as the thoughtless masses, and a discourse that bypasses the personal experiences of the individual, that Nooteboom is free to explore his own being in a world.

Yet, Nooteboom in imagining the conditions of a more authentic belonging than that which prevails in modernity, wants to look nostalgically back in history towards a homogeneous world, united by the single overwhelming worldview of Christianity, as the model of community. In the historic city of Soria Nooteboom meditates upon the profuse religious imagery that still abounds upon its buildings,

all those stories and admonitions and decorations that were carved a thousand years ago by master craftsmen and that survive here in the dry, harsh climate of Soria, they are truly worthy of pilgrimage [...] The decorations are often miniatures in stone, and if you want to read what the images have to say, you must come armed with a dictionary of Biblical and Christian icons and symbols. I confess to a heartfelt irritation when I cannot interpret precisely what the pictures are trying to tell me. What used to be common knowledge is now the preserve of experts. (Nooteboom 1992: 25)

---

4   Said also notes that "the pathos of exile is the loss of contact with the solidity and the satisfaction of earth" (Said 2001: 142).

Yet, as the journey of exploration he undertakes to reveal it progresses, the real essence of belonging becomes apparent, and it is not that of the traditional ideal of community, of shared beliefs and a shared discourse. As a man of modernity Nooteboom is infected with an awareness of an individual selfhood that he cannot rid himself of and which is challenged by such a community. The journey is as much an exploration of the self as it is of the European heritage that Nooteboom perceives a defining Spain.

Why Spain?

There is also the question of why, of all the countries Nooteboom is familiar with should it be Spain that he imagines himself as belonging to? It could be argued that Nooteboom's attachment to Spain reflects upon him personally in two distinct ways. Firstly, in the context of Europe as a mosaic of national identities it can be explained as the allure of the exotic Other which, with its dramatic scorched landscapes and traditional cultural association with extremes of passion, would likely capture the imagination of a northern European living in the relatively benign landscape of a restrained Protestant Holland. The Spanish character Nooteboom identifies draws upon a familiar stereotype, with his descriptions of Spain as "brutish, anarchic, egocentric, cruel" and "chaotic, dreamy," and "irrational." (Nooteboom 1992: 5) Also, through his own Catholic upbringing and education, Nooteboom has been provided with the vocabulary giving him access into a Spanish culture so infused by Christian ideas and imagery. Certainly, the Spain Nooteboom uncovers embodies the essential elements of the European cultural heritage he subscribes to:

A reckless thought: if you took hold of Spain by the edges and dragged it with giant's strength over the Pyrenees to lay it on top of France, much of what now remains hidden from most people would be suddenly part of the treasure house that is the European cultural heritage. (Nooteboom 1992: 44)

And which allows him to state that "sometimes it is as if Spain is out to preserve the past for the rest of Europe" (Nooteboom 1992: 40).

Is there, though, a connection to be made between his choice of Spain as the locale for his pilgrimage and the methodology of exploration Nooteboom follows. There is the other Nooteboom to the one who thinks of himself as located so centrally within the European cultural heritage. There is the inveterate traveller who has spent most of his adult life wandering across the globe. He is a constant pilgrim, in permanent exile from any place that could claim to define his identity. And it is the proposition that the essential basis of Nooteboom's identification with Spain derives not from a desire to re-engage with his childhood Catholicism or from a romanticized attraction to a stereotype of a Mediterranean naturalness, but from his life as a pilgrim that is to be explored. Could it be that Nooteboom the pilgrim is drawn to Spain because he perceives the Spanish sense of community such that he identifies with it not as a European national but as a figure of exile?

Spain as a Pilgrimage Community

It is significant that for Nooteboom the city that most encapsulates the essence of Spain should be neither Madrid, the geographical and political center, nor Toledo, for many centuries, the historical capital, but Santiago de Compostela, together with Jerusalem and Rome one of the three principal sites of pilgrimage in European history. What does designating a pilgrimage site as a symbolic capital signify with regard to how Spain is characterized as a nation? Spain as a country is made of many different parts. Apart from considerable variations of geography, several different languages are spoken, Castilian, Valenciano, Catalan, Galego and Vasco, and in its history it has absorbed civil war and eight hundred years of Muslim occupation. Nooteboom does not gloss over the heterogeneity of Spain: "The love of each man and woman for the native soil, the affinity with the region, its language – all these things transcend the idea of nationhood. That's the way it is now and that is the way it was in the past." (Nooteboom 1992: 19) Yet he insists upon the virtue of its unity which it becomes his task to affirm, and as an outsider it is he who has the vantage point from which to recognise the continuity and connections that make a national identity. He is constantly observing the unchanging nature of practices and places in Spain. Within Spanish buildings different architectural styles representing distinct European epochs harmonise to a coherent whole:

The notions one might entertain about architectural purism, which invariably arise when someone tries to put an office block up next to a seventeenth-century canal house, do not function in this sort of space. The exterior of the building is Romanesque, the cross-vaults are Gothic, the tomb of Don Lupo Marco is a masterpiece of Renaissance art, the sacristy door is particularly exuberant baroque, but still the eye does not balk. (Nooteboom 1992: 11)

What is at issue then is the question of what gives to Spain its unity? For Nooteboom an important element of the unity of Spain is to be found in a cultural heritage that takes its vocabulary from the twin pillars of European culture – the Greco-Roman classical inheritance and Christianity, a heritage with which, in his mind as being first and foremost a Western European, he identifies personally. Recollecting from his youth being taught the classics of Cicero, Livy, Caesar and Ovid, he admits, "I can't conceive of my life without Latin, I feel as if the part of me that stayed behind in that world is actually growing more robust as I get older. Who knows, the slow homecoming has already begun." (Nooteboom 1992: 209) But what gives special force to this cultural identity in Spain is an underlying *ethic* of belonging.

More than any other country in Western Europe Spain is unified by a single expression of faith. With the conclusion of the Christian re-conquest of the peninsula in the fifteenth century the Jews and Muslims who had refused to convert to Christianity were expelled from the country and the Inquisition was installed to ensure that those that remained were true to their new faith. To be Spanish was to adhere to the Catholic religion, which gave to a Spanish notion of identity a moral imperative. Spanish art, music and culture were not closed to influences from outside – there even emerged a particular architectural style, termed Mozarabic, incorporating Islamic styles within Christian religious buildings. The difference that could not be tolerated within Spain was that of another religion, a difference not of an identity so much as a principle of community.

The close association of a national identity with a religious doctrine gives to that identity an added moral imperative. Throughout his travels through Spain Nooteboom retains the sensibility of a stranger, yet only with his account of his stay in the Basque country does this translate into a state of acute discomfort, of a consciousness of not belonging as a danger. This is not simply accounted for by a reflection upon the activities of Eta, rather Nooteboom is sensitive to a difference that resists identification within the broader church that is Spain. The Basque sense of a separate identity crosses a line for Nooteboom: to refuse to participate within an ecumenical debate of what it means to be Spanish is a form of heresy.

But Nooteboom conceives of the essence of Spanish identity not simply in terms of adherence to the doctrine of the Catholic Church. It is not the superimposition of a Christian identity upon a pre-formed national entity. Rather, it is the pilgrimage tradition lying at the hcart of Christian doctrine as the allegory for earthly life itself that is the defining means by which Nooteboom engages with the Spanish identity and which makes of his experience of Spain an imagining of a radically distinctive kind of community.

Suggestive of the development within Nooteboom's narrative of a representation of Spain as an altogether differently conceptualized national community is his ambivalent attitude towards Spain's relationship with Europe. Despite Nooteboom's evident appreciation of the deep infiltration of Spanish culture by European ideas and styles in religion, art, architecture, and literature, he insists that "Spain has never really been a part of Europe". If Spanish identity is recognized to be profoundly indebted to a European cultural heritage how is it that Spain is not to be regarded as a European country? And, if it is that this insistence upon an estrangement from Europe is to be explained by Nooteboom's emerging consciousness of a different basis for communal identity within Spain to that of the predominant European model of the nation-state, the question arises as to how this other conceptualization of community is configured.

It has already been noted how the theme of the stranger is central to the book. It is not only that Nooteboom actively seeks solitude for himself but that he observes as characteristic indifference on the part of the Spanish he encounters towards his presence. He knocks repeatedly to gain entrance to a chapel but is kept waiting: "At long last a distrustful little old woman opens the door and sells me a ticket, muttering to herself all the while." (Nooteboom 1992: 36) And at Albarracín he sees a priest in the church, "we look at each other, have nothing to say [...]" (Nooteboom 1992: 44). And as if in response to his being constantly received so dispassionately by those he meets they are only granted an appearance in the text as background, as curators of a historical landscape rather than real, living individuals. But it is consistent that the Spanish refusal to welcome his presence should confirm to Nooteboom his belief that Spain is the place where he belongs. It is not to demonstrate the breakdown of his relation with the Spanish people but represents a necessary act of disengagement that preludes any authentic act of communion.

Disengaged from the social, Nooteboom's re-engagement with the world takes place at the most elemental level. As a foreigner in a strange country Nooteboom has a heightened awareness of the very physical presence of Spain: "I often think I should have been born here, but perhaps it is the other way round: the very circumstances of my birth in the marshy green lowlands has made me sensitive to the temptations of harshness and stone." (Nooteboom 1992: 271) As he states of the religious imagery adorning Christian churches and cathedrals, "how much stronger is an image conjured up by words than the words themselves, when that image is capable of transcending its own verbal origins" (Nooteboom 1992: 104). The image works upon the conscious mind through the body. The text remains in the abstract world of discourse, whilst the image emerges to be a part of the physical world that impacts upon the individual in their corporeal presence. For much of the text Nooteboom is in dialogue with images – with paintings, sculptures, carvings and photographs. His journey through Spain is testimony to his conviction that he will get closer to the truth of an event if he is himself proximate to the place or physical representation of that event. In the northern mountains, Nooteboom comes across the remains of a church of the early Middle Ages, and imagines the scene of its consecration by Gennadius of Astorga:

Bishop, mitre, staff, an autumn day, chilly mountain air. They consecrate a church, a man carves an inscription in stone, the event must be recorded. That sounds active, and the result is passive: I take part in that historical event and reactivate it by imparting it. (Nooteboom 1992: 233)

When the text and present reality coincide, as in the case with his reading of a copy of *La Vanguardia* left to be picked up in a café, he avoids the text. Instead he concentrates upon describing the report of the murder of a senior military figure in the Spanish army by ETA through a detailed description of the photographs printed in the newspaper. Through the lens of the camera Nooteboom is able to dissect the story imagining the events through the vision of his own eyes.

It is reason that renders discourses as compelling: their persuasiveness derives more essentially from an internal coherency than a relation to the physical. But pilgrims journey to a site to bear witness themselves to the truth of an event that had been transcribed in a text. The pilgrim, through the embracing of poverty and hardship, the exposure of their body to the elements, experiences the physical world as a non-world, what the Greeks termed *physis*. *Physis* would translate into the modern term 'nature' but this would not capture the essential lack of structure to the Greek understanding of *physis*. Standing in opposition to *nomos*, the order of reason and law, *physis* represents a primeval chaos that persists beneath the order of a world transcribed as a discourse. Important to the pilgrimage's purpose of the experience of the truth is maintaining this connection to the openness of *physis*. And it is at the site of this openness to the physical world that there is the common ground of the community of humanity. It is the intimacy of this engagement with the earth that is the measure of the truth of the human community, not the superstructure of a cultural discourse which has, in modernity in particular, become distanced from this authentic moment of exposure. Pilgrimage is the chosen way of finding oneself not only because it is analogous to the journey of life, but also because it is to escape from an estranged discourse, a discourse of a society that has become disengaged from a deeper reality of an essential humanity.

Nooteboom's descriptions of Spain link Spanish culture to a primal relation of *nomos* to *physis*. Spain is described as a primordial country; the forms of the landscape have not been able to contain the forces of nature:

The mountains themselves look like sightless, savage beasts, the earth is grey, black, brown, yellow, the wind blows where it pleases and buffets the car, the weather is determined to wear down these mountains, a crazily contorted tree clings precariously to the grey rock face, spectres, figures roaming in the mist, black stripes against the mountainside, "the devil has shat here," the peaks are hidden in the clouds scudding along at the same speed as my car, greasy and gaunt, there the Beast cooks his infernal stew. (Nooteboom 1992: 203)

The Spanish land and climate is harsh, savage and hostile to human life, foretelling the excesses of a Spanish history marked by conflict and violence. Nooteboom actively avoids the experience of a benign Spain. He seems only to visit the verdant north in the winter, when it is exposed to the wind and the cold, and similarly, his appearances in the south occur in the intense heat of the summer. There is an intimacy of the relationship between the physical structures of civilization in Spain and the land: buildings emerge from the natural terrain as a direct response to it, continuing in dialogue as they stand:

> Your field of vision seems to be filled with nothing but earth. And then you notice a shape in the landscape, which at first you take to be a natural mound or outcrop, then it looks like a gigantic inanimate body sprawled on a hill or in the fold of a mountain [...] a bastion, a castle, a fortress, pierced by the wind and eroded by time.

Monasteries and churches are presented as sanctuaries from land they inhabit, their cool, dark and calm interiors contrasted with the intense heat and brightness of the Spanish day. In the province of Soria, the epitome of Spain's austere landscape, Nooteboom confesses, "I seek refuge from the heat in the monastery of Veruela. It's like slamming the door on the plain behind you and stepping into a different, cooler, world." (Nooteboom 1992: 9)

The timelessness of Spain is expressed through this linkage to nature:

> the mass of the land remains unperturbed, lies there patiently, pushes trees and wheat skyward, submits to fishing, hunting and the waging of wars, consents to be called kingdom, province, country, see, caliphate, free state, allows itself to be divided by those arbitrary, rarely geographical, man-made and hence illusory yet existing boundaries that are frontiers, giving in to a succession of name changes while remaining true to itself. (Nooteboom 1992: 38-39)

Objects made of wood rather than aluminium, or a "lamplight tawny with tobacco smoke instead of soul destroying neon", symbolize a Spain prior to the material progress of modernity "messed up so much of what was old and authentic" (Nooteboom 1992: 21-22). The authentic in Spain is that which has retained this connection to the way of being of its antediluvian beginnings.

And the people too are a product of this landscape, a humanity that is raw, coarse, stripped to its bare essence. The Spanish people he encounters communicate with glances, gestures, grunts, reminiscent of a time before language; he is met by a monk visiting a monastery "with a vague wave [...] he doesn't speak" (Nooteboom 1992: 10). Twice he recalls hearing the meaningless sounds of the shouts of a madman. On each occasion only he is disturbed by it. Those around him do not react to the noise, they do not think of it as sufficiently extraordinary to warrant their attention. On each occasion Nooteboom moves out into the open in search of the origins of the noise, and he becomes aware of his own estrangement from his surroundings, as though he is listening to an echo from a primeval, pre-linguistic past that only he can hear.

I head in the direction of the lowing sound and then I set eyes on him, in the middle of a Renaissance patio: a lonely self-absorbed imbecile spinning around in circles like a giant, earth-bound butterfly among the columns, shouting incessantly. The palace he lives in is an asylum, the locals are evidently used to the noise because they walk by without a glance in his direction, only I stop and look at him and at the others, who return my look from a world in which mine counts for nothing. But what is nothing? For in my consciousness, too, this lowering noise now belongs to the world, and when I reach the end of the street I still hear it, but it also spreads over the landscape lying below ... out across the hillside, and the shouting is part of it all. (Nooteboom 1992: 280-81)

The amorphous, incoherent vocal utterances of the madman represent the essence of language: the word at its very origin in search of a meaning. In the same way, as he closes upon his destination in Santiago, he admits of the power of "the sound of a name [...] to lure me off my course": "Burgos, Castrojeriz, Frómista, Carrión de los Condes, Valencia de Don Juan, León, the Panteón de los Reyes, each name a temptation and a memory, like sirens they rise up on either side of the road to seduce me."

The pilgrim, embracing hardship, walking, ideally barefoot, is restored to an essential relation to the earth; to a re-engagement with the origins of cultural discourse, when words emerged to name physical objects and the chaos of *physis* would challenge the human being to the instigation of an explanatory ordering discourse of *nomos*. The Spanish has a peculiar relation to the land because the land is so hard and primeval, so abstract, so physically present, which is the experience of the world of pilgrimage itself. It is what gives to being in the world the feeling of exile, of being ejected from Eden.

But one has to be aware that the mad in literature are often possessed of great insight. The incoherent cries of the madman are of the sounds of the earth, and the wisdom that lies behind them is the recognition of the impossibility of the finite human being at home in the physical world. What is required is to make of such cries a nomenclature, to create a discourse as an escape from the sense of alienation in an unknowable world. But all such discourses must be contingent, which brings us, as Derrida observed, to the "crisis of decision" of "the choice and division between the two ways separated by Parmenides [...] the way of logos and the non-way, the labyrinth, the *palintrope* in which logos is lost; the way of meaning and the way of non-meaning; of Being and of non-being." (Derrida 1978: 62) Which is no choice at all. Yet, as Roughley shows, Derrida thinks philosophers and writers such as Husserl and Joyce imagine the possibility of returning to this origin of all beginnings: Both writers

Husserl through univocity and Joyce through equivocity sought to escape the limited "factual historical structure[s]" of their respective traditions in order to return to the "common origin" of the "zero point," where all "determined contradictions, in the form of given, factual historical structures, can appear, and appear as relative to this zero point at which determined meaning and nonmeaning come together in their common origin." (Derrida 1978: 56)

This connection to the time of the decision for being in the presence of non-being finds its most striking expression in the work of his favorite artist Zurbarán. Contemplating Zurbarán's paintings in the sacristy of the monastery at Guadalupe Nooteboom is transported to the moment of creation:

And suddenly I dream of the silence which must have reigned here while Zurbarán was painting the silence of the monastery, the silence of the village which was even smaller at the time, the silence of the empty countryside all about. The only noises are those made by the animals, the wind, the human voices, the monastery bells, the monk's chant. (Nooteboom 1992: 144)

The silence is of the absence of discourse, the sounds are the background noises of life being lived as it is. Zurbarán does not turn this silence into discourse but into images which do not close off this reality of the past, but in some way capture the essence of the world as it is present. And in this way, Zurbarán's art is profoundly spiritual. And Zurbarán's palette reinforces this sense of communion with the physical reality of his surroundings. Zurbarán paints with the colors of the earth, his red is the color of blood, his blue of the magpie. And it is a richer palette than that provided by manifestation of the Christian discourse that dominated the medieval perception of reality. He notes how Zurbarán brings attention to the profusion of resources available to reality to presence itself beyond the simple shades of text upon parchment and paper:

The plethora of monks sometimes makes you forget there are other colours besides brown and grey and white and black, until he himself reminds you with the green and blue and another blue and yet another blue and gold and red and pink in *The Adoration of the Magi* at Grenoble. (Nooteboom 1992: 133)

But it is an excessive reality that it is inclined to be retreated from. Throughout the work Nooteboom contrasts the darkness of the interiors of buildings with the light of the outside world. Visiting Leon he reflects upon a European cultural heritage of which an authoritative account could be contained within the works of one man, Saint Isidore of Carthage:

In the Romanesque church that bears his name I sit and think it all over. Visigoths, exegetes, the mysteries of the tetramorph, lion, bull, eagle, man, which are called the 'four living creatures" of the Apocalypse in the Book of Revelation, the church around me, the royal tombs below, the mutually fortifying reflections which are so potent in this place and which will forfeit their validity in the bustling world outside, while that world would not exist without this ancestry, and yet, when I step out into the street it is as if I am falling through a trap door into the light, a light that is brilliant and effervescent. (Nooteboom 1992: 216)

The darkness of the interiors resemble the settings of the scenes of many of Zurbarán's paintings; an enveloping blackness that gives to the paintings a purity of discourse. Enacted upon an amorphous backdrop the images in the painting stand clear and comprehensible, there is nothing to distract the eye from the central narrative. And it is this coherency of discourse that is the allure of belonging to the pilgrim traveller. But the darkness is also suggestive of a dreamlike quality to the story being told. The dream is a familiar theme in pilgrimage narratives; it links the experience of pilgrimage to the metaphysical, to the unchaining of the possible from a deference to a received determination of the world. The darkness also signifies that for a discourse to emerge there is a necessary process of separation from the physical world; a discourse is an act of creation for which the human being as creator must take responsibility. The tension of the moment of either being or non-being, of Derrida's "crisis of decision" is not to be resolved here but accepted as of the essential condition of existence.

But, as Nooteboom becomes aware, the "factual historical structures" of one's tradition are an integral part of who one is. It is as the book nears its end that he begins to reference his homeland and the inescapable impression it has made upon him. He refers to the history of Holland as "*my* history", as "the history of my native country" (Nooteboom 1992: 127) as he is forced to admit that "My home is not Castile, nor is it León. One does not choose the country of one's birth." (Nooteboom 1992: 310) No matter how often or how far he departs from Holland a part of him will always remain there, he cannot escape the consequences of his Dutch identity, as signified by the memories he holds of the landscape and his childhood education. The realization as he journeys through Spain that it must of necessity remain elusive as a destination, never fully attainable as a place for his selfhood to be, is foreshadowed at the beginning of the book by his refusal, stood within the Cathedral of Santiago, to claim for himself the status of a true pilgrim of the Camino: "in grasping that pillar I have never felt the emotion that comes after walking for more than a year to arrive. I was not a man of the Middle Ages, I was not a believer, I arrived by car." (Nooteboom 1992: 3) His journeying by car symbolizes an essential alienation from Spain, both as a person out of time, and as a foreign national who could never belong to the country as someone who has walked through its landscapes from birth.

However, there is a level in which he still imagines an identity with Spain, stating of Spain and Holland, "I am at home and not at home in both," (Nooteboom 1992: 295) There is a sense in which Nooteboom imagines European nations as representing different constitutive elements of a complete personality. He writes, for example, of Italy as representing the spirit of the heart, Holland the reason of the mind, Spain the passion of the soul. But Nooteboom is not simply saying that by belonging to Spain as well as Holland he is embracing the passionate side of his personality. Spain as it appears in his Journey is not simply one nation amongst many. Rather Spain represents an idea, a way of being, that transcends simplistic notions of national stereotypes. In a Spain where the past is not severed from the present, where time lapses "into an infinitely slower measure", (Nooteboom 1992: 310-11) Nooteboom imagines the possibility of a different kind of identity. To be at home in Holland is to recognize that one exists within a given discourse. To be at home in Spain is to reclaim a self from within this determinative context, to experience the world in its physical presence is to experience the self in its radical individuality. But this experience of an absolute self manifests itself as a profound obligation to take responsibility for the discourse that makes of the experience of the world a meaningful whole. Nooteboom, like many pilgrims, translates the experiences of his journey into text.

There is a profound unity to the pilgrim communion. Past and present merge as pilgrims follow in each other's footsteps, and allegorically, the footsteps of the original journey of Christ's passion. On the pilgrimage journey the transience of existence is underscored, it is in part a re-enactment of the journey of life. But this becomes a necessary prologue to the pilgrim's realization of a higher identification of the self within the community of humanity as a whole: the city of man supplanted by the city of God as the true home of the soul. On the pilgrimage route the pilgrim experiences the transcendence of the self: that the self is not secure immured within the fixed identities founded upon a place within the world but deprived of the full possibilities of its being. Delimited worldly communities such as the nation choose to forget that they are constructed identities and close off an essential relationship with the physical world that is also of the essence of the corporeal human being. Nooteboom's decision to remain as Other within an historically and physically grounded Spain is the recognition that it is his life as a traveller that gives him access to an originary consciousness of belonging, of the authenticity of being at home in homelessness.

Conclusion

Pilgrimage narratives introduce us to a different idea of community. The book begins with the author placing his hand in the impression of a splayed hand on the pillar at the Cathedral of Santiago de Compostela. It is a symbolic act of affiliation to the pilgrimage commune and he admits, writing of himself in the first person, that he is not as yet deserving of such a claim. He remains an individual, alone within himself, which, in contemporary terms, is as a Dutch national in a foreign land. The book concludes with his repeating the act. He has come to relinquish the aspiration of proving that his authentic self is as a Spanish national. But he does achieve a belonging to Spain, not as a nation, but as a symbol of pilgrimage, through the pillar at Santiago which connects him spiritually to all humanity which in their true essence as pilgrims.

The narrative explores on several levels notions of departure and arrival. Any journey involves a simple movement from place to place, but with the pilgrimage there is also a departure from a specific framework of meaning correlated to a fixed society. This does not necessarily suggest a break with the prevailing discourse of truth associated to that framework but it does imply the detachment of such a discourse from the familiar social and physical landscape constitutive

                              John Outhwaite

of the selfhood of the individual. In such a circumstance a foundational discourse of existence retains its authority through its association with the norms and precepts of that environmental framework, but, as a free-floating discourse, it exists contingently. Such a discourse can only command adherence by virtue of its being re-grounded in timeless and universal principles.

The pilgrimage is just such a discourse. It is the communion of strangers: the condition of belonging to the pilgrimage is to essentially exist as a stranger, both to every other and the world. It is through the recognition of the condition of being a stranger that the essential commonality of being is exposed. Difference is neutralized as a differentiating force; rather it directs us to the true condition of commonality. Nooteboom's is a journey of exclusion; he embraces the solitude that affirms his status as a pilgrim/stranger. His is the Christian notion of sojourning upon the earth, who conceives of his true being in the metaphysical realm of the kingdom of heaven. Thus, to sojourn on the earth as a pilgrim, to be at home in homelessness, is the authentic condition of belonging of the human being.

Bibliography

Anderson, B.R. 1983. *Imagined Communities: Reflections on the Origin and Spread of Nationalism*. London: Verso.

Bhabha, Homi K. 1990. *Nation and Narration*. London: Routledge

—. 1994. *The Location of Culture*. London: Routledge.

—. 1996. 'Cultures in Between' in S. Hall, Paul du Gay (eds.) *Questions of Cultural Identity*. London: Sage.

Derrida, Jacques. 1978. Cited in: Roughley, Alan. 1999. *Reading Derrida, Reading Joyce*. Florida: University of Florida Press.

Nooteboom, Cees. 1992. *Roads to Santiago*. London: Harvill Press

Said, Edward. 2001. *Reflections on Exile and Other Literary and Cultural Essays*. London: Granta.

Schama, S. 1995. *Landscape and Memory*. London: HarperCollins.

Turner, Victor and Edith. 1978. *Image and Pilgrimage in Christian Culture*. Oxford: Basil Blackwell.

Weill, Simone. 2002 (1952). *The Need for Roots*. London, New York: Routledge.

5. Catholic Approaches to Jerusalem:
Fragmentation and Continuity of Identities – Evelyn
Waugh's *Helena* and Muriel Spark's *The Mandelbaum
Gate*

Martin Potter

Evelyn Waugh's historical novel *Helena* and Muriel Spark's novel of
intrigue and adventure *The Mandelbaum Gate* both portray protagonists with complex identities – identities which mirror in important
ways the identities of the authors – in quests for self-understanding
and resolution of inner unrest through travel. Their journeys consist in,
or culminate in, pilgrimages to Jerusalem and the surrounding holy
sites. In each case, the complexity and fragmentation within the character of the protagonist (reflecting that in the author) is compared with
the complexities and layerings in the identity of Jerusalem, while ultimately, through the notion of pilgrimage, a unified sense of identity
is achieved, both for the protagonists' view of the city and for the protagonists' view of their own selves. In this achieved sense of identity,
the various historical strands are affirmed as part of a spiritual whole.
I shall explore first the complex and to some extent parallel personal
webs of identity which each author creates for the protagonist, showing how issues of religious identity and nationality intersect and come
into conflict in similar ways for both authors and their protagonists. I
shall then examine how in each novel Jerusalem, at first approach,
presents conflicts and layerings of identity which echo those of the
protagonists and lead to an encounter in which the protagonists must
decode an elusive Jerusalem, as well as reflect on themselves. Finally,
I shall discuss how the idea of pilgrimage offers, through this encounter of personality and place, a way to the reconciliation and fulfillment
of identities which the protagonists of both novels eventually achieve.[1]

---

[1]   Recent Catholic thinking has explored two important notions, that of sacra-
       mentality (the way that the spiritual and physical worlds interact) and that of

Issues of personal identity and conflicts or feelings of irresolution within the self are key elements of both novels. The importance of these problems for both novelists can be related to their status as members of the Catholic minority in the United Kingdom. This minority has felt itself to be marginalized since the Reformation, and falls outside the dominant state churches, the Church of England and the Church of Scotland, which, since the Reformation, have been central to the formation of national identity, whether English, Scottish, or British. Twentieth-century Catholic British writers have regularly taken the stance of writing against the majority Protestant culture in Britain, often seeing it as not only non- and anti-Catholic, but also suspecting it of being largely secular.[2] The sense of marginalization and non-inclusion is felt particularly poignantly by those whose Catholicism does not result from a Catholic ethnic background, and who therefore cannot resolve the conflict between their British identity and their Catholicism with the help of an alternative Catholic national identity. Many of the most prominent twentieth-century British Catholic writers have been in this situation (e.g. G. K. Chesterton, Evelyn Waugh, David Jones, Muriel Spark, Graham Greene), which has been the result of their being converts. Being a convert raises further complexities, since converts have grown up with another religious background, which remains part of their personal history, and they may also feel themselves to be a minority within a minority among Catholics, the majority of whom are not converts. Some of these writers have sought a reconciliation between their religious and national identities by reconnecting with a pre-reformation past (e.g. Chesterton with medieval Catholic England, and David Jones with early Welsh and British history). On the other hand, others (such as Graham Greene, Muriel Spark, and, to some extent, Evelyn Waugh) have em-

---

the development of traditions, and the necessity of understanding those traditions in narrative form. Thinkers such as David Jones, Alasdair MacIntyre and Charles Taylor work with these ideas. The ideas of sacramentality and of a narrative of the dynamic development of traditions and identities allow one to connect the arrival at the pilgrimage site, its place, and the departure from it, with personal spiritual development, and the development of cultural traditions, since spiritual realities must both be enacted, and embodied in physical action – as I explain further below.

2   For British Catholics' sense of being an "alien minority" see Woodman 1991: xiii.

phasized a cosmopolitan atmosphere in much of their writing, taking advantage of their sense that British Catholics can more easily understand the non-British world, and are more internationally oriented, than their Protestant counterparts. Evelyn Waugh, in particular, explored in some of his writings the culture of English recusants, that is, those English Catholics belonging to families which remained Catholic continuously since the Reformation, forming a very tightly knit circle of their own. In *Helena* and *The Mandelbaum Gate* Waugh and Spark transpose their own British Catholic convert identities in adapted form onto their protagonists, whom they then take out of Britain and send into a cosmopolitan world.

Evelyn Waugh's *Helena*, published in 1950, is a historical novel, in which the legendary mother of the Emperor Constantine, in the fourth century A.D., sets out to find the True Cross in the Holy Land, although much of the novel covers her early life. She does not arrive in the Holy Land until late in the novel, when she is already old, being more than seventy when she goes to Rome, which is before she goes to Jerusalem (Waugh 1963: 90). This is a comparatively late novel of Waugh (who was born in 1903), and he chooses St. Helena as a figure whose early life is obscure historically, so he can take advantage of the traditional British legends which present her as being British-born, although there are other versions of her origins. Waugh, who was a convert of English background, thus represents himself in a woman of British background, who grows up as a pagan in late Roman Britain, and who is converted to Christianity later in life. The first two chapters of the novel portray Helena as a young woman who has grown up at the court of a local king, in Colchester, now in the East of England. Helena's growing up as a pagan parallels Waugh's non-Catholic childhood, while Waugh presents the society in which she grows up as non-Christian, but with some Christians present, again forming a parallel with the mainly non-Catholic environment in which Waugh grew up in early twentieth-century England, in which there would nevertheless have been some Catholic presence. By placing Helena's childhood in a location which is now in England, but in a period before England existed, and when the area would have been inhabited by the Britons, who are the cultural ancestors of the Welsh, Waugh creates a potential ambiguity in her national identity, from the point of view of setting up correspondences with the twentieth century. He exploits this ambiguity by introducing anachronisms which suggest both modern

English and modern Welsh identity. Waugh admits that he is going to use anachronisms "as a literary device" in the preface (Waugh 1963: 9), and these anachronisms, in linking the third- and fourth-century action with a twentieth-century atmosphere, make the contemporary relevance intended by Waugh all the clearer, as well as perhaps contributing a humorous effect.[3] Helena's passion for horse-riding and hunting suggests a twentieth-century English young person of an aristocratic background. Her plain-speaking and practicality, as well, are likely to represent aspects of modern English identity. On the other hand, Waugh acknowledges the Welsh association in making Helena's father a patron of singing and poetry. In calling Helena's father "King Coel", Waugh fuses the Welsh and the English associations by spelling in a Welsh way the name of a legendary ancient British king, who features in an English nursery rime as 'Old King Cole'. Her being red-haired (Waugh 1963: 13) also emphasizes her Britishness.

After marriage to Constantius the Roman, Helena leaves Britain and is introduced into the cosmopolitan world of the continental Roman Empire, where she is not shown to have any contact with other people of British origin. She is portrayed adapting well to the various locations in the Roman Empire where she lives, such as Trier, Dalmatia, and Rome. She even considers settling permanently on the Dalmatian coast after she has been divorced by Constantius, when he is declared future successor of the Emperor of the West, although by the end of the novel she regards Rome as home and wishes to be buried there (Waugh 1963: 158). So Helena exemplifies the ease with being abroad and outside British society which British Catholic novelists and their protagonists often show. An example is Evelyn Waugh's Guy Crouchback in the *Sword of Honour* novels, who has grown up partly in Italy and is fluent in Italian, and, like Helena, performs a partially autobiographical function for Waugh. However, the features of Englishness which she retains throughout are her practicality and her skepticism, both redolent of associations with British empiricism,[4] which shape her rejection of pagan mystery cults, as when she derides the fashionable Neo-Platonic theories of her ex-tutor Marcias in Chapter 6 (Waugh 1963: 81-85). Another example of her skeptical empiricism appears when, having arrived in Jerusalem and summoned ex-

---

[3]	On anachronisms in *Helena* see also Patey 1998: 294-95.

[4]	See Wykes 1999: 162.

perts in order to gather information relevant to her search, she is impatient with fanciful accounts of the origins and composition of the Cross (Waugh 1963: 140-41). It is her receiving definite answers to her when- and where-questions on Christianity (Waugh 1963: 85), which she had been unable to obtain in relation to pagan religion – when asking Constantius about the cult of Mithras (Waugh 1963: 66-67), or Marcias about Neo-Platonism (Waugh 1963: 83-84) – that precedes and seems to contribute to her conversion. After her conversion, she is seen as having gained a sense of belonging to a new community, the Church, and attends liturgy as an ordinary member of the congregation – despite being Empress Dowager – both in Rome, at the Lateran basilica (Waugh 1963: 93), and in Bethlehem, at the shrine of the Nativity (Waugh 1963:92). While in Jerusalem, she lives in a convent and shares the tasks of the nuns (Waugh 1963: 138). Helena's finding a sense of religious community with people in various locations outside Britain reflects the experience of twentieth-century British Catholics abroad, who are able to feel a sense of belonging in places which for their Protestant counterparts are culturally inaccessible. Helena's attendance at the shrine in Bethlehem at Epiphany, the feast of the Three Kings, is also used by Waugh to emphasize her convert status, and he has her, in her prayer, describing the Three Kings as "my especial patrons ... and patrons of all late-comers" (Waugh 1963: 145) – therefore also Waugh's patrons.

In her 1965 novel *The Mandelbaum Gate*, Muriel Spark creates a protagonist, Barbara Vaughan, whose correspondences with herself are more direct than those of Helena with Evelyn Waugh, and who exhibits sharper conflicts of identity than Helena.[5] The novel is set at the same period when it is published, and Barbara is of a similar age to Spark, visiting the Holy Land at the same time that Spark did herself. Like Waugh, Helena, and Spark herself, Barbara is a convert, but unlike Waugh and Helena, and like Spark, Barbara has one Jewish and one non-Jewish parent.[6] Spark slightly adjusts Barbara's background compared with her own by giving her a Jewish mother from England

---

[5] Bold notes that there is more emotional content in *The Mandelbaum Gate* than in Spark's other novels, and that this led to her having misgivings about the novel later (Bold 1986: 78).

[6] Spark's mother had some Jewish background, through Spark's grandmother's father. The extent of Spark's Jewish background was later the basis of a controversy between her and her son – see Stannard 2009: 518.

and an English father, and has her grow up in England, whereas she herself had a Scottish-Jewish father and an English mother, and grew up in Scotland. So Spark's Scottish-English-Jewish background is simplified to an English Jewish one, while, on the other hand, Barbara's having a Jewish mother, rather than, like Spark, a Jewish father, creates an extra complexity, in that she could, from a Jewish point of view, regard herself as fully Jewish, as an Israeli guide of Polish-Jewish background points out to her on one of her tours of holy sites (Spark 1967: 27). This possibility, which has been open to Barbara, to regard herself as completely Jewish emphasizes that it has been her decision not to simplify her identity, but to insist on both elements, as she explains to an Israeli friend in Jerusalem:

My Gentile relations tried too hard to forget I was a half-Jew. My Jewish relations couldn't forget I was a half-Gentile. Actually, I didn't let them forget, either way. (Spark 1967: 37)

During flashbacks, Spark describes and contrasts Barbara's childhood holiday stays with each set of relatives: her urban Jewish relatives, the Aaronsons, in Golders Green, London, and her fox-hunting English relatives, the Vaughans, in Worcestershire, in the English countryside. Barbara finds that in Israel her conversion to Catholicism is seen as simply her choosing the Gentile rather than the Jewish side of her identity. After failing to explain herself to the Polish-Israeli guide, she is at pains to explain to her Israeli friend in Jerusalem that, to her, becoming a Catholic does not signify becoming a Gentile, and that she sees Catholicism as having Jewish origins (Spark 1967: 39-40). What would be less likely to be clear from an Israeli point of view than it would be from a British point of view is that, by becoming a Catholic, she has taken on an identity not seen as similar to their own by her Church of England relatives, and they might even regard it as the most un-English move she could make.[7] Spark repeatedly hints at the lack of comprehension a Catholic may meet with in British society. She does this both by emphasizing the way her British contacts have trouble understanding, and do not sympathize with, her difficulty in marrying Harry Clegg, the archaeologist, without his receiving an annulment from the Church of his previous marriage, and by mentioning

---

[7]   For the outsider status "par excellence" of Catholics in England, see Poitou 1985-86: 19.

anti-Catholic views expressed by Barbara's friend Miss Rickworth, with whom she has been working at a girls' boarding school in England, and by an English acquaintance, Ruth Gardnor, who looks after Barbara while she is hiding in Jordan and convalescing from scarlet fever. Spark's frustration possibly with her own experience of anti-Catholic attitudes is put into Barbara's thoughts has accused Catholics of narrow-mindedness and gullibility: after Ruth Gardnor

This was nothing new to Barbara: ever since her conversion she had met sophisticated women who, on the subject of Catholicism, sneered like French village atheists, and expected to be excused from normal good manners, let alone intelligence, on this one subject. (Spark 1967: 265)

Barbara also feels "irritation when Ricky [Miss Rickworth] let fall a remark about some Catholic dogma which revealed not only her disapproval, but a muddled notion of what the dogma was" (Spark 1967: 161). There is a social acceptability of anti-Catholicism in British circles indicated here, as well as a lack of knowledge about Catholicism, which makes the Catholic feel isolated and misunderstood. So Spark emphasizes that Barbara's decision to become a Catholic is neither an opting for the English-Anglican side of her identity, nor a rejection of her Jewish side. Spark hints at her sense of the Jewish content in Catholicism, and the connection of this with her own identity, when Barbara, recalling Dante, mentions the two testaments of the Bible "bound by love into one volume" (Spark 1967: 26).[8] Also, Barbara's detailed recollections of her experiences of celebrating Jewish Passover with her Golders Green relatives, during the same period when she was celebrating Easter with her Worcestershire relatives, can be interpreted as anticipating her later attachment to the Catholic mass, especially when she emphasizes the role of the unleavened bread. (Spark 1967: 33)[9]

As well as the divisions in her national and religious identity, Barbara also feels a conflict of personality between a calm intellectual side and a passionate side. Before visiting the Holy Land, Barbara has tended, outwardly, to display her intellectual, non-passionate side, to

---

[8] Edgecombe argues that Barbara's childhood experiences with the two sets of relatives can be compared to the two testaments of the Bible as seen by the Church Fathers (Edgecombe 1990: 74).

[9] See Sproxton 1992: 33.

the extent that her friend, Miss Rickworth, headmistress at the girls' school where she works, is convinced that Barbara will never marry, and that Barbara will eventually set up household with her. However, Barbara has been having a secret and passionate affair with an archaeologist, Harry Clegg,[10] and is frightened of revealing this to Miss Rickworth,[11] as well as hesitating about whether to marry Harry. Harry has previously been married and would need an annulment, which it is uncertain if he could obtain, to marry again from a Catholic point of view. This situation is unresolved when she starts her journey to the Holy Land. Harry Clegg is actually, at the same time, working at the Dead Sea Scrolls site on the Jordanian side of the border, but she is irresolute as to whether to visit him there, given the impasse in their relations. Barbara sees a connection between the two sides of her personality and her Jewish-Gentile division, relating her passionate side to her Jewish identity (Spark 1967: 43), although she is not sure why – it may be because of the conspicuous lack of passion which she sees in her non-Jewish English relatives. For example, her cousins, with whom she is staying, in England, when she starts her affair with Harry Clegg, fail to suspect that anything is happening, despite the clear evidence, a fact which gives Barbara a frustrated sense that they cannot understand her whole self. This misunderstanding on the part of her cousins also leads her to reevaluate her appearance and to realize "that her self-image was at variance with the image she presented to the world" (Spark 1967: 39). Barbara's divisions of character can be summed up in an oft-quoted phrase, when she describes herself as "a Gentile-Jewess, a private judging Catholic, a shy adventuress" (Spark 1967: 164), a description which Spark, in fact, uses to sum up Barbara's incipient feelings of the reconciliation of the opposites. This happens at a point well into her stay in the Holy Land, when she has just entered Jordan, but a British diplomatic friend induces her to leave her hotel in the Old City in the middle of the night, convinced that she is in danger, as I shall discuss further below. In this case, it is a recollec-

---

[10]   Kermode points out the link between Harry being an archaeologist, and truth being hidden under layers of accumulation in the novel – whether this is the truth of Barbara's or Jerusalem's identities, or the facts about the annulment process (Kermode 1971: 274-75).

[11]   Walczuk sees Barbara's need to escape from a false identity imposed on her by Miss Rickworth as a key reason for her journey to the Holy Land (Walczuk 2005: 73-74).

tion of the eccentricity of her father's English family which allows her to achieve a sense of the reconcilability of the seeming opposites in her character. So Barbara bring with her a feeling of multiple, unresolved divisions in her identity when she arrives in the Holy Land.

Both Helena and Barbara bring their personal sense of unresolvedness with them to Jerusalem, and in both cases they discover that the personal complexities they bring with them are matched by complexities of identity of place which Jerusalem presents to them. In each case, Jerusalem turns out not to be one place but a coexistence of different places, each claiming to be Jerusalem, lying side by side or even one on top of another. Barbara and Helena are faced with untangling the multiple faces of the Jerusalem they find, as they endeavor to identify Jerusalem, just as they have been trying to identify themselves.

In *Helena*, the action does not move to Jerusalem until the last three of the twelve chapters, and Helena herself is not there until the eleventh and twelfth, the tenth concentrating on the background to and anticipation of Helena's visit through the eyes of Macarius, Bishop of Jerusalem. Even though Helena starts her pilgrimage in 326 (Waugh 1963: 129), and is therefore much closer to the events of the New Testament than is Barbara Vaughan, the complexity in Jerusalem's identity as a place which she confronts is to a large extent due to the historical layerings which have already taken place in the intervening three centuries. The Jewish city of the New Testament has been destroyed by the Romans and replaced by a Roman city called Aelia Capitolina, built over the ruins. However, by the time Helena arrives, this pagan city is already beginning to give way to a Christian city, the basilica over the Holy Sepulchre already being under construction, by order of the Emperor Constantine, Helena's son. The reader learns through Macarius' recollections that the sites of the Crucifixion and Resurrection had been buried during Hadrian's building of the new city, and were known to be more or less underneath a temple of Venus, in the center of the new city. The new city had been designed as a flat rectangle laid over the hills and valleys of the previous city and environs, obliterating any trace of the sites, and obscuring their previous location outside the walls of the city (Waugh 1963: 132-33). Under Constantine's orders the whole area is excavated, the valley is emptied of the rubble with which it had been filled in, and two hills are found, one being Golgotha, the site of the Crucifixion, and the other containing Christ's tomb in its slope (Waugh 1963: 134). The exposure of the site in something like its original state, though, is short-lived, as under the plans of Constantine's architect, the hill of Golgotha is turned into a cube of rock, and the hillside around the tomb is cut away, turning it into a kind of house. (Waugh 1963: 136) This has all already happened by the time Helena arrives, and it is in a building site that she has to attempt to locate the Cross, the object of her pilgrimage. So Helena has to negotiate three historical Jerusalems in her search to locate the events of the New Testament in Jerusalem. She encounters Jewish elements (for example Antonia Tower, from Herod's palace – Waugh 1963: 137) and Roman elements (for example Pontius Pilate's praetorium) in Jerusalem, and contributes Christian elements of her own, commissioning new basilicas (at the Mount of Olives, as well as in Bethlehem – Waugh 1963: 138-39). In fact, the tripartite Jewish-Roman-Christian layering in Jerusalem reflects a similar layering in Helena, who has grown up in a Romano-British family, with stress laid both on the Celtic ancestry and the superposed citizenship of Rome, and has recently capped both with her Christian conversion. The fact that Christian Jerusalem is just beginning to be built can be seen as a parallel to Helena's late conversion, and her status (and Waugh's) as "late-comer". The discovery of the identity of place in *Helena* is presented archaeologically, digging being required to find the holy sites of the Crucifixion and Resurrection under Aelia Capitolina, and digging being required for Helena to find the True Cross under the building site of the new basilica. Helena expresses an interest in digging for identity of place right at the beginning of the novel, when as a young woman she discusses Troy with her tutor, Marcias, and insists that the site should be excavated to find remains of the ancient city. (Waugh 1963: 15) In this case also, identity of place connects with her personal identity, both in terms of her name, because Troy was the city of Helen (Waugh 1963: 15), and because there is a legend of the Britons' descent from the Trojans, as Helena mentions (Waugh 1963: 14).

Barbara Vaughan's Jerusalem is even more divided and complex than Helena's. This is partly because of the many additional historical layers accumulated since Helena's times, such as Byzantine, Arab, Ottoman, Latin Crusader, British Mandate, States of Israel and Jordan. In 1961, the year of Barbara's (and Muriel Spark's) visit, the Holy Land and Jerusalem itself are divided between Israel and Jordan.

Passage between the Israeli and Jordanian sides is via the Mandel-baum Gate, a checkpoint after which the novel is named.[12] Pilgrims aiming to visit the Christian holy sites must visit both Israel and Jordan. Nazareth is in Israel, whereas Bethlehem is in Jordan. In Jerusalem, the Church of the Holy Sepulchre and the Mount of Olives are on the Jordanian side, but the Church of the Assumption and the traditional site of the Last Supper are on the Israeli side. So Barbara is faced both with locating the Jerusalem of the Bible among the traces of the many subsequent historical layers, as well as negotiating the hostile status of the two states.

Like Helena, Barbara finds a Jerusalem and a Holy Land, which, despite their importance from a Christian point of view, are not dominated by Christians, and in which many people are pursuing other religions, or indeed none at all. On the Israeli side, the concerns relating to the building up of the newly-founded state of Israel dominate the consciousness of most of those with whom Barbara comes into contact. Barbara's first two hired guides prove uninterested in Christian shrines and keen to show her the practical achievements of the new state. Others encourage her to attend the trial of a German war criminal which is underway. In Beersheba, Barbara tells the Polish-Israeli guide, "I'm really only interested in the Beersheba of Genesis" (Spark 1967: 23), after having been shown a completely new town, to which he responds, "This is the Beersheba of Genesis." (Spark 1967: 24) While, on the one hand, Barbara partly solves this problem by hiring a car without a guide for her next tour, on the other hand, the guide's assertion that the modern town and the Old Testament site are the same place looks forward to the sense of reconciliation which eventually emerges from the novel.[13] As well as the practical face of the emerging state, Barbara also encounters those who are dedicated to religion – but not to Barbara's religion – in the Orthodox Jewish population of Jerusalem, who disapprove of her attire (Spark 1967: 14), and who would only share her interest in some of the shrines, but not others. On the Jordanian side, Barbara also finds that most people are not Christian, and her tour guide there, who is of Moslem back-

---

[12]   Malin notes that by the end of the novel the Mandelbaum Gate also represents the unity lying below the surface of division, as, unlike the gates in the walls of the Old City, it is not a real gate (Malin 1970: 107).

[13]   Edgecombe argues that it is "an imagination activated by faith" which Barbara needs to see the biblical Beersheba in the modern city (Edgecombe 1990: 69).

ground, knows the shrines in a professional way but is vague about their religious meaning. The atmosphere on the Jordanian side is one of Arab nationalism and political intrigue, the shrines themselves are surrounded by commercial opportunism, and there are even factional rivalries between the Christian groups within the shrines. At the Church of the Holy Sepulchre, for example, there is a sense of unease between the Catholic and Orthodox groups saying mass at adjacent altars simultaneously, the quieter Catholic mass being drowned out by the more musical Orthodox one. Moreover, the English priest celebrating the Catholic mass irritates the Italian custodians by giving a sermon, against instructions, holding up the program for the day. Thus, multifarious modern distractions threaten to stand between Barbara and the religious meaning she is looking for.

As already mentioned, Barbara's Jerusalem is not only divided vertically, through history, like Helena's, but also horizontally, through a geographical division between states running through the city, and for Barbara this presents particular difficulties. Barbara has arrived in Israel first, and is planning to cross from there into Jordan, which is the opposite direction from that usually taken by Christian pilgrims (Spark 1967: 68). The Jordanians do not allow people with Jewish ancestry to enter Jordan, and may think she is a spy if she does not admit to a Jewish background when she enters and they subsequently discover it, especially as she has entered from Israel. She is at risk of discovery, as she is known about by someone on the Israeli side whose family is on the Jordanian side (in fact, the brother of her Jordanian tour guide), and also because she has met an Israeli journalist who is reporting on the war crimes trial, to which a cousin of Barbara's has been summoned as an expert. Barbara worries that the journalist will mention her in an article in a way which reveals that she is partly Jewish and is planning to enter Jordan, and, in fact, the journalist does. The danger which Barbara may be in once she has entered Jordan then forms the basis for the plot of a large part of the novel – a British diplomatic acquaintance, Freddy Hamilton, fearing for her safety, "rescues" her from her Jerusalem hotel, and then hides her near Jericho, with the cooperation of the Jordanian tour guide, Suzy Ramdez. She then has to lie low near Jericho for a couple of weeks, convalescing from the scarlet fever she has caught in the hotel. As a result of this adventure, Freddy Hamilton fortuitously manages to break up a spy ring, but then afterwards mysteriously forgets the entire episode, and does not know what has happened to Barbara, who is thought to have disappeared, until she returns to West Jerusalem, on the Israeli side, helped by her tour guide and her tour guide's brother. While this episode illustrates the hostile division in the Jerusalem of the time – a hostility capable of producing fatal consequences, and felt so strongly that in Jordan even the word "Israel" may not be pronounced (Spark 1967: 11) – nevertheless underlying unities emerge. Examples of such unities are the fact of the family of Barbara's tour guide being located on both sides of the border and communicating regularly, though unofficially; the existence of archaeological work of Jewish interest, i.e. the Dead Sea Scrolls excavations, on the Jordanian side; the continued residence of a substantial Arab population on the Israeli side; the common historical background of both sides up to the end of the British Mandate; and, of course, the distribution of religious shrines on both sides. The danger that Barbara may be in, on the Jordanian side, due to her half-Jewishness highlights the fact that she is really part of the contemporary political scene, or at least could be, despite her professed disinterest in anything post-biblical. She also makes one strong friend on the Jordanian side, Suzy Ramdez, her tour guide, to balance her friend on the Israeli side, the archaeologist Saul Ephraim.

Jerusalem is a major Jewish, Christian and Islamic destination of pilgrimage, and as a Christian destination its holy sites are first recorded mentioned as holy sites in a letter by the Emperor Constantine to Bishop Macarius (Morris 2005: 50). I have so far enumerated and discussed the parallel divisions in the identities of the protagonists of the two novels, and in the identity of the city of Jerusalem. I shall now turn to examining the way that the idea of pilgrimage brings in a religious and Christian perspective which contributes to a sense of the achievement of resolution, both in the personalities of the protagonists, and in their sense of their understanding of Jerusalem, in the two novels. In the Catholic tradition, the approach to spirituality is sacramental, which means that the material world corresponds to and represents a spiritual reality, and that the material world constitutes a means through which human beings can arrive at spiritual understanding, being themselves a material-spiritual composite, as Catholics understand them.[14] So the Catholic pilgrimage is not one in which the physical world is left behind as the spirit soars to a completely unrelated level, but rather one in which the material world reveals the spiritual world, when perceived with spiritual eyes, and the spiritual world shines through it.[15] There is also a tradition of talking of the celestial life as a heavenly city, which, building on the psalms, is employed in St. Paul's Epistles and in the Book of Revelation, and is continued by St. Augustine in *The City of God*. This city is often identified with Jerusalem, although St. Augustine is also thinking of Rome as the earthly counterpart of the heavenly city. In the light of this tradition, the Catholic pilgrim's task on arriving in a city of pilgrimage such as Jerusalem or Rome is to see whichever earthly city it is in such a light as allows the spiritual vision of the heavenly city to shine through it. For Helena and Barbara (and Waugh and Spark), a working out of the way the various identities and strata of the earthly cities they visit can be united – legitimated under the umbrella of the spiritual vision which the cities enable – goes hand in hand with a new understanding of how their personal spiritual identity and purpose can gather up and legitimate the different strands of their earthly identity and history.[16]

---

[14]   There are many Catholic discussions of the concept of sacramentality. See for example Jones 1959. The concept of 'place' is important in a sacramental understanding, because spiritual realities are communicated through physical realities, which must be specific physical realities, thus occupying a location. Theorist of sacramentality, David Jones, thus emphasizes the local, explaining that the artist, in attempting to show the presence of incorporeal realities in corporeal realities, a process which he believes art is, must work with a local scene familiar to the artist – see, for example, Jones 1972: 24-25.

[15]   See, for example, Balthasar 2004: 60-61.

[16]   In the Catholic tradition, there is a concept of the development of doctrine in the Church, made explicit by Newman in his *An Essay on the Development of Christian Doctrine*, which is then applied beyond this sphere by other Catholic thinkers, such as Alasdair MacIntyre, who sees all intellectual endeavors as needing to be understood as narratives of their own developing tradition (see MacIntyre 2006), and Charles Taylor, who sees all kinds of human understanding as taking narrative form (see Taylor 1989: 46-48). Of course, understanding the spiritual development of the individual as a process, and a story, has long been important in the Christian tradition. Given a sacramental approach, according to which spiritual realities inform and are manifested through spiritual realities, the arrival at the place of pilgrimage, and departure from it, can be understood as a physical reality informed by an episode of spiritual development – the approach towards the facing up to a conflict, and the coming away from the conflict after resolution and growth. Barbara's arri-

For Helena, who is already an older person when she visits Rome and Jerusalem, it is seeing the cities with the eyes of her new faith that makes these visits pilgrimages rather than journeys. In Rome, her attitude to the crowds in the world's biggest city is transformed from what it would have been before: "There was not hate in her now and nothing round her was quite profane" (Waugh 1963: 92). What is more, anyone in the crowd might also be a member, together with her, of the Church, the "Mystical Body" (Waugh 1963: 93): "There was no mob, only a vast multitude of souls, clothed in a vast variety of body, milling about in the Holy City, in the See of Peter." (Waugh 1963: 93) This new vision which Helena has is a vision of the same physical sights which inspired in Horace a hatred of the mob, whose famous poem commemorating his sentiment is used by Waugh as a pagan counterpoint to Helena's new-found perception (Waugh 1963: 92). It is not inspired by any beauty of the city, which Waugh claims "would come later," the classical city being "gross and haphazard" in Waugh's reconstruction (Waugh 1963: 92). As mentioned above, the Jerusalem Helena visited is one in which much of the city in which the events of the New Testament happened has been covered with an ordinary Roman provincial town: "It might have lain in Britain or Africa; a standard, second-century garrison-town." (Waugh 1963:133-34) What is more, the site of the Crucifixion and Resurrection has been turned into a building site, one in which Macarius the Bishop can no longer picture to himself the scenes of the New Testament events (Waugh 1963: 136). Helena has, however, come with a clear objective, which is to find the True Cross. Before achieving this, she gets to know important sites which have not been obscured by the new Roman town, such as the Mount of Olives and the Cave of the Nativity, where she commissions new basilicas, as mentioned above. Also, on her first day she orders the staircase of the building where she is supposed to be staying to be taken to Rome, on the basis that the building might have been Pilate's Praetorium, in which case the staircase might have been the one which Jesus descended on the way to the Crucifixion. Waugh portrays her, on hearing this, climbing the

---

val in the Holy Land is the facing up to her conflicts, and her departure her personal growth having confronted them and resolved them in some way. Helena's arrival at Jerusalem is the determination to face up to fulfilling an unaddressed ambition, even vocation, and her departure is the completion of this task, to which her life had been building up.

staircase on her knees, in the way that pilgrims to Rome have since done (Waugh 1963: 137-38). However, her first sight of the future site of the Church of the Holy Sepulchre, in the vicinity of which the True Cross might eventually be found, is of a huge building site, the same one mentioned above in connection with Macarius. Waugh describes it again and in more detail when he narrates Helena visiting it in the company of Macarius, concentrating on the mundane details (Waugh 1963: 143), none of which intimidate Helena, despite Macarius' doubts, although, in the end, in Waugh's narrative, it takes a divinely inspired dream to enable Helena to find the Cross.

So, as in Rome, Helena is not put off by the prosaic nature of much of what she sees, but nevertheless she does insist that the physical world she is looking at is genuinely connected to the spiritual world – and that is the significance of her quest for the Cross.[17] Helena, as I have mentioned, has throughout the novel been portrayed as skeptical of the mystery religions of the time, which do not show definite, identifiable correspondences with places and times in the physical world. In seeking, and eventually, finding, the Cross, she is affirming her faith in the reality of the events of the New Testament, and thereby in the real significance of the physical world, which can bear spiritual meaning, just as later pilgrims to Jerusalem, by going to the specific place, affirm the spiritual-physical correspondence. In addition, Helena achieves her own spiritual purpose by finding the cross: throughout the novel, Helena seems to be preparing for something, without knowing what it is. As a young woman before marriage, she imagines visiting Troy and Rome, and excavating Troy, and yet as a middle-aged woman, she still has not even been to Rome and is not expecting to go. In her conversation with her ex-tutor Marcias in Trier before her conversion, it emerges that she has not achieved what she had wanted, but has accepted what has come her way. (Waugh 1963: 84) It is after her late conversion and then her invitation to Rome by her son that she begins to fulfill the obscure ambitions of her youth. Evelyn Waugh is associated in his fiction with the idea that every individual has been created for a specific purpose, and in looking back over Helena's life in the novel, it becomes apparent that each ingredient in her identity and every stage of her development was necessary

---

[17]   On the True Cross representing the meaning carried by everyday objects, see McCartney 1992: 153-54.

for her to accomplish that task and achieve that spiritual purpose which she alone was meant to achieve. Like the Three Kings, she is a late comer, but there is nevertheless a place and purpose for her, as there is for them (and, as Waugh would hope, there is for him), which makes sense of everything which has contributed to her life.[18] Equally the pilgrimage cities, such as Rome and Jerusalem, have needed to be places of contradiction and conflict in order to become places of spiritual significance, as Waugh implies when he has Constantine, portrayed as a superficial person in the novel, complaining that Rome will always be heathen, and that it is only considered holy because St. Peter and St. Paul were martyred there: he says this to justify his founding of Constantinople as a completely Christian city, with churches dedicated to Wisdom and Peace (Waugh 1963: 125). Helena expresses the ethos of the novel when she expresses her disapproval of the idea of a cleaned-up "New Rome", as Constantinople was called, and also of dedicating churches to ideas rather than people (Waugh 1963: 126).[19] It is in and through the untidiness of the physical world, according to the novel, that the road to the spiritual meaning and identity of people and places is found.

Barbara's pilgrimage has a less clear initial objective than Helena's. She has come to an impasse in her relationship with Harry Clegg, and she is not sure if she wants to meet him at the Dead Sea Scrolls site. She does not want to face her friend Miss Rickworth (who in fact pursues her to the Holy Land in an effort to find her) and tell her that she is considering getting married, thus cancelling their plans for sharing a household together in the future. She is trying to resolve a feeling of contradictions in her identity, between the Jewish and non-Jewish sides, and between the passionate and methodical, intellectual sides. However, the journey is still a pilgrimage, and her main occupation while there, when not recuperating from scarlet fever, is visiting all the sites that a Catholic pilgrim would. The reconciling effect of Barbara's pilgrimage works on her gradually. After two difficult experiences with tour guides, in which one guide challenges her on her identity, she drives herself to Mount Tabor, possible site of the Transfiguration, and it is while sitting on a wall on the hill, looking at

---

[18]   See Guillamet 2005: 221-22.

[19]   For Waugh's favoring of the concrete Rome over the ideal Constantinople, see Davis 1981: 230.

the Holy Land – both the Israeli and the Jordanian sides – spread out beneath her, that she reflects on her identity (these flashbacks give the reader the bulk of the information on her background early in the novel). In fact, the chapter which consists of her reflections and memories while sitting on Mount Tabor is called "Barbara Vaughan's Identity". It may be significant that it is at this site that she sits down to reflect on her identity, because the Transfiguration is the event in which Jesus reveals his divine identity to two of the apostles. Barbara is here working towards a vision of her own spiritual identity, which will transfigure all the worldly strands of which she is made up.

Much of her self-discovery, however, seems to take place during the later, Jordanian leg of the pilgrimage. The novel's major theoretical statement on the significance of pilgrimage takes place while Barbara is in the Church of the Holy Sepulchre, on the Jordanian side, in the sermon of an English priest: Barbara is suffering from the effects of scarlet fever, and in disguise, while she hears the sermon, and appears unable to listen to it (Spark 1967: 202). Barbara, like Freddy, the other main character, is taken up by a sense of adventure when he comes to fetch her from her convent-hotel (St. Helena's Convent) in the middle of the night, on her first night in Jordan. As mentioned above, her consciousness of her eccentric English ancestry ("unself-questioning hierarchists, anarchistic imperialists, blood-sporting zoophiles, skeptical believers", Spark 1967: 164) seems to her capable of making sense of the oppositions in her identity.[20] However, whereas Freddy cannot sustain the adventure, and later suffers from amnesia, Barbara continues, recovers from scarlet fever, and afterwards completes her pilgrimage to the Jordanian holy places in disguise. The reason why, for Barbara, the adventure is ongoing, whereas for Freddy it is a thrilling aberration, seems to be that she, unlike Freddy, has "the beautiful and dangerous gift of faith" (Spark 1967: 23), which she has mentioned earlier in the novel. This stage of the pilgrimage affords Barbara the opportunity to make her own statements about her understanding of the religious significance of what she is doing, explaining it to her guide, Suzy Ramdez. Barbara responds to Suzy's remark that Barbara, unlike other pilgrims she has guided, does not restrict herself to religious conversation in the intervals between visiting shrines, and defends the place of the profane within the total religious picture:

---

[20]   See Poitou 1985-6: 21.

Well, either religious faith penetrates everything in life or it doesn't. There are some experiences that seem to make nonsense of all separations of sacred from profane – they seem childish. Either the whole of life is unified under God or everything falls apart. (Spark 1967: 283)

So, as for Helena, the mundane is not something to be kept apart from a spiritual understanding, but rather it is an essential part of that life through which, as in a pilgrimage, spiritual understanding is achieved.

The obstacles to Barbara's marriage to Harry Clegg are particularly difficult for her to negotiate spiritually. From before her arrival in the Holy Land, Barbara has been insisting that Harry must go through official church channels to try to obtain an annulment of his previous marriage, and that if he does not succeed she will not marry him. However, this resolve seems to waver once she is in the Holy Land. She decides that she will marry Harry whatever the result, and tells him so on the telephone while he is in Rome on an inconclusive trip in pursuit of the annulment (Spark 1967: 181). The novel provides a surprising solution to this problem, by having Miss Rickward, Barbara's friend who is against the marriage, come to the Holy Land looking for Barbara. She meets and eventually marries the father of Barbara's Jordanian guide, and then plots to sabotage the chances of Barbara's marriage by having a birth certificate for Harry Clegg faked, so that it states that he was baptized Catholic (Harry doesn't know whether or where he was baptized). She mistakenly assumes (on the basis of information from Barbara's guide's brother) that this will prevent Harry from obtaining an annulment, but in fact the reverse is the case. So Barbara does not have to marry outside the Church, despite her stated willingness to do so. She nevertheless doubts whether she would have been able to continue outside the Church permanently, even if she had gone through with a civil marriage: "I would have married you anyway. But it would have taken courage to continue being out of the Church. It's the keeping it up I was afraid of." (Spark 1967: 244) She follows this admission up with the statement: "With God everything is possible" (Spark 1967: 244). This statement suggests a kind of providential interpretation for what has happened, that is, that God has rewarded her for her religious faith, and her faith in love, even if that has threatened to take her out of the Church's discipline.[21] From this point of view, Spark would resemble Graham

---

[21]   See Caporaletti 2000: 300.

Greene in wanting to explore the way that love might justify actions on the edge – or beyond the edge – of the Church's usual moral code. However, another light is thrown on the issue right at the end of novel, when Barbara's life after the events of the novel is described in somewhat unsentimental terms: "Barbara and Harry were married and got on fairly well together ever after." (Spark 1967: 303) While this is a happy ending, it is not so ideally happy as to suggest that romantic love is the highest aim. Talking to her Jordanian guide Suzy about her affair with Harry, Barbara says that "it now seemed that she had been living like a nun without the intensity and reality of a nun's life" (Spark 1967: 278).[22] So, what her experience of romantic love has done has been to take her out of herself, in the way that a nun's life of devotion might, but her unmarried life of self-devotion was not doing. This looking outwards is a necessary part of the religious attitude, so her love for Harry is a stage in her religious development, but not its ultimate expression. Like Waugh in *Helena*, Spark is suggesting that the journey to spiritual understanding passes through difficult and un-tidy worldly territory, territory which is nevertheless valuable, as without it there would be no journey.

The English priest who preaches at the mass in the Church of the Holy Sepulchre, at which Barbara is present but affected by scarlet fever and unable to pay attention, includes biblical references to the heavenly Jerusalem from St. Paul's Epistle to the Hebrews and the Book of Revelation in his sermon, and seems to sum up the novel's theory of pilgrimage. He starts by describing how the act of pilgrim-age is an act that humans engage in by instinct, and is an end in itself, like a work of art (Spark 1967: 195-96).[23] This might be seen as put-ting pilgrimage in the Aristotelian category of acts which humans do because it is in the nature of humans to do them, as described, for ex-ample, in the *Nicomachean Ethics*. The priest reminds his congrega-tion that physical annoyances and commercialism have always ac-companied pilgrimages, even in New Testament times, and that partly in consequence of this the pilgrims should not rely on having exalted

---

[22]   Edgecombe argues that Barbara wants to escape from "non-sacramental" celi-bacy with Miss Rickward, that is, a state involving no dedication to anything outside herself (Edgecombe 1990: 84).

[23]   Sproxton sees Barbara's instinct to visit the Holy Land as arising from a spir-itual need which nothing else can fulfill, even her love for Harry (Sproxton 1992: 148-49).

feelings at each shrine, or insist on visiting every one, but that the right disposition is enough (Spark 1967: 196-97). These points made by the priest, even though Barbara has not been listening, apply strongly to Barbara's pilgrimage: as I have mentioned above, the reasons why Barbara has come are mixed, and going ahead with the Jordanian stage of the pilgrimage is risky, but she nevertheless completes the pilgrimage. She has sometimes been underwhelmed in terms of feelings at particular shrines, and has on occasion not even had the energy to see minor shrines when in the area, such as the house of Simon the Tanner in Jaffa, or the "Mensa Christi" in Nazareth, if there was some slight obstacle (Spark 1967: 25). Nevertheless, she continues with the pilgrimage, and, later, her Jordanian guide, Suzy, remarks that she spends comparatively little time in each shrine, considering the trouble taken to reach them. Barbara explains, "It's an act of presence, [...] as when you visit a bereaved friend and there's nothing to say. The whole point is, that a meeting has materialized." (Spark 1967: 283) So Barbara has the pilgrimage instinct, and she has an attitude of faith, rather than an emotional exaltation. The priest goes on to tell the pilgrims that whether the shrines are in exactly the right places is not important (Spark 1967: 198-99), but that there is a relation between the Jerusalem they are visiting and the heavenly Jerusalem:

For there is a supernatural process going on under the surface and within the substance of all things. In the Jerusalem of history we see the type and shadow of that Jerusalem of Heaven that St John of Patmos tells of in the Apocalypse. [...] This is the spiritual city which is involved eternally with the historical one. [...] It is the New Jerusalem which we seek with our faith, and which is the goal of our pilgrimage to this old Jerusalem of history. (Spark 1967: 199)

What is emphasized here is the same concept which underlies *Helena* – which is that a pilgrimage expresses the idea that spiritual reality is reached through physical reality, and that each physical reality, however apparently imperfect, corresponds to an aimed for perfection in the spiritual world, and is the way to it. The priest rounds off the sermon with some comments on doubt, which, again, seem relevant to Barbara. He recommends doubt in any uncertainty which lies outside the creed, and asserts: "Doubt is the prerogative of the believer; the unbeliever cannot know doubt." (Spark 1967: 199) He adds the qualification, however: "But in whatever touches the human spirit, it is better to believe everything than nothing." (Spark 1967: 199) These statements perhaps put Barbara's hesitations about marriage to Harry Clegg in a religious context: if she has had struggles of conscience, it is because she has believed something, and if she has erred, it has been in a generous direction, and Providence seems to have stepped in on her behalf.[24] However, the novel overall suggests that it is not emotional highs, whether romantic or religious, which are the pilgrim's genuine objective, but contact with a spiritual reality which is not less real than the physical, which gives meaning to the physical, and to which the physical offers a way.

In this paper I have been discussing how both Evelyn Waugh and Muriel Spark, through their protagonists St. Helena and Barbara Vaughan, explore personal problems of human identity and purpose. In both cases they approach the resolution through a process of seeking an objective perspective on which to map the personal realm. This is done partly by comparing the complex and divided nature of the protagonists' personal histories with the equivalently complex histories of places, places which are also destinations of pilgrimage. Jerusalem is particularly suited to be the geographical counterpart to the human identity in this process of comparison, being a major, for many the major, destination of pilgrimage, and having a particularly complex and divided history. However, another level of objectivity is brought in with the religious dimension, which, from a characteristically Catholic point of view, posits a realm which is as real as the physical realm, and which corresponds with it, giving it direction and purpose. It is this sense that the person of faith sees the eternal realm as well as the physical realm as absolutely real, which gives both novels a pragmatic and emotionally restrained atmosphere, one which the reader might be surprised to find in novels of spiritual discovery and fulfillment. From a Catholic point of view, what characterizes the religious attitude is not passing moments of illumination or fleeting experiences of ecstasy, although these may occur, but a steady conviction of the spiritual meaning in all material things. Barbara and Helena's quests often lead them to be misunderstood by those around them, misunderstanding which their creators Waugh and Spark will have been familiar with as British Catholics. However, the spiritual reality which gives them spiritual identities under which to unify their historical identities, and which guarantees their value as individuals, also

---

[24]   See Whittacker 1982: 46, 75.

guarantees the value that they must see in all other individuals, including those who misunderstand them, as well as in every place, whether a destination of pilgrimage, or any other place of human habitation and history. Arrival in Jerusalem, therefore, from a Catholic perspective, as expounded by Evelyn Waugh and Muriel Spark, is not a rejection of worldly identities in favor of the spiritual, but an arrival at a sense of the inclusion of the physical and spiritual worlds in each other.

Bibliography

Balthasar, Hans Urs von. 2004. *Epilogue* (trans. Edward T. Oakes). San Francisco: Ignatius.

Bold, Alan. 1986. *Muriel Spark*. London: Methuen.

Caporaletti, Silvana. 2000. *A World in a Grain of Sand. I romanzi di Muriel Spark*. Lecce: Milella.

Davis, Robert Murray. 1981. *Evelyn Waugh, Writer*. Norman, Oklahoma: Pilgrim.

Edgecombe, Rodney Stenning. 1990. *Vocation and Identity in the Fiction of Muriel Spark*. Columbia: University of Missouri Press.

Guillamet, Ma. Eulàlia Carceller. 2005. 'Religion and Reconciliation in *Helena*' in Carlos Villar Flor and Robert Murray Davis (eds.) *Waugh without End: New Trends in Evelyn Waugh Studies*. Bern: Lang.

Jones, David. 1972. *The Anathemata. Fragments of an Attempted Writing*. London: Faber.

—. 1959. 'Art and Sacrament' in Grisewood, Harman (ed.) *Epoch and Artist*. London: Faber.

Kermode, Frank. 1971. 'The Novel as Jerusalem. Muriel Spark's *Mandelbaum Gate*' in *Modern Essays*. London: Fontana.

MacIntyre, Alasdair. 2006. 'Epistemological Crises, Dramatic Narrative, and the Philosophy of Science' in *The Tasks of Philosophy: Selected Essays*, vol. 1. Cambridge: Cambridge University Press.

Malin, Irving. 1970. 'The Deceptions of Muriel Spark' in Melvin J. Friedman (ed.) *The Vision Obscured: Perceptions of Some Twentieth-Century Catholic Novelists*. New York: Fordham University Press.

McCartney, George. 1992. 'The Being and Becoming of Evelyn Waugh' in: Alain Blayac (ed.) *Evelyn Waugh: New Directions*. Basingstoke and London: Mac-Millan.

Morris, Colin. 2005. *The Sepulchre of Christ and the Medieval West. From Beginnings to 1600*. Oxford: Oxford University Press.

Newman, John Henry. 1989. *An Essay on the Development of Christian Doctrine*. Notre Dame, Indiana: University of Notre Dame Press.

Patey, Douglas Lane. 1998. *The Life of Evelyn Waugh. A Critical Biography*. Oxford: Blackwell.

Poitou, Marc. 1985-6. 'La rage d'être autre: *The Mandelbaum Gate* de Muriel Spark' in *Cycnos* 2 (Hiver 1985-6).
Spark, Muriel. 1967. *The Mandelbaum Gate*. London: Penguin.
Sproxton, Judy. 1992. *The Women of Muriel Spark*. London: Constable.
Stannard, Martin. 2009. *Muriel Spark. The Biography*. London: Weidenfeld and Nicholson.
Taylor, Charles. 1989. *Sources of the Self. The Making of Modern Identity*. Cambridge: Cambridge University Press.
Walczuk, Anna. 2005. *Irony as a Mode of Perception and Principle of Ordering Reality in the Novels of Muriel Spark*. Krakow: Universitas.
Waugh, Evelyn. 1963. *Helena*. London: Penguin.
Whittacker, Ruth. 1982. *The Faith and Fiction of Muriel Spark*. London: MacMillan.
Woodman, Thomas. 1991. *Faithful Fictions. The Catholic Novel in British Literature*. Milton Keynes: Open University Press.
Wykes, David. 1999. *Evelyn Waugh. A Literary Life*. London Basingstoke: MacMillan.

6. Colonus Heterotopos.
Theatre as Tragic Inversion of Ritual Order

Gert Hofmann

We begin with Blanchot, and with a cascade of discourses leading us down to place of Oedipus' arrival at Colonus, a *deme* or district of the *polis* of Athens, which is in fact the place of origin of Sophocles himself, the author of the so-called Theban Plays *Oedipus at Colonus*, *Oedipus Tyrant*, and *Antigone*. The *polis* of Thebes is the place where tragic fate commences, Colonus, however, the place of ultimate conclusion and *katharsis*. Oedipus had been ostracized by his political community, ritually expelled as a scapegoat – as a *pharmakos* or *homo sacer* – in order to purify the city from catastrophic conflict, and he had been thrown onto a path of uncontainable suffering, helplessly exposed to any violent assault on his person. Colonus is the place of arrival for the journey that follows his ostracism, which could be interpreted, from the protagonist's viewpoint, as an inverted pilgrimage, originating in a moment not of approved but *failed* faith in the possibility of redemption, implemented through an act of suspended social and religious protection, and terminating not in a state of sublimated life but accomplished death. The *topos* of his arrival, the neither sacred nor profane, but in a curious way counter-sacred garden of the Eumenides, which exemplifies in fact many of the characteristics of a Foucaultian "other space" or "heterotopia" (Foucault 2002), marks the moment of his death. Opposite to the oriental ancient garden which, according to Foucault, celebrated in microcosmic abbreviation cosmos as a benign world dedicated to the living,[1] Sophocles' garden of the

---

[1] "The traditional garden of the Persians was a sacred space that was supposed to bring together inside its rectangle four parts representing the four parts of the world, with a space still more sacred than the others that were like an umbilicus, the navel of the world at its center (the basin and water fountain were there); and all the vegetation of the garden was supposed to come together in this space, in this sort of microcosm." (Foucault 2002: 234)

Eumenides is dedicated to the dead, as a terrifying ante-chamber to the Other-world.

Blanchot

Maurice Blanchot wrote an amazing text entitled "L'Instant de ma mort" (Blanchot 1994) (The Instant of my Death; Blanchot 2000), a brief autobiographical fragment where he reflects on the early most defining moment of his life as an "encounter of death with death". (Blanchot 2000: 5) In 1944, suspected of having supported resistance fighters, the young Blanchot had been facing a Nazi firing squad ordered to execute him, already pointing at him with their rifles, when the commanding officer of this Nazi gang was distracted by a nearby skirmish, giving Blanchot the chance to escape.

It is interesting that Blanchot calls this "instant" – occurring to him while waiting for the imminent "fire" command – "encounter of death with death," not of *life* with death. Does he want to point out, that in this moment *death had already crossed the threshold of his conscious life* (initiating a kind of *epilogue* to his life) and induced an ecstatic state of mind which is, in spite of a "feeling of lightness", utterly self-contradictory:

He was perhaps suddenly invincible. Dead – immortal. Perhaps ecstasy. Rather the feeling of compassion for the suffering humanity, the happiness of not being immortal or eternal. (Blanchot 2000: 5)

The strange dynamic of this conceptual mayhem defines precisely the confounding complexity of the conscious threshold of death: Being *dead* but still on the side of the living means being *immortal*; *staying alive* on the side of death, being conscious in death, however, equals the joy of "not being immortal" motivating a potentially infinite compassion with human suffering, and marking *death* as the confirmed condition of ultimate relief.

Since the two sides of this threshold are not complementary, but incompatible, the place, the *topos* of the threshold of death in human life remains a *non-topos* in time and space; "dying", so Blanchot in *L'Écriture du désastre*, is not only inconceivable, "because it doesn't have a presence, but because it doesn't have a place, and be it in time, in the temporality of time". (Blanchot 1980: 181) Derrida perceives this remark as an attempt to provoke the threefold thought of the three 'irreconcilable' assertions of death: death is ever imminent, essentially impossible – and has yet already arrived. (Derrida 2000: 31)

The moment death encounters *itself*, […] at this moment both inescapable and improbable, […] this arrival of death that never arrives and never happens to me – at this instant lightness, elation, beatitude remain the only affects that can take measure of this event as an "unexperienced experience." […] Dying will finally become possible – as prohibition. All living beings have an impossible relation to death; at the instant death, the impossible, will become possible as impossible. (Derrida 2000:65)

These forcefully experiential but otherwise inconceivable certainties of the presence of death in human life remain irreconcilable, because of their conceptual incompatibility: being irrefutably present and ultimately absent, categorically impossible and absolutely factual at the same time; the threshold of death in life marks a categorical abyss; neither side can ever become an argument for the other. The sense of living cannot truthfully anticipate death, and the notion of death in its detached absoluteness – because it is always the death of the *Other* – can never motivate life.

But there is a way to anticipate death and configure the incompatible and irreconcilable: the way of tragic fiction as truly taboo-free *experimentum de hominis naturae*. While tragedy can generally be perceived as a propedeutic approach to death, *Oedipus at Colonus* can be seen as Sophocles' tragic play that most explicitly sets out to configure into performative image the threshold-space in between of living and dying. It visits the *hetero-topos* of death within the realm of the living – and acknowledges the presence of the 'underworld' as *other*-world within this world.[2]

If the dramatic play re-enacts Oedipus' arrival at the garden of the Eumenides, it also re-creates the inverted sacredness of this exceptional site in the space of theatre. The affinity of both sites becomes manifest. The theatre is the place of arrival of the god Dionysus in the human realm of mortality. It is dedicated to the celebration of his messianic status and redemptive power (to re-establish the forlorn Golden

---

[2] According to Foucault (2002: 233), this capacity of theatre highlights one of the privileged powers of the heterotopic space: "The heterotopia is capable of juxtaposing in a single real place several spaces, several sites that are in themselves incompatible. Thus it is that the theater brings onto the rectangle of the stage, one after the other, a whole series of places that are foreign to one another."

Age of eternal youth, and of cohabitation of divine and human life),
but actually it bears the god's contamination with death and completes
his human metamorphosis in the play of the tragic mask as a product
of human artistry (*poiesis*). In other words, the Athenian theatre of
Dionysus is the place of an epochal struggle between divine inspiration (Dionysus is *musagetes*, the leader of the Muses) and human poetical self-invention (Dionysus is the god of theatre as an all-art
event), or between *mythos* and *logos*, authoritative monologue (of the
rhapsodic singer) and argumentative dialogue (of drama, philosophy
and politics) as two controversial types of human cultural meta-
narrative.[3]

Euripides calls Dionysus the "arriving god". For the ancient
Greeks Dionysus features as the *delayed* god, the messianic god
whose advent actually never happens, even though his arrival remains
always imminent. He is the god of a utopian religion in which the future *never* arrives. With Dionysus' arrival, a *Threshold Space* of an
ever expected, but permanently postponed epiphany of the mythical
itself opens up at the site of the theatre – a typically heterotopic space
of crisis in which both sides of the threshold, the sacro-mythical of the
past, and the logical, poetical and political of the future, appear ques-
tionable and fragile.

In the classical period of Athens Dionysus had thus become a
type of post-religious *supplement* to reason. He does not embody *the
irrational,* rather he reflects such crises of reason as arise in the course
of its political realization, and lends expression, in the context of the
tragic *agon* (the tragic competition), to the conflict between religious
tradition and rational political vision. As Jean Pierre Vernant pointed
it out, it is the *tragic theatre* which serves as the primary location, the
topos – with Foucault we are able to say, the *heterotopos* – for such a
critical argument:

---

[3] About the *mythos-logos* opposition in the context of early Athenian tragedy cp.
Vernant 1990. Regarding the developing discourse of philosophy at the same time,
Plato's dialogue *Timaios* is most representative. Jacques Derrida, in his interpretation
of *Timaios*, was the first to discover the meaning of *khōra* as a kind of discursive in-
between space, discourse defining, but in itself non-identifiable: space of a third kind,
"that exceeds or precedes, in an order that is, moreover, alogical and achronic, anachronistic too, the constitutive oppositions of mytho-logic as such, of mythic discourse
and of the discourse on myth". (Derrida 1995: 112).

It confronts heroic values and ancient religious representations with the new modes of thought that characterize the advent of Law within the city-state. [...] The tragic turning point thus occurs, when a gap develops at the heart of the social experience. It is wide enough for the oppositions between legal and political thought on the one hand and the mythical and heroic traditions on the other to stand out quite clearly. Yet it is narrow enough for the conflict in values still to be a painful one and for the clash to continue to take place. (Vernant 1990: 26)[4]

What emerges here is not just a new political system, it is a new anthropology, a *liminal* anthropology, a new way of thinking "human", which on one hand heightens human awareness of mortality – as being subjected to mythically acknowledged, natural and divine powers – but on the other hand employs human intellectual power as the sovereign source of a (trans-mythical) vision of humanity that transcends any given time and tradition. The threshold presence of death in human life, and the human ways of approaching and confronting death as the ultimate limit of sovereign self-articulation become the core questions in this anthropological endeavor.

Sophocles' garden of the Eumenides, and the tragic Athenian theatre as a cultural institution are crucial venues of this confrontation. Sophocles' Oedipus breaches the taboo sphere of the Eumenides' garden and violates the border between the sacred and the profane, which defines divine Law in its absoluteness and also draws the line between mortal and immortal life. But he does so not in order to redeem the human from the burden of mortal fate, but to celebrate human fatality as the very source of human grandeur. The inverted messianic meaning of Dionysus' arrival in the theatre, which makes him succumbing to the human crises of mortality rather than overcoming them, follows

---

[4] The text continues: "The tragic consciousness of responsibility appears when the human and divine levels are sufficiently distinct to be opposed while still appearing to be inseparable. The tragic sense of responsibility emerges when human action becomes the object of reflection and debate while still not being regarded as sufficiently autonomous to be fully self-sufficient. The particular domain of tragedy lies in this border zone where human actions hinge on divine powers and where their true meaning, unsuspected by even those who initiated them and take responsibility for them, is only revealed when it becomes a part of an order that is beyond man and escapes him." Cf. also Cartledge 1997: 6. According to Cartledge, Dionysus, as the mythical embodiment of the end of myth, serves as "a device for defining Athenian civic identity", making room for the yet undefined to present itself, for "exploring and confirming, but also questioning what it was to be a citizen of a democracy, this brand new form of popular self government".

a similar logic. In both cases the sacred seems to be exposed in its innermost affinity with the abject.[5]

As the "god of arrival" who incorporates the divine among humans, and as the *mortal* god who is bound to dying and being reborn three times in any cycle of his life, Dionysus dwells on this very threshold and realizes his *messianic* status only in his theatrical and tragic epiphany, where his mythic-eschatological promise proves essentially self-contradictory.

The theatrical cult of Dionysus invokes his presence by alluding to his absence. The theatre stage becomes the venue of his constant artistic displacement where emphasis on the fictional and illusory character of the god's arrival overrides his failure to appear as the divine redeemer. The absence of his eschatological advent motivates his poetic appropriation. His perception switches slowly from the mythic to the poetic and from the sacred to the profane.[6]

With Dionysus' arrival in the Athenian Dionysus Theatre, where the god himself was to be sacrificed *in effigie* of the tragic hero, his actual exposure to the human condition of mortality becomes effective in a playful sphere of both anthropological crisis and responding poetic criticism. What manifests itself to human mind on the theatre stage is the fundamental liminality of the human experience: the caesuras of life and death, the threshold experiences and in-between stages of order and chaos, the absences and unconscious states between living and dying – in short all those moments in which the totality of life, literally speaking, is to play for. Those crisis moments occur in the theatre as an exclusive and poetic space of deferred mythic signification, synchronizing absence and presence of the god, where metamorphoses of human cultural awareness occur, whose interpretations still remain to be delivered.

---

[5] The Eumenides, the divine spirits of terror, protect the Underworld against human trespassers. Potential affinities of the sacred and the abject that both share the power of terror ("Pouvoirs de l'horreur") have first been explored by Julia Kristeva (Kristeva 1980).

[6] "Playing" as a way of 'profanizing' and humanizing the sacred has been phenomenologically analyzed by Giorgio Agamben (Agamben 2007). Cf. esp. the chapter on "In Praise of Profanation".

The Tragic Mask as Heterotopic Site

In theatre the mask was no longer to be understood as an attribute, rather as the materialization of Dionysus' ambiguous essence. The god *is* the mask, and the mask is the focus of the tragic performance: the mask conjures both presence and absence, presents a front, while hiding what lies behind, presence and pretense, proffered identity and lack of authenticity – face to face.[7] The mask is the membrane of a merely *illusory* identity above an actual abyss of disillusionment, which serves again as the inexhaustible reservoir of character possibilities for the theatrical play. The mask becomes the surface of a dual projection and presents itself as the heterotopic site of two mutually exclusive epochal spaces, crossing each other: the ambiguous figures of a disappearing mythological time appear through its reverse side, the front side by contrast, reflects the configurations of a power of imagination which has ceased to be mythical and imposed by divine inspiration. This new intellectual power of imaginative self-awareness articulates itself in a political and *poetical* way (i.e. as crafted by humankind).

So in the conflict of the tragic performance it becomes clear that the messianic expectation towards Dionysus' coming can only be fulfilled in an inverse and anti-redemptive fashion. The yearned for arrival of the divine as a power which, in the sphere of the human, conquers time and mortality can only be realized in the tragic event – in the form of disempowerment – and in the non-authentic, hybrid form of its masked appearance. Each tragic hero mirrors and reconfigures yet again the mortal essence of the tragic god, while at the same time the theatrical ability to restage, repeat and vary the dramatic masked performance allows the human mind to take possession of his re-birthed metamorphoses. According to Giorgio Agamben tragic theatre thus allows for the embodiment of "the limit concept of religious experience in general, the point in which religious experience passes beyond itself and calls itself into question". (Agamben 1998: 56)

Theatre mirrors the crisis of mythic and religious interpretive authority. At the same time it establishes art, *poiesis*, which discredits

---

[7] The mask therefore figures as divine presence in the human face. Cf. Emmanuel Levinas' thought of the human face as "actus purus", act of pre-linguistic, ethically foundational communication: Levinas 2003: 36. Cf. also Vernant and Frontisi-Ducroux 1990: 202.

the arriving messianic god as a heteronymous impostor, and questions with him all transcendent redemptive meta-texts, submerging them into the finite and conflict-bound realm of the human interpretive discourse. Nonetheless, based on a sovereign approach to mortality as a form of genuine human dignity, tragic theatre is able to reclaim for itself something of the divine; namely the *crisis* and *exception* character of its uncontrollable playfulness and metamorphic dynamic which exceeds any pre-set boundaries of established human life.

Bare Life and the Topography of Human Arrival

The tragic inversion of the Messianic represents a perversion, seen from a religious perspective. It transmits, against all interpretive authorities, to the art and philosophy of theatre the blasphemous power of tragic powerlessness as *the* human form of sovereignty which is based on nothing but emphatic acknowledgment of human mortality. In the theatrical gestures of such blasphemy the tragic heroes place themselves on a par with the divine. One example suffices to illustrate this:

King Oedipus chooses to blind and condemn himself to banishment in an act of powerless rebellion against the god Apollo. Challenged about the violation of his eyesight, which always carries the presumption that he was punished by Apollo, the god of light, he only replies: "Not by his hand; *I did it.*"

The subversive nuance in this response converts the act of violence against him into an act of sovereignty in the face of all worldly and divine judicial authorities. By his own decision and on the strength of the sovereign dignity conferred on him through his self-imposed banishment, Oedipus commits himself to the unprotected existence of a *homo sacer* or *pharmakos*, i.e. to the "bare life" of an uncontainable suffering, which eventually transcends the political and juridical meaning of his time. (Cf. Agamben 1998: 114)[8] Consequently, when he reaches the end of his journey, he finds exclusive shelter and acceptance only in the garden of the *Eumenides*, among

---

[8] "In our culture the meaning of the term 'sacred' continues the semantic of *homo sacer* and not that of sacrifice [...] What confronts us today is a life that as such is exposed to a violence without precedent precisely in the most profane and banal ways."

the gods of the underworld, of whom Dionysus is one. Here Dionysus is associated with *Zeus chthonios*, Hades, and thus represents one of the most significant metamorphic versions of his being. Colonus, the mythical place, the garden of the Eumenides, and the theatre play that revisits it, configure a Heterotopia of crisis in the terms of what defines human sovereignty in principle, be it sacred or profane. Oedipus, representing Dionysus, fulfills at Colonus in a truly blasphemous position the messianic promise, to come. He enters the sacred garden which is forbidden to humans and thus crosses the threshold between divine and human, mortal and immortal – but not in a move towards ultimate divinization and redemption from death, but towards a sovereign human act of accomplishing and adopting death and dedicating his life to the human condition of mortality.

The threshold is not actually being crossed, but becomes, as a niche of exception, the erratic *sign* of Oedipus as an archetype of humanity: "It was fated, and this is the sign" (Sophocles 1974: 73, v47) he replies with tenacity when being asked to remove himself from a rock, situated in the middle of the Eumenides' grove, where he finally had taken seat in order to rest.

Seating himself on this throne-like rock of the Eumenides, which represents his fate, he confers on it the status of a symbol of human sovereignty which equals that of the immortal gods but is based instead on fateful mortality. As such a symbol it determines the Eumenides' garden as the ultimate destination of his solitary wanderings as a *Pharmakos*. At this point he manifests himself as the tragic human epiphany of the god Dionysus, however in that earthly associated and, in terms of divine power, subversive way, which leads only to the re-entanglement of the long-yearned for, messianic presence of the divine, in mortal affairs.

As a self-determined *Pharmakos*, he is the manifestation of that irreducible dignity of "bare life," which can only be seen in human life, insofar as we can assume that human *reflective awareness* of mortality means aggravation as much as elevation of the suffering associated with it. We remember how Blanchot described his sensitized state of awareness in the moment of his death: "Rather the feeling of compassion for the suffering humanity, the happiness of not being immortal or eternal." Agamben has shown that such awareness, though it remains powerless, never falls subject to the *vitae necisque potestas* of all sovereign power, be it political or religious. Banished bare life, exposing human mortality, and sovereign power over death and life, meet each other in that same *frame of exception* – or Heterotopia of ultimate crisis – which falls outside of the due processes and the laws of the political and mythical cosmos.

According to Agamben the "bare life" of the *homo sacer* is ever to be killed, but never to be sacrificed; he can be killed, because *he is already essentially dead*, and he cannot be sacrificed, because he has already acquired, and be it in an inverted and subversive capacity, sacred status. We remember: Blanchot had described his own near-death experience in front of the Nazi firing squad as a moment where *death encountered death*. (Death had already taken possession of his life, like of *homo sacer's* life.) Also Oedipus, when arriving at Colonus and taking his residence in the Eumenides' garden, considers himself only "the shadow, no more the man"! (Sophocles 1974: 75, v119) Eventually, in performing his own death ritual in form of a libation sacrifice (85), Oedipus claims again his humane sovereignty over the threshold of life and death, which even supersedes the political sovereignty of king Theseus, who was prepared to grant Oedipus Athenian citizenship, but then simply becomes the sole witness and companion of Oedipus' self-governed act of dying – each a sovereign of his own kind, but on par within theatre as heterotopic sphere of exception from both political and religious rule.

The theatrical topography of Oedipus' arrival at Colonus is marked by the heterotopic threshold-site between life and death, where human awareness of "bare life", banished life exposed to limitless suffering, invokes an inversion of the distinction between divine and human, mortal and immortal and suggests a form of human sovereignty which lays ground for an initial perception of humanity, rooted in a liminal awareness of bare life, which is previous to any mythical, ritual, or political act of foundation.

Bibliography

Agamben, Giorgio. 1998. *Homo Sacer. Sovereign Power and Bare Life* (trans. Daniel Heller Roazen). Stanford: Stanford University Press.
—. 2007. *Profanations*. New York: Zone Books.
Blanchot, Maurice. 1980. *L'Écriture du désastre*, Paris: Gallimard.
—. 1994. *L'Instant de ma mort*. Saint Clement: Fata Morgana.

—. 2000. 'The Instant of my Death' in Maurice Blanchot, Elizabeth Rottenberg, Jacques Derrida. *The Instant of my Death*. Stanford: Stanford University Press.

Cartledge, Paul. 1997. 'Deep Plays: Theatre as Process in Greek Civic Life' in Easterling, P. E. (ed.) *The Cambridge Companion to Greek Tragedy*. Cambridge: Cambridge University Press.

Derrida, Jacques. 1995. 'Khōra' in Derrida, Jacques. *On the Name*. Stanford: Stanford University Press.

—. 2000. 'Demeure: fiction and testimony' in Maurice Blanchot, Elizabeth Rottenberg, Jacques Derrida. *The Instant of my Death*. Stanford: Stanford University Press.

Foucault, Michel. 2002. 'Of Other Spaces' in Mirzoeff, Nicholas (ed.) *The Visual Culture Reader*. London: Routledge.

Kristeva, Julia. 1980. *Pouvoirs de l'horreur: essay sur l'abjection*. Paris: Éditions du Seuil.

Levinas, Emmanuel. 2003. *Humanism of the Other*, trans. Nidra Poller. Chicago: University of Illinois Press.

Sophocles. 1974. 'Oedipus at Colonus' in *The Theban Plays* (trans. E.F. Watling). London: Penguin.

Vernant, Jean-Pierre. 1990. 'The Historical Moment of Tragedy in Greece' in Vernant, Jean-Pierre and Pierre Vidal-Naquet (eds.) *Myth and Tragedy in Ancient Greece*. New York: Zone Books.

Vernant, Jean-Pierre and Françoise Frontisi-Ducroux. 1990. 'Features of the Mask in Ancient Greece' in Vernant, Jean-Pierre and Pierre Vidal-Naquet (eds.) *Myth and Tragedy in Ancient Greece*. New York: Zone Books.

7. Reading the Other.
Bakhtin and the Topography of Arrival in Literature

David Buchanan

This chapter describes the topography of arrival in a literary work as determined by the coordination of time and space. Following upon a brief account of the existential meeting of Self and Other in *The Epic of Gilgamesh* (c. seventh century BCE), an exploration of the chronotopic changes in romance from Xenophon of Ephesus's *An Ephesian Tale* (c. second century CE) to Walter Scott's *The Heart of Midlothian* (1818) as outlined by Mikhail Bakhtin demonstrates how synchronic influences lead to significant diachronic changes in an otherwise consistent literary form. Then, a reading of Anton Chekhov's *Lady with the Dog* (1899) shows how variations in social space effectively reconstruct the topography of arrival. The result is a historical map of literary works that complicates the reading of difference in existential terms by illustrating the chronotopic manipulation that frames arrival.

The demigod Gilgamesh is the young, unruly king of the city of Uruk. He meets the wild man Enkidu and attempts to overcome him in battle. The two are reconciled and become the best of friends. Gilgamesh and Enkidu set off to the Forest of Cedar to earn fame by slaying the guardian Humbaba and to destroy the sacred forest for timber. Gilgamesh later refuses the advances of the goddess Ishtar. In retaliation, a great bull is sent to wreak havoc in Uruk. It is killed by the combined efforts of Gilgamesh and Enkidu, but Enkidu dies shortly after as a result. Distraught, Gilgamesh wanders in search of immortality to Uta-napishti the Distant. On his journey, he imposes his will on others, but at the ends of the world, his mortality is revealed. Gilgamesh returns home to inscribe his journey on clay tablets and continue his reign as king over the city and people of Uruk.

This ancient tale contributes to an understanding of the topography of arrival as the existential meeting of Self and Other in several ways. First, Gilgamesh's discovery of the unknown at the ends of the

world is emphasized in the prologue: "[Gilgamesh] saw what was secret, discovered what was hidden, / he brought back a tale of before
the Deluge." (Anon 1993: 2) The stress placed on the 'secret' and
'hidden' coincides with reference to the preservation of the tale in
writing and instructions to "read out / the travails of Gilgamesh [...]
Who scoured the world ever searching for life, / and reached through
sheer force Uta-napishti the Distant" (Anon 1993: 2). Second, Gilgamesh meets subjects, rivals, nature and animals, foreigners and a goddess in Uruk and on his travels. In each case, the young king affirms
the priority and seeming invincibility of his own existence through
violence. It is only when Enkidu dies that Gilgamesh faces that which
cannot be conquered. But Gilgamesh, confronted with death, attempts
to prevail over his own mortality anyway. Exhausted by his endless
travels, he arrives at the ends of the earth, stripped of his royal robes,
worn out and alone. Uta-napishti the Distant makes it clear that the
divide between Self and Other cannot be overcome: "No one at all
sees Death,/no one at all sees the face [of Death,] / no one at all
[hears] the voice of Death,/Death so savage, who hacks men down."
(Anon 1993: 86) The meeting with Uta-napishti reveals an ultimate
displacement of the Self in relation to an Other that cannot be imposed
upon. As such, Gilgamesh's arrival at the ends of the earth may be
viewed as the revelation of an existential human condition.

   Gilgamesh ends with a repetition from the prologue: "O Ur-
shanabi, climb Uruk's wall and walk back and forth! / Survey its
foundations, examine the brickwork! / Were its bricks not fired in an
oven? / Did the Seven Sages not lay its foundations? / A square mile is
the city, a square mile date-grove, a square mile is / clay-pit, half a
square mile the temple of Ishtar: / three square miles and a half is
Uruk's expanse." (Anon 1993: 99) Gilgamesh's final arrival is a return to Uruk, the return of an impetuous, wandering king to the wall
that cannot be built alone, to the Seven Sages who commune with the
gods on behalf of mortals, to a city centered about a place of worship
and to the act of inscription. The topography of this final arrival continues to describe the transcendent displacement of Self in relation to
that which precedes, that which is unchanging, to the divine and to
language. As such, there is an emphasis on the timeless difference between Self and Other, however defined. Despite this, the return from
Uta-napishti the Distant is also to a city made of brick, with clear di-

mensions and recognizable spaces, which brings into question the chronotopic balance that informs the topography of arrival.

In "Forms of Time and of the Chronotope in the Novel", Bakhtin provides a means of describing the topography of arrival in terms of the construction of time and space, beginning with the ancient Greek romance. The external form of Xenophon's *An Ephesian Tale* is simple: boy meets girl, there are plans for marriage, an interruption follows, a series of adventures take place, boy and girl return home to marry. The vast majority of the story occurs between meeting and marriage, but regardless of the real time required to complete the intervening adventures, meeting and marriage follow as if not a single second had elapsed. Bakhtin summarizes the sense of time by stating that

> all the action in a Greek romance, all the events and adventures that fill it, constitute time-sequences that are neither historical, quotidian, biographical, nor even biological and maturational [...]. In this kind of time, nothing changes: the world remains as it was, the biographical life of the heroes does not change, their feelings do not change, people do not even age. This empty time leaves no traces anywhere, no indications of its passing. (Bakhtin 1981: 91)

This static time is complimented by a sense of space that is entirely abstract. The adventurers of *Ephesian* reach distant seas and high mountains, foreign cities and hazardous caves, but there are no indications of time passing. Particular social and political structures, specificities of culture and history, fail to ground the tale in a recognizable historical moment. As such, "[a]ll adventures in the ancient Greek romance are thus governed by an interchangeability of space" (Bakhtin 1981: 100).

On the inside, between the book-ends of meeting and marriage, a series of paratactic events governed solely by fate, chance or the gods occur 'suddenly' or 'instantaneously' to create a vertical structure oriented towards infinite time. Events are not connected linearly by way of cause and effect. Everything in an ancient Greek romance is isolated and unique. A kidnapping may follow a shipwreck, but it could just as easily happen in reverse without effect to the outcome of the tale. Every episode, like every space, is exchangeable. There is a sense of unity in such a tale, but it is tied solely to the dominance of fate. The hero does not take any initiative and the world is merely a backdrop to events. The introduction of progressive time and localized space would have serious consequences:

[It] would introduce its own rule-generating force, its own order, its inevitable ties to human life and to the time specific to that life. Events would end up being interwoven with these rules, and to a greater or lesser extent would find themselves participating in this order, subject to its ties. This would critically limit the power of chance; the movement of the adventures would be organically localized and tied down in time and space. (Bakhtin 1981: 101)

But at no point in *Ephesian* does the hero's arrival, including his return home, alter the sense of identity or the world. The abstract chronotope of ancient Greek romance leaves no trace of or possibility for progression. Despite the seemingly desperate action of the adventure episodes, nothing "is destroyed, remade, changed or created anew. What we get is a mere affirmation of the identity between what had been at the beginning and what is at the end" (Bakhtin 1981: 110). The topography of arrival, then, no matter where or how that arrival takes place, at the entrance to a mysterious cave across the sea or at the altar of a local temple, is one that reaches vertically without taking root.

The topography of arrival changes in two significant ways with *Metamorphoses* (c. 170 CE) by Lucius Apuleius. First, the main character Lucius undergoes two transformations – he is turned into an ass and then back into a human. Second, transformation is connected to wanderings throughout a recognizable world. Bakhtin notes that "what strikes us first of all is the mix of adventure-time with everyday-time" (Bakhtin 1981: 111). The emphasis on static self-affirmation and fate in Greek adventure-time gives way to an individual becoming linked to critical events attached to real places and progressive time. In this way, "[m]etamorphosis serves as the basis for a method of portraying the whole of an individual's life in its more important moments of *crisis*: for showing *how an individual becomes other than what he was*" (Bakhtin 1981: 114-5). Most striking about this form is how the journey and personal transformation become intertwined. *Metamorphoses* "fuses the course of an individual's life (at its major turning points) with his actual spatial course or road – that is, with his wanderings" (Bakhtin 1981: 120). There is a concretization of the local that is absent from *Ephesian*. As such, "[s]pace becomes more concrete and saturated with a time that is more substantial: space is filled with real, living meaning, and forms a crucial relationship with the hero and his fate" (Bakhtin 1981: 120). Chance still plays a significant role, but the logic of chance is subordinated to the limits of everyday life. Lucius's descent to the harsh Roman world and his subsequent ascent or rebirth is grounded in individual responsibility that emerges within the limits of the concretization of place. Lucius experiments with magic, takes the wrong potion and turns into an ass. He must then find his own way back to the form of man. Ascension, return to the norm, is not simply a matter predetermined by fate, although fate and the gods are always involved to some extent, but requires that the hero act consciously to alter his being-in-the-world. Bakhtin comments: "The series of adventures that the hero undergoes does not result in a simple affirmation of his identity, but rather in the construction of a new image of the hero, a man who is now purified and reborn." (1981: 117) This change in chronotope from *Ephesian* to *Metamorphoses* is reflected by an alteration of the topography of arrival towards spatial or material integration. The world itself remains unaltered. The metamorphosis remains individual and unproductive in terms of effect on the world. The everyday world does not 'become' with the hero, but remains fixed or largely absent. There is no change in this sense from the Greek romance, but Lucius goes through a metamorphosis that is *constructed or framed by the real world*, not solely imposed by fate. Every arrival along his path is, or is potentially, self-transformative. The topography of arrival, described in chronotopic terms, does not yet include anything approaching historicity, although a significant shift towards a new balance between time and space emerges such that arrival is no longer strictly divine, but dependent on interaction with concrete space.

The introduction of biographical time in literary works such as Voltaire's *Candide, ou l'Optimisme* (1759) clears the way for the further integration of historical time and space. *Candide* is as much a formulaic romance as *Ephesian*, but at the end of the many adventures that again occur between meeting and resolution the characters do not emerge unaffected by their journey. Attitudes change, but more importantly, the characters have aged. The events of *Ephesian* could only have occurred over the course of many years, but at the end the hero and the heroine are united in marriage, still young and beautiful with an entire lifetime ahead of them. In contrast, the arrival at the final garden in *Candide* is by no means the return to an unchanged paradise. Candide and the others, in their lifetime, must make something of the garden they have before them. There is no direct sense of history, but *Candide* sets forth a sense of diachronic time and adds to a notion of personal responsibility that carries on from *Metamorphoses*. Further, the arrival of Candide and all the other characters at the final garden is not only personal, but collective. The self is not affirmed (or reborn) by the decree of fate or by a personal relation to an abstract world, but by recognition of the co-existence of self and others in the world. Critically, it is not merely Candide who returns or ascends, as with Gilgamesh and Lucius. Candide and the others are assembled together; the arrival in this instance is inclusive.

The topography of arrival is altered further with the introduction of natural, or cyclical, time throughout the Enlightenment, culminating with Jean-Jacques Rousseau's *Confessions* (1782-89), which presents a view of people in relation to pristine Nature. Of importance, this portrayal brings Nature into the description of a journey that sets forth the meeting of and distance between Self and Other. When Rousseau sets out on a journey, he always does so in relation to his natural surroundings and a view of Nature as faultless and infinite. Arrival becomes a relation of Self to a sense of time beyond human grasp. Rousseau recognizes and co-exists with a sense of the immortality of Nature at every arrival along the path of his journey. The ephemeral materiality of Paris or Geneva is offset by the infiniteness of Nature. In contrast, Gilgamesh travels to the Forest of Cedar to find lumber; in this case, nature is a destination to be attained and trees, like divine bulls, women or boatmen, are to be overcome as the affirmation of one's own existence. This difference suggests that the literary construction of existential Otherness is also chronotopic.

It is Johann Wolfgang von Goethe, according to Bakhtin, who assimilates Rousseau's sense of natural or infinite time with the continuity of man-made spaces. In "The *Bildungsroman* and Its Significance in the History of Realism" Bakhtin writes of Goethe's *Italian Journey* (1816-17): "Terrestrial space and human history are inseparable from one another in Goethe's integrated concrete vision. [...] It is in Rome that Goethe experiences especially keenly this impressive condensation of historical time, its fusion with terrestrial space" (Bakhtin 1986: 40). Goethe's sense of time sets forth an entirely new chronotope:

It is history, above all, that one reads quite differently [in Rome] from anywhere else in the world. Everywhere else one starts out from the outside and works inward; here it seems to be the other way around. All history is encamped about us and all history sets forth again from us. This does not apply only to Roman history, but to the history of the whole world. [...] My experience with natural history is repeating itself here, for the entire history of the world is linked up with this city, and I reckon my second life, a very rebirth, from the day when I entered Rome. (Bakhtin 1986: 40)

Rome, for Goethe, is a great chronotope of *human* history. Arriving at Rome, he does not merely enter into a city of the present, but into the coexistence of times that stretch from past into future at one point in space.[1] Bakhtin notes that "[t]he space of Rome, revealed for Goethe the 'fullness of time'" (1986: 41) and summarizes his mode of visualizing time described in *Italian Journey* in the following way:

[E]verything is intensive in Goethe's world; it contains no inanimate, immobile, petrified places, no immutable background that does not participate in action and emergence (in events), no decorations or sets. On the other hand, this time, in all its essential aspects, is localized in concrete space, imprinted on it. In Goethe's world there are no events, plots, or temporal motifs that are not related in an essential way to the particular spatial place of their occurrence, that could occur anywhere or nowhere ('eternal' plots and motifs). Everything in this world is a *time-space*, a true *chronotope*. (Bakhtin 1986: 42)

The topography of arrival thus described has changed dramatically. In contrast to an ancient Greek journey by which the hero displaces nothing, Goethe sketches the self in relation to the synchronic and diachronic transformations of a concrete, human place. Whereas *Gilgamesh* dwells on the transcendent relation of Self and Other, *Italian Journey* clearly introduces a historical frame of reference.

This shift in the topography of arrival from ancient Greek adventure-time to the 'true chronotope' set out in Goethe's reflections on his journey to Rome reaches full expression in European literature with Scott's *The Heart of Midlothian*. Many of the symbols and motifs of *Ephesian* remain in *Midlothian*, for both are essentially of the romance genre, but time and space merge in a new way. In Scott's his-

---

[1]   The concept of the chronotope set forth by Bakhtin and elaborated upon in this chapter reminds of "heterotopology" as outlined by Michel Foucault in a March 1967 lecture titled "Des Espace Autres" in which he describes heterotopias in terms of the "simultaneously mythic and real contestation of the space in which we live", describing six key aspects, including the juxtaposition of spaces and the multiplicity of times (Foucault 2002).

torical romance, "the concrete wholeness of the real world is sensed in each of its images" (Bakhtin 1986: 46). The landscape is not abstract, but distinctly Scottish. The heroes are not governed wholly by fate, but are enabled and motivated within the limitations of a real world carefully situated in historical time. The concrete complexities of Scotland in relation to England, Europe and America in the middle of the eighteenth century are set forth not as a backdrop to events, but as integral to and inseparable from the development of the tale. As a chronotope populated at least in part by real historical figures, places and events, "this is a piece of human history, historical time condensed in space. Therefore, the plot (the sum of depicted events) and the characters do not enter it from outside, are not invented to fit the landscape, but are unfolded in it as though they were present from the very beginning" (Bakhtin 1986: 49). As such, it is not merely a picture of the past, but a connection between past and present that projects a particular range of subsequent possibilities into the future. Scott's fusion of past and present in real space is a powerful means of expression because it connects directly to an audience. As a result, every fictional arrival in *Midlothian* speaks to the imagination of things otherwise in the real world. Bakhtin writes of Goethe what is certainly no less true of Scott:

The world and history did not become poorer or smaller as a result of this process of mutual concretization and interpenetration. On the contrary, they were condensed, compacted, and filled with the creative possibilities of subsequent *real* emergence and development. Goethe's world is a *germinative seed*, utterly real, visibly available, and at the same time filled with an equally real future that is growing out of it. (1986: 50)

In this light, the journey of the Scottish heroine Jeanie Deans from Edinburgh to London to save her sister from execution involves a chronotopic integration of historical time that sets forth political possibilities. Jeanie follows the word of God to the point that she will not say an untrue word to save her sister in court, but her arrival in London, as the typical Scottish lass outfitted in tartan, an outsider seeking favor from the king, is not only dependent on personal initiative, but steeped in the historical moment. Her arrival in London is the meeting of Scotland and England, a relation determined by the 1707 Act of Union, but also one challenged by the Edinburgh riots of 1736. The word of God guides Jeanie on a personal level, yet her actions occur within a concretely outlined historical continuum that precedes and determines possibilities, enabling the pardon for her sister and framing her return to Scotland. Unlike *Gilgamesh*, which describes a return to an ancient, unchanging and sacred city, this is a return with a clear difference rooted in the historical moment. Jeanie faces Queen Caroline, challenging political authority and bringing into question the destiny of a Scottish nation subordinated to foreign rule. The displacement that takes place as a result of these events, followed by the description of Jeanie's place in an emerging, middle-class community in rural Scotland, is personal, national, and situated within changing circumstances particular to the modern world. A 'new' community emerging from 'ancient Highland sources' within the complex, real limitations of broad historical context shapes the possibilities of a recovered Scotland and an emerging Britain. The final journey is an arrival/return that caps a journey to the Other so as to suggest the displacement of an entire nation's future; it is not only Jeanie that is transformed, but Scotland. Scott ensures that Jeanie's journey speaks to the consciousness of an entire nation, and the realities of an emerging nation state, by embedding her arrivals and departures in a complex, overlapping series of social and political fields filled out by the material and economic concerns of a particular time and space. Metamorphosis takes on a whole new aspect, linking the individual with the nation, and the topography of arrival emerges as the displacement of self in relation to history such that the manipulation of the latter seems wholly within reach of the former. The intensive time of Goethe in Scott's hands is the means of setting forth the realization of an active self and the imagination of a collective Self (Scotland/Britain) that exists in a constructed and historical world of Others (nation states and empires).

Chekhov's short story *Lady with the Dog* is nothing like the historical romance of Scott. The integration of historical time plays no role. In fact, time seems strangely absent. However, the story is useful within the framework of this chapter because it emphasizes variations in the construction of medial spaces that re-describe the topography of arrival. There are four significant spaces in *Lady*: Moscow, Yalta, the theatre and the Bazaar. The story begins in Yalta. People are "telling one another that a newcomer had been seen on the promenade – a lady with a dog" (Chekhov 2002: 1524). The circulating gossip, however, reveals only a superficial description of a typical woman on holiday with a Pomeranian at her side. In contrast, a man with a full name, distinguished from the crowd, accustomed to the ways of Yalta, then "catches sight" (Chekhov 2002: 1524) of the newcomer. Dmitri Dmitrich Gurov watches 'the lady with the dog' from a distance, thinking to himself that "it wouldn't be a bad idea to make her acquaintance" (Chekhov 2002: 1524). But before Gurov and the lady with the dog meet, Gurov's wife in Moscow is introduced. She is described almost entirely in abstract terms connected to language. She is a self-proclaimed thinker, a great reader, a progressive writer and particular in her pronunciation. As such, the initial contrast between Moscow and Yalta is set out in terms of women and language. Moscow refers to the wife and to the use of language for specific purposes. Yalta indicates an unnamed woman and the fluid movement of words associated with idle conversation. Moscow is also connected to family, employment and society, whereas Yalta suggests sexuality and liberation. The movement from Moscow to Yalta, then, is the simultaneous departure from the space of order and arrival at the space of freedom.

In Yalta, Gurov claims to be a philologist (he is actually a banker) and advances upon the lady (as yet) without a proper name. He starts from a distance by reading the lady with the dog: "Her expression, gait, dress, coiffure, all told him that she was from the upper classes, that she was married [...] alone and bored." (Chekhov 2002: 1524-5) He sizes up the unknown woman, reading her appropriateness for sexual conquest. But Gurov's approach continues *within* language that precedes and overwhelms him: "stories of easy conquests [...] came back to him, and the seductive idea of a brisk transitory liaison, an affair with a woman whose very name he did not know, suddenly took possession of his mind." (Chekhov 2002: 1525) Gurov appears set to employ language to undermine his wife's authority in Moscow by possessing another woman, to temporarily escape his marriage bond and satisfy his personal desire. However, he is not in complete control; there is an uneasy tension between direct and indirect forms of language that leaves the nature of the situation uncertain.

Upon meeting Gurov, the lady with the dog lowers her eyes, blushes and does not look at him when speaking. She seems willing to succumb to Gurov's advances, but the conversation then begins through the dog. The questions are generic and the replies might be addressed to anyone. Gurov and the lady refer to the boredom of Yalta, then go "on eating in silence, like complete strangers" (Chekhov 2002: 1525). Gurov explains something of his life, but the description deteriorates, as indicated in the text by ellipses. She tells him that she grew up in Petersburg, married and lives in the town of S., but is incapable of explaining her husband's position. Gurov learns that her name is Anna Sergeyevna, but this is not her married name. The elusiveness of the words exchanged at this initial meeting in Yalta is critical to the topography of arrival set out in *Lady*. Neither character seems able to communicate much of anything. In contrast to the strict commands of the wife in Moscow, ambiguity and silence dominate the conversation between Anna and Gurov. An irreducible space lingers between them.

The words and thoughts of Gurov and Anna seem to exist in separate cages, residing side-by-side in the text, yet never bringing the two characters together. As such, Moscow (wife/Gurov) and Yalta (Gurov/Anna) seem entirely different. The first is a space of intentionality, the second of co-existence or ambiguity. The difference between these spaces (north/south) can be further described in Nietzschean terms. The Apollonian refers to clarity, appearance/illusion, boundaries, self-control and perfection; the Dionysian to nature, instinct, the wholeness of existence and the dissolution of boundaries. In the north, Gurov is dominated by his wife and Anna by her husband. Each lives within limits set by social and political structures that define norms of behavior. In the southern resort of Yalta, Gurov and Anna seek escape from the territorialized space of 'cultivated' society and from the 'civilized' idea of how they should or should not exist. Arrival, then, is a departure from order, from intentionality and inhibition. In Yalta, there are no acquaintances, no wives, husbands or children. Everyone is anonymous, free to take on new professions and names. Arrival in Yalta is a rebirth, of sorts. But this renewal of Dionysian freedom occurs by way of the northern construction of a south, a relative space that re-determines identity and relations.

Oreanda is a small seaside resort on the outskirts of Yalta to which Gurov and Anna go to escape detection. It is an important place for several reasons. First, it represents a return to nature: "When they got out of the carriage [at Oreanda] [...] the grasshoppers chirruped, and the monotonous hollow roar of the sea came up to them, speaking of peace, of the eternal sleep lying in wait for us all." (Chekhov 2002: 1528) Descriptions of nature are used repeatedly throughout *Lady* to represent the sublime – majestic beauty free of human constraint, a release from the city, displacement in relation to the infinite monotony of nature. Second, and more importantly, it is not simply that the south, or Yalta in particular, represents the Dionysian. In Yalta, Gurov and Anna are aware of the threat of someone seeing them together. Anna's husband is constantly expected from the north. The imposition of others, the threat of judgment, weighs heavily. As such, Yalta is not a definite or exclusive space of freedom. The transgression of self, holding open the Dionysian space of desire, requires perpetual movement, one journey after another, not a particular place. Oreanda does not represent the final destination, for here too they are seen by others. Thus, there are two aspects to consider: first, the movement from the perceived rigidity of space or imposition of order (Moscow, then Yalta); second, the construction of the new space in which they locate themselves. At Yalta, they walk on the beach between sea and city. At Oreanda, they sit between the sea and a nearby church:

> The roar of the sea came up to them, speaking of peace, of the eternal sleep lying in wait for us all [...] and it may be that in this continuity, this utter indifference of life and death, lies the secret of our ultimate salvation, of the stream of life on our planet, and of its never ceasing movement towards perfection. (Chekhov 2002: 1528)

Between city and sea, and between sea and the sacred, they pursue a dwelling that is uncertain. The literary construction of arrival involves language (the opposition between direct and indirect forms), the movement between Apollonian and Dionysian forces and *the construction of in-between spaces* – each of which locates the meeting of individuals between finite and infinite.

Intentional language re-enters the story by way of a letter from Anna's husband in the north indicating that he will not come to Yalta because his eyes are troubling him and that she should return home at once. Significantly, Anna refers to the letter as "the intervention of fate" (Chekhov 2002: 1529). There is something of the Greek romance in the abrupt arrival of the letter and the quick parting that follows. Gurov, too, returns to his home in the north, but Gurov's memory of Anna does not fade: "He would pace up and down his room for a long time, smiling at his memories, and then memory turned into dreaming, and what had happened mingled in his imagination with what was going to happen." (Chekhov 2002: 1530) A memory suggests something that can be recalled, but one does not consciously bring back a dream, which hints at the unconscious, that which exceeds control, much like the sea, God, love, desire, the Dionysian. However, for Gurov the dream is of Anna. A process of individuation, whereby the undifferentiated tends to become individual, takes shape. The desire for life – the south, perpetual transgression – tends toward an undifferentiated whole in Gurov's mind, in the form of Anna. In Yalta, Gurov seemed to be escaping Moscow and boundaries by way of leisure and sexual freedom. Back in Moscow he is steeped in an urban life, "Frantic card-playing, gluttony, drunkenness, perpetual talk always about the same thing [...] discussing the same thing over and over again and there was nothing to show for it all [...]" (Chekhov 2002: 1531). Gurov seems to balk, not at order, but at an excess of Dionysian forces. He turns Anna into a single Apollonian entity, a fixation around which he redefines his existence. The Apollonian and Dionysian seem to meet in Anna. It might be expected that the return to Moscow is the return to binding laws, duties and expectations. However, it seems to be a mingling of the Apollonian *and* the Dionysian in two ways, home and life in Moscow, individuation and desire in Anna. As such, every arrival is dependent on a departure, that is, the relationship between two spaces. The relation between the space departed from and the space arrived at re-determines identity, as well as the spaces involved. The relation between Gurov and Moscow outlined in Yalta that contributed to the development of his relationship with Anna cannot be the same after Yalta.

Suffering from insomnia, sick of family life, bored of the excesses of Moscow, filled with the thought of and desire for Anna, Gurov travels to the town of S. to find her. At the hotel, there is a "carpet of gray military frieze" and outside Anna's house "a long gray fence" (Chekhov 2002: 1531). Gurov must wait, "hovering in the vicinity of the fence" (Chekhov 2002: 1531) which separates him from Anna. In his hotel room he uses "the cheap gray quilt, which reminded him of a hospital blanket" (Chekhov 2002: 1532). The movement to the anonymous town, emphasis on the color gray, waiting and hovering, indicate a shift. Gurov may still be pursuing Anna, but his arrival no longer has the accompanying feeling of conquest it did in Yalta. Gurov finds Anna at the theatre. They "wandered aimlessly along corridors, up and down stairs; figures flashed by in uniforms of legal officials, high-school teachers and civil servants, all wearing badges [...]" (Chekhov 2002: 1533) They have no single destination in mind and notice none of the artificial trappings of society that designate rank or power. Gurov thinks: "What on earth are all these people, this orchestra for?" (Chekhov 2002: 1533) A half-consciousness seems to carry them forward on a journey without a destination, but the scene is not without a spatial frame. It is clearly indicated that their meeting on "a dark, narrow staircase" takes place in the middle of the staircase: "On the landing above there were two schoolboys, smoking and looking down [...] Someone was ascending the stairs." (Chekhov 2002: 1533) In other words, they meet in the shadows of stage and audience, arriving between the upper and the lower, suspended between public and private. The space is at once particular and indeterminate, specifically located, yet emphasizing movement. The space of arrival in *Lady* is clearly not one of resolution or clearly defined borders, but every (medial) space redefines the relationship between Anna, Gurov and society. Yalta, Oreanda and the theatre stairway make up a series of locations that emphasize the perpetual reconstruction of boundaries. This continues when Gurov and Anna meet in Moscow at Slavyanski Bazaar.

The bazaar traditionally represents a place of exchange or flow, anonymity and otherness, in which, neither order nor freedom dominate completely. In reference to the square or the bazaar in the thirteenth and fourteenth centuries in Europe, Bakhtin writes: "It was a remarkable chronotope, in which all the most elevated categories, from that of the state to that of revealed truth, were realized concretely and fully incarnated, made visible and given a face." (Bakhtin 1981: 132) In *Lady*, the Bazaar is a hotel room isolated from the public sphere. Two anonymous foreigners in their own city, Anna wearing gray and Gurov with his graying hair, meet to hold open the possibility of a new life together, but also a means of interrupting the closed, known lives each leads away from the other. Of Gurov, Chekhov discloses the following:

He led a double life – one in public, in the sight of all whom it concerned, full of conventional truth and conventional deception, exactly like the lives of his friends and acquaintances, and another which flowed in secret [...] He began to judge others by himself, no longer believing what he saw, and always assuming that the real, the only interesting life of every individual goes on as under cover of night, secretly. Every individual existence revolves around mystery [...] (2002: 1534)

The arrival at the Bazaar is the final crossroads at which public and private space meet. Both Gurov and Anna face an Other in the form of society from which they must hide, but there is also the public and the private between Gurov and Anna, the space between them indicated by their inability to communicate or resolve their situation. The meetings of Anna and Gurov at Yalta, Oreanda, the theatre and the Bazaar represent the infinite series of Dionysian transgressions, as well as the mediality of spaces, that make possible the desire between people without ever allowing for complete communication with another or total knowledge of one's self.

In antiquity, "[t]o be exterior meant to be for others, for the collective, for one's own people. A man was utterly exteriorized, but within a human element, in the human medium of his own people. Therefore, the *unity* of a man's externalized wholeness was of a *public* nature" (Bakhtin 1986: 135). This is entirely opposite to Gurov's world. Every new space, from Yalta to the Bazaar, is an arrival defined by escape from others, from the public and his own public persona, and also the potential staging ground for a new balance between private and public that would allow for the union of private desire, the love of Gurov and Anna, with public acceptance. In Moscow, they meet at the Bazaar, but it is not a public place. It is a private hotel room and it is in this enclosed space that their real selves are revealed, however incompletely, as well as their plans to enter back into public life on their own terms. For the ancient Greek citizen, as in *Ephesian*, "[t]here is no mute or invisible core to the individual himself: he is entirely visible and audible, all on the surface" (Bakhtin 1981: 134). In contrast, *Lady* depicts an interior space that is always present, but never wholly revealed. Further, it is the perpetual re-creation of the space shared by two individuals that holds open the possibility of a balance between internal Self and external Other. *Lady*, then, not only sets forth the unknowable Other, but does so through the specific and immanent spatial construction of every meeting.

In conclusion, two vivid images provided by Franz Kafka summarize the central contrast of this paper. First, in "An Imperial Message" the messenger travels through vast, infinite crowds; he is powerful, tireless and carries the sign of the sun. But,

how vain are his efforts [...] he will never get to the end of them; and even if he did, he would be no better off; he would have to fight his way down the stairs; and even if he did that, he would be no better off; he would still have to get through the courtyards; and after the courtyards, the second outer palace enclosing the first; and more stairways and more courtyards; and still another palace; and so on for thousands of years [...] (Kafka 1976b: 159)

The journey continues without conclusion. It is, in some way, the story that runs throughout the history of literature, from *Gilgamesh* to *Lady*, an endless procession of arrivals and departures holding open the separation of Self and Other described in so many ways. Second, in "Before the Law" a man from the country travels to the doorkeeper to gain access to the Law. He is not denied entry, but not given it either. He waits and waits. While doing so, he asks questions of the gatekeeper and makes every attempt to gain entry. Years pass by as he waits and wonders uncertainly. Finally, near death, the man asks, "Everyone strives to reach the Law, so how does it happen that for all these many years no one but myself has ever begged for admittance?" (Kafka 1976a: 149). The doorkeeper answers: "No one else could ever be admitted here, since this gate was made only for you. I am going to shut it now" (Kafka 1976a: 150). The journey may be endless, and the existential difference insurmountable, but every arrival is particular; the literary construction of identity depends on the historical coordination of time and space.

Bibliography

Anon, 1993. *Sha naqba īmuru* (c. seventh century BCE); Engl.: *The Epic of Gilgamesh* (trans. George, Andrew). New York: Penguin.

Bakhtin, M.M. 1986. *Bildungsroman i ego znachenie v istorii realizma*; Engl.: 'The Bildungsroman and Its Significance in the History of Realism' (trans. McGee, Vern W.) in Emerson, Caryl and Holquist, Michael (eds.) *Speech Genres and Other Late Essays*. Austin: University of Texas.

—. 1981. *Formy vremeni i khronotopa v romane* (written 1937-8); Engl. 'Forms of Time and of the Chronotope in the Novel' (trans. Emerson, Caryl and Holquist) in Holquist, Michael (ed.) *The Dialogic Imagination : four essays*. Austin: University of Texas Press.

Chekhov, Anton. 2002. *Дама с собачкой* (1899); Engl. 'The Lady with the Dog' (trans. Litvinov, Ivy). in Lawall, Sarah et al. (eds.) *Norton Anthology of World Literature*, vol. E. New York: W.W. Norton.

Foucault, Michel. 2002. 'Of Other Spaces' in Mirzoeff, Nicholas (ed.) *The Visual Culture Reader*. London: Routledge.

Goethe, Johann Wolfgang von. 1994. *Italienische Reise* (1816-7); Engl.: *Italian Journey*. Princeton: Princeton University Press.

Kafka, Franz. 1976a. *Vor dem Gesetz;* Engl.: 'Before the Law' in *The Penal Colony: Stories and Short Pieces* (trans. Muir, Edwin and Muir, Willa). New York: Schocken.

—. 1976b. *Eine kaiserliche Botschaft;* Engl.: 'An Imperial Message' in *The Penal Colony: Stories and Short Pieces* (trans. Muir, Edwin and Muir, Willa). New York: Schocken.
Rousseau, Jean-Jacques. 2000. *Les Confessions*; Engl.: *Confessions*. Oxford: Oxford University Press.
Scott, Walter. 2004. *The Heart of Midlothian* (1818). Edinburgh: Edinburgh University Press.
Voltaire, 2006. *Candide, ou l'Optimisme* (1759); Engl.: *Candide and other stories*. Oxford: Oxford University Press.

8. From Exile to Escape:
Frame Narratives of the *Decameron* and the *Heptameron*

Irina Dzero

Exile and the change of location are the plot devices in the frame narratives of Boccaccio's *Decameron* (a collection of one hundred stories, began in 1350, finished in 1353). Margaret of Navarre repeats this structure when she writes a French version of this book, called the *Heptameron* (first published in 1558) because she only completed seventy-two novellas. The storytellers in these two Renaissance works must leave the city and go to the countryside to produce and enjoy fiction, and they go there in spite of themselves, only because they must. These are the two aspects that I would like to study here. How do we interpret that they literally walk from one place to another? And secondly, why must there be a plague (in *Decameron*) or a flood (in *Heptameron*) to make the characters invent, tell, and enjoy stories?

The frame narratives of the *Decameron* and the *Heptameron* have received various interpretations. Critics attempted to uncover a moral message of the works. For example, Angelo Lipari supposed that "Boccaccio intended the *Decameron* […] for the instruction of his fellow-poets" (Lipari 1945: 102). Victoria Kirkham suggests that the ten storytellers of the *Decameron* represent ten virtues and the book as a whole advances "a point of view that approves of rational behavior and disapproves of irrational behavior. [...] reason should control the appetites, not the other way around" (Kirkham 1985:18). For Gerard Defaux and Edwin Duval the conversations of the storytellers *Heptameron* show the supremacy of the Gospel over human stories (Defaux 2002: 40 and Duval 1993: 60), and for Paula Sommers they "reveal [...] an essentially Pauline perspective" (Sommers 1984: 793). Feminist critics focus on identifying oppressive gender hierarchies in the interactions of the storytellers. Marilyn Migiel examines "the strategies used to control discourses about women, their agency, and their sexuality" in the *Decameron* (Migiel 2003: 4). Patricia Cholakian examines how in the *Heptameron* "preexisting male narratives have been written over" (Cholakian 1991: 5). But the question of the force majeure in the frame narratives remains unanswered. Why characters cannot simply gather together in the city for their literary pastime? I would like to show that this "in spite of oneself" production and enjoyment of fiction illustrates the establishment of literature as a legitimate practice.

Let me consider the first aspect of the frame narratives, that the storytellers walk from one place, the city in which they have a real life, to another place, in the countryside, in which they produce and enjoy fictional life. My goal is to show that this forced change of location illustrates the experience of reading. The storytellers of the *Decameron* must go away from the city for the same reason that people read fiction, to forget their present troubles. In the beginning of the *Decameron*, seven ladies, later to be joined by three gentlemen, meet in the church. One of the ladies (Pampinea) explains to the rest that they must leave the city. If they do not, they shall die, either from the plague which ravages Florence, or from melancholy. Everywhere they turn, they find desolation. Pampinea complains:[1]

[W]e remain here [in the church] for no other purpose than to witness how many bodies are buried [...] If we leave this church we see the bodies of the dead and the sick being carried about. Or we see those who had been exiled from the city by the authority of the laws for their crimes, deriding this authority because they know the guardians of the law are sick or dead and running around the place. Or we see the dregs of the city battening on our blood and calling themselves sextons, riding about on horseback in every direction and insulting our calamities with vile songs. On every side we hear nothing but "So-and-so is dead" or "So-and-so is dying." [...] But if I go home there is nobody left there [...] Whether I go or sit at home I seem to see the ghosts of the departed, not with the faces as I knew them but with the dreadful looks which terrify me (8).[2]

---

[1] The references to the *Decameron* are from the following edition: Boccaccio, Giovanni. 1949. *The Decameron* (trans. Richard Altington). Garden City, NY: Doubleday.

[2] "Noi dimoriamo qui, al parer mio, non altramente che se essere volessimo o dovessimo testimonie di quanti corpi morti ci sieno alla sepoltura ... E, se di quinci usciamo, o veggiamo corpi morti o infermi trasportarsi dattorno, o veggiamo coloro li quali per li loro difetti l'autorità delle publiche leggi già condannò ad essilio, quasi quelle schernendo, per ciò che sentono gli essecutori di quelle o morti o malati, con dispiacevoli impeti per la terra discorrere, o la feccia della nostra città, del nostro sangue riscaldata, chiamarsi becchini e in strazio di noi andar cavalcando e discorrendo per tutto, con

Thus, the storytellers-to-be need to leave because everything they see – in the church, in the street and in their own homes – fills them with fear and despair. In the church they witness a continual burial service for the dead. In the streets outlaws and criminals are having a ball. At home they are greeted by a solitude inhabited by the ghosts of the loved ones who died of the plague. In other words, Pampinea concludes, "I am ill at ease here [in the church] and outside of here and at home" (8).[3] They leave because their real life has become intolerable.

Upon their arrival to the countryside, the storytellers find that they left too much of themselves within the walls of the plagued city, in the real life. One of the three men who joined the seven ladies (Dioneo) sets forth an ultimatum: "I do not know what you are thinking of doing with your troubles here, but I dropped mine inside the gates of the city when I left it with you a little time ago. Therefore, either you must make up your minds to laugh and sing and amuse yourselves with me [...], or you must let me go back to my troubles and stay in the afflicted city" (11).[4] And thus is born the idea to tell stories.

Thus, storytelling is designed to entertain those who are forced to leave their real life behind. The fictional life will allow them to subsist until they can return to the city and assume their usual selves. The storytelling site is not the countryside villa where they live, but the meadow nearby, "a lawn of thick green grass entirely shaded from the sun" (13).[5] Why storytelling rather than other diversions? Because

---

disoneste canzoni rimproverandoci i nostri danni. Né altra cosa alcuna ci udiamo, se non: - I cotali son morti, - e - Gli altrettali sono per morire [...] E, se alle nostre case torniamo, [...] io, di molta famiglia, niuna altra persona in quella ... trovando, impaurisco e quasi tutti i capelli addosso mi sento arricciare; e parmi, dovunque io vado o dimoro per quella, l'ombre di coloro che sono trapassati vedere, e non con quegli visi che io soleva, ma con una vista orribile, non so donde il loro nuovamente venuta, spaventarmi" (19-20). The references to the original text are from the following edition: Boccaccio, Giovanni. 1967. Bari: Editori Laterza.

3   "Per le quali cose, e qui e fuori di qui e in casa mi sembra star male" (20).

4   "Io non so quello che de' vostri pensieri voi v'intendete di fare; li miei lasciai io dentro dalla porta della città allora che io con voi poco fa me ne uscì fuori; e per ciò, o voi a sollazzare e a ridere e a cantare con meco insieme vi disponete [...] o voi mi licenziate che io per li miei pensieri mi ritorni e steami nella città tribolata" (25).

5   "uno pratello, nel quale l'erba era verde e grande né vi poteva d'alcuna parte il sole" (28).

other pastimes, such as games, cannot fill the thoughts of all company at once, explains Pampinea.

Here it is cool and lovely, and, as you see, there are games of chess and draughts which everyone can amuse himself with, as he chooses. But, if my opinion is followed, we shall not play games, because in games the mind of one of the players must necessarily be distressed without any great pleasure to the other player or the onlookers. Let us rather spend this hot part of the day in telling tales, for thus one person can give pleasure to the whole company. (13)[6]

Thus the storytellers spend their ten-day exile producing and enjoying ten stories a day. Not surprisingly, they grow to love their exile more than the place which they had to leave. They begin to like the fictional life which they produce more than the real life they left in Florence. Thus, the exile becomes an escape.

Margaret of Navarre in her unfinished imitation of the *Decameron* called the *Heptameron* (it unexpectedly breaks off on Novella 72), replicates the force majeure condition of storytelling and the change of location. She restores the gender balance between the narrators: five ladies and five gentlemen. While Boccaccio's storytellers gather together because of the plague, Margaret's narrators are driven to their place of exile by a flood. As a number of members of the French court were relaxing at the baths of the Pyrenees at Cauterets, heavy autumn rains flooded the river and barred the passage back. This calls to mind the biblical flood, with which God attempted to reform human nature by drowning all the sinners. Margaret alludes to this attempt at making a tabula rasa out of human nature: "there fell such excessive and extraordinary rains that it seemed as though God had forgotten His promise to Noah, and was again about to destroy the world with water." (1)[7] Thus, the flood cuts the storytellers off from

---

[6]   "Qui è bello e fresco stare, e hacci, come voi vedete, e tavolieri e scacchieri, e puote ciascuno, secondo che all'animo gli è più di piacere, diletto pigliare. Ma se in questo il mio parer si seguisse, non giucando, nel quale l'animo dell'una delle parti convien che si turbi senza troppo piacere dell'altra o di chi sta a vedere, ma novellando (il che può porgere, dicendo uno, a tutta la compagnia che ascolta diletto) questa calda parte del giorno trapasseremo." (28)

[7]   The quotations from the Heptameron come from the following edition: Navarre, Margaret of. [1558] 1984. *The Heptameron of Margaret, Queen of Navarre* (trans. P.A. Chilton). New York: Penguin Books. The quotations from the original French text come from Navarre, Marguerite de. [1558] 1999. *Heptaméron* (ed. Renja Salminen). Geneva: Droz. The original French version for

their homes and their real life at the French court. At first, they will make every attempt to get home. Many of the vacationers perish, many of them make it back, but ten of them gather at the monastery of Notre Dame de Serrance. The first person to arrive there, an old and pious woman, goes there on purpose. She finds there two young ladies who have taken refuge there after being attacked by a bear, and a gentleman who has nearly drowned when trying to cross the river to get back home. Then five more people arrive at the monastery, after some extraordinary adventures. Two married ladies and their husbands got in trouble with robbers and one of the husbands got killed. Fortunately the two admirers of these ladies kill the robbers. Then, the group of three men and two ladies also go to the monastery of Notre Dame de Serrance. Thus, five men and five women, of different age, marital status, and intelligence are brought together in an unfamiliar setting, quite in spite of themselves, although they are glad to see each other alive and well.

In spite of the force majeure – the flood that expulsed them from their normal life, they want to get back to it. One of them (Simonault) nearly loses his life in the attempt. All of his servants drown when he tries to cross the river, because he was "tired of waiting that the river should subside" (5).[8] Time and again, the entire company impatiently inquires if they can go home and they are upset when find out they cannot. "After the company had heard mass and dined, they sent to see if it were possible to pass the Gave river, and were in consternation at hearing that the thing was impracticable" (5).[9] They finally resolve to sponsor the construction of a bridge in order to return home. "After dinner they sent to know if the waters were fallen, but finding, on the contrary, that they were still higher, and that it would be a long time before they could pass safely, they resolved to have a

---

this quotation is: "vindrent les pluyes si merveilleuses et si grandes, qu'il sembloit que Dieu eut oblyé la promesse qu'il avoit faicte à Noé de ne destruire plus le monde par eaue" (1).

[8]   "ennuyé de la longue demeure quel faisoit la riviere à s'abaisser" (6).

[9]   "Après qu'ilz eurent oy la messe et disné, envoyerent veoir s'il estoit possible de passer la riviere du Gave, et, congnoissans l'impossibilité du passaige, furent en merveilleuse craincte." (5)

bridge made" (6).[10] However, the workmen who undertake to construct this bridge announce that it will take from ten to twelve days. The company realizes that they are stuck in the monastery with nothing to do, and begin "to grow tired" (7).[11] So they ask the old pious woman, who alone among them had planned to get to this monastery (Oisille), to "devise some amusement to mitigate the annoyance we shall suffer from so long a delay, for unless we have something agreeable and virtuous to occupy us, we are in danger of falling sick" (7).[12] But the pious old woman knows of no better entertainment than the Scriptures. "You want me to invent an amusement which shall dissipate your ennui. I have been in search of such a remedy all my life long, and I have never found but one, which is the reading of the Holy Writ. It is in such reading that the mind finds its true and perfect joy" (7).[13] Although pious, the company begs for a more diverting pastime. As one of them (Hircan) puts it, "we are not yet so mortified [...] we have need of some amusement and corporeal pastime. When we are at home we have the chase and hawking, which make us forget a thousand bad thoughts; the ladies have their household affairs, their needlework, and sometimes dancing, wherein they find laudable exercise." (8)[14] They come up with a solution to accommodate the need for piousness and for entertainment. They decide to read and listen to the Scriptures in the morning, but in the afternoon they will tell stories, as the characters of Boccaccio *Decameron*. Yet, as in Boccaccio, the telling of tales is not an end in itself. Margaret's storytellers have re-

---

10 "Après disner envoyerent sçavoir si les eaues estoient poinct escoulées, et, trouvant que plustost elles estoient creues et que de longtemps ne pourroient seurement passer, se delibererent de faire ung pont." (7)

11 "commença fort à s'ennuyer" (8).

12 "quelque passetemps pour adoulcir l'ennuy que nous porterons durant notre longue demeure; car, si nous n'avons quelque occupation plaisante et vertueuse, nous sommes en dangier de devenir malades" (8).

13 "ung passetemps qui vous puisse delivrer de vos ennuyctz; car, aiant chergé le remede toute ma vye, n'en ay jamais trouvé que ung, qui est la lecture des sainctes lettres en laquelle se trouve la vraie et parfaicte joie de l'esprit" (8).

14 "nous sommes encore si mortiffiez qu'il nous fault quelque passetemps et exercice corporel; car si nous sommes en noz maisons, il nous fault la chasse et la vollerye, qui nous faict oblier mil folles pensées; et les dames ont leur mesnaige, leur ouvraige et quelquesfois les dances où elles prennent honneste exercice" (10).

course to it "whilst waiting for the completion of our bridge" (10),[15] while waiting impatiently to return to their real life.

However, Margaret's storytellers, as Boccaccio's, also enjoy the fictional lives that emerge in front of them on the empty meadow. The virgin nature turns out to be the best place to enjoy the experience of engrossing oneself in the life of others. In contrast to the villa or the monastery, there is nothing in the field that would remind them of their status and situation. There are no paintings, no crucifixes, no familiar objects that could return the imagination to their real selves. Thus, at the end of the first day of storytelling the very lady who had recommended the Scriptures as the best possible entertainment (Oisille) confesses that although she had heard the call to vespers, she said nothing to stop the narrator. She says, "vespers have been rung at the Abbey this long time. I did not tell you so before, because I was less desirous to hear vespers than to know the end of the story" (105).[16] Even the monks of the monastery come to listen to the stories. They also want to live the lives of others. At the end of the third day, when the fascinating and shocking story of a double incest is over (Novella 30) and the audience starts discussing it from a religious point of view, one of the storytellers notices that the monks did not care to listen to it. He says, "whilst we were telling our stories the monks who were behind that hedge did not hear the vesper-bell; but no sooner did they hear us talk of God than away they went, and now they are ringing the second bell" (291).[17]

Thus, both Boccaccio and Margaret of Navarre insist that the storytellers leave their real lives only because they have no choice. But why would they want to stay in this fictional realm after spending only a short while there? Boccaccio explains it in the proem to *Decameron*. He begins the book with "Tis humane to have compassion upon the unhappy" (i).[18] Boccaccio intends to cure suffering souls

---

[15]   "actendant que nostre pont soit parfaict" (11).

[16]   "oyez la cloche de l'abbaye, qui, long temps a, nous appelle à vespres, dont je ne vous ay point advertiz; car la devotion d'oyr la fin du compte estoit plus grande que celle d'oyr vespres" (105).

[17]   "tant que nous avons racompté noz histoires, les moynes, derriere ceste haye, n'ont poinct ouy la cloche de leurs vespres, et maintenant, quant nous avons commencé à parler de Dieu, ilz s'en sont allez et sonnent à ceste heure le second coup" (287).

[18]   "Umana cosa è aver compassione degli afflitti" (3).

with his book. He knows about suffering from experience, as he relates that in his youth he was so deeply in love with a lady that he nearly died. Now, cured from this love, he intends to offer some solace to other sufferers. In his opinion, ladies need more distraction and consolation than men, so it is to the ladies that he dedicates his *Decameron*. Their real lives are boring and miserable for, having no profession, they must sit idly in their room. Ladies' real lives are also full of fear because everyone has a right to boss them around: mothers, and all male family members:

[W]omen are restricted by the authority of fathers, mothers, brothers and husbands. They spend most of their time shut up in the narrow circuit of their rooms, sitting in almost complete idleness, wanting and not wanting a thing in the same hour, turning over different thoughts which cannot always be gay ones. Now if the melancholy born of fierce desire should enter their minds, they must be forced to remain in sadness unless it is driven away by new discourse (vi).[19]

Boccaccio continues to explain why it is harder for a woman to bear the annoyances of the real life. Women cannot distract themselves even for a short while, cloistered at home and without a profession. Men, on the contrary, can do many things to banish depressive thoughts and to renew their mental and moral strength.

If men are afflicted with melancholy or heavy thoughts, they have many ways of lightening them or avoiding them; whenever they wish, they can go out and hear and look at things, they can go hawking, hunting, fishing, riding; they can gamble or trade. By these means every man can divert his mind wholly or partly, and free it from uneasy thought, at least for a time; and thus in one way and another consolation comes to him or the anguish grows less. (vi)[20]

---

[19]   Original Italian version: "ristrette dà voleri, dà piaceri, dà comandamenti de' padri, delle madri, de' fratelli e de' mariti, il più del tempo nel piccolo circuito delle loro camere racchiuse dimorano e quasi oziose sedendosi, volendo e non volendo in una medesima ora, seco rivolgendo diversi pensieri, li quali non è possibile che sempre sieno allegri. E se per quegli alcuna malinconia, mossa da focoso disio, sopravviene nelle lor menti, in quelle conviene che con grave noia si dimori, se da nuovi ragionamenti non è rimossa" (5).

[20]   Original Italian: "Essi, se alcuna malinconia o gravezza di pensieri gli affligge, hanno molti modi da alleggiare o da passar quello, per ciò che a loro, volendo essi, non manca l'andare a torno, udire e veder molte cose, uccellare, cacciare, pescare, cavalcare, giucare o mercatare: de' quali modi ciascuno ha forza di trarre, o in tutto o in parte, l'animo a sè e dal noioso pensiero rimuoverlo almeno per alcuno spazio di tempo, appresso il quale, con un modo o con altro, o consolazion sopraviene o diventa la noia minore." (5)

Boccaccio shows that women suffer more psychologically because, unlike men, they cannot vent their emotions. Only in their minds can they forget about their actual existence, devoid of meaningful activities and fully dependent on the good graces of other people. Yet did not Boccaccio begin by confessing that he himself nearly died of love? None of the activities to which his gender entitled him could help him divert his mind from his real-life troubles. In short, in the proem Boccaccio makes three points: that the real life of a person, regardless of the gender, can be boring or miserable, or both at once, that everyone needs to escape from it, and that the best escape from real life is the world of fiction.

Margaret of Navarre was a pious person. In her poetry she draws inspiration from Evangelism and Lutheranism, which emphasize faith and the Gospel. This is why her countryside escape is situated beside a monastery. This is why the storytellers spend the first part of the day reading and listening to the Scriptures. The *Heptameron*'s religious dimension is Marguerite's major innovation and corrective to the *Decameron*. Yet, the *Heptameron* shows that even the most pious person needs a mental escape from his or her real life. Thus, even though the monastery seems to provide the storytellers with all they need: lodging, food, and spiritual counsel, they still leave it and engage in the production and enjoyment of fiction. The dwellers of the monastery, the monks follow the storytellers to the meadow to eavesdrop on the fascinating fictional lives. At the end of the second day, the storytellers are late for the evening service because they were too absorbed by the last story. They are surprised to find that the clerics also missed it:

[The storytellers went] into the church, where they found that although the bell had been rung for vespers there were no monks to say them. The fathers had been apprised of the agreeable manner in which the company spent their time in the meadow, and being fonder of pleasure rather than of their prayers, they had gone and crouched down there in a ditch behind a very thick hedge, and had listened to the tales with so much attention that they had not heard the vesper-bell. The consequence was that they came running in with such haste that they were quite out of breath then they should have begun vespers. After service, some of the company inquiring of them why they had come in so late and chanted so badly, they confessed the cause; and for the future they were allowed to listen behind the hedge, and to sit at their ease. (190)[21]

---

[21]   "entra dedans l'eglise, où ils trouverent vespres très bien sonnées, mais ilz n'y trouverent pas ung religieux pour les dire, pource qu'ilz avoient entendu que

Thus, Boccaccio and Margaret make a point that men and women, secular and pious, married and unmarried, all need a mental vacation. This is why the unwanted, forced exile from the real life transforms into an escape. After immersing themselves into the fictional life for a few days, the storytellers realize that they do not want to go back. In the *Decameron* they only resolve to go back to Florence lest their acquaintances find out about their escape in the world of fiction and come to disrupt it with real-life connections, memories, and plans: "our being together is already known round about, and so our company might be increased in such a way as to destroy our pleasure" (556).[22] In the *Heptameron*, they actually begin to dread the day when the bridge over the flooded river would be completed. "After mass they took a little walk while waiting for dinner, anticipating as agreeable a day as the preceding one. Saffredent said that he was so charmed with the good cheer they made and the recreation they enjoyed, that he could wish it might be a month yet before the bridge was finished (352).[23] Thus, the unwanted exile becomes a desirable escape. Yet, why must it have begun as exile?

Let me now examine the second aspect of the frame narratives. Why, indeed, do the storytellers go into the space where they can enjoy fictional life in spite of themselves? Why must there be a force majeure to expulse them from their ordinary life and from the city?

---

dedans le pré s'assembloit ceste compaignye pour y dire les plus plaisantes choses qu'il estoit possible; et, comme ceulx qui aymoient mieulx leurs plaisirs que les oraisons, s'estoient allez cacher dedans une fosse, le ventre contre terre, derrière une haye fort espesse. Et là avoient si bien escouté les beaulx comptes, qu'ilz n'avaient poinct oy sonner la cloche de leur monastere. Ce qui parut bien, quant ilz arriverent en telle haste, que quasi l'alaine leur failloit à commencer vespres. Et quand elles furent dictes, confesserent à ceulx qui leur demandoient l'occasion de leur chant tardif et mal entonné, que ce avoit esté pour les escouter. Parquoy, voyans leur bonne volunté, leur fut permis que tous les jours assisteroient derriere la haye, assiz à leurs ayses" (193).

[22]   "la nostra brigata, già da più altre saputa dattorno, per maniera potrebbe multiplicare che ogni nostra consolazion ci torrebbe" (562).

[23]   "Après la messe oïe et s'estre ung peu pourmenez, se meirent à table, promectans la Journée presente debvoir estre aussi belle que nulle des passées. Et Saffredent leur dist qu'il vouldroit que le pont demorast encore ung mois à faire, pour le plaisir qu'il prenoit à la bonne chere qu'ilz faisoient" (343).

Why could not they have organized a sort of a reading club, a sort of a literary Friday, to take place at a certain location in the city, at a set time? It is important to realize that the frame story occupies a place in the work where it is expected of the author to explain how and / or why the fiction that will follow came about. I would like to suggest that in placing their storytellers in force-majeure circumstances to start enjoying fiction Boccaccio and Margaret invent another excuse that hides the agency of the writer, adding to the excuses which existed before them: the discovery and translation of an ancient book, the recording of the ideas of a patron, of a vision, or of a dream.

Authors deny their agency in having invented a story: they have written something *in spite of themselves*, not on their own initiative. Thus, Christine de Pizan in *The Duke of True Love* (1403-5), claims to have written a love story to obey to a patron, who also told her what to write: "it is his [my patron's] pleasure that I recount, even as he has told them unto me, the grievous distresses, the joys, and the strange adventures, through which, during many bygone years, he has passed [...] and with his consent, I will relate on his behalf the facts even as he has set them forth." (Pizan 1966: 2)

In the same vein, the famous poet Chrétien de Troyes claims in the beginning of famous romance *Lancelot* (1176-81) that both the subject matter and the treatment of the story belongs to Marie de Champagne, his patroness. "Here Chrétien begins his book about the Knight of the Cart. The material and the treatment of it are given to him by the Countess, and he is simply trying to carry out her concern and intention." (Troyes 1928: 270)

The appearance of Chrétien's romance *Cligés* (1176) is due to a lucky find of an ancient book. "This story, which I intend to relate to you, we find written in one of the books of the library of my lord Saint Peter at Beauvais. From there the material has been drawn of which Chrétien has made this romance. The book is very old in which the story is told, and this adds to its authority." (Troyes 1928: 91) Chrétien adds that he did no more but translate it. Luce de Gast, the author of *The Romance of Tristan* (1230-1240), similarly writes, "I have read and re-read the great Latin book many a time [...] and I am amazed that no worthy man has undertaken to translate it from Latin into French [...] I have taken it upon myself to translate a part of this story" (Troyes 1928: 3). Marie de France in the prologue to her *Lays* (end of the 13th century) realizes that all of the stories have already been written, and so she sets out to work on the ancient Breton fables. "Many a one, on many a day, the minstrel has chanted to my ear. I would not that they should perish, forgotten, by the roadside. In my turn, therefore, I have made of them a song, rhymed as well as I am able." (France 1932: 2)

Christine de Pizan, in the prologue to her *Book of the City of Ladies* (1405) defending the female sex from misogynist attacks, has a vision. As she sits in her study, brooding over the sad lot of women, three imposing-looking ladies appear before her. Christine writes: "So occupied with these painful thoughts, my head bowed in shame, my eyes filled with tears, leaning on the pommel of my chair's armrest, I suddenly saw a ray of light fall on my lap, as though it were the sun ... And as I lifted my head to see where this light was coming from, I saw three crowned ladies standing before me" (Pizan 1982: 6). Christine records her conversation with them during which they erect a city of and for, virtuous, smart, and courageous women.

Finally, medieval authors often relate a dream. The narrator of the famous allegorical poem *The Romance of the Rose* by Guillaume de Lorris and Jean de Meun (mid-13th century) falls asleep at the opening of the poem: "I lay down one night, as usual, and slept very soundly. During my sleep I saw a very beautiful and pleasing dream ... Now I wish to tell you this dream in rhyme, the more to make your hearts rejoice" (Lorris 1995:31). The narrator sleepwalks through his allegorical journey to the rose and wakes up in the last verse: "Straightway it was day, and I awoke" (Lorris 1995: 354). Christine de Pizan in her *Advision Cristine* (beginning of 15th century) also falls asleep, so that her spirit can leave her body, soar in the air, and teach her God's eternal truths (Pizan 2001: 11).

To summarize, medieval authors hide their agency in the act of translating an old book or recording the story dictated by a patron, a dream or a vision. These excuses are designed to make us believe that authors produced a book *in spite of themselves*. The exile and force majeure circumstances in *Decameron* and *Heptameron* replicate the same in-spite-of-oneself production and enjoyment of fiction. The storytellers of Margaret and Boccaccio are brought to it by the plague and the flood. They did not choose to come to the site where they can only live in their imagination: they were exiled from real life. Yet in contrast to the medieval narrators, the storytellers of the two Renaissance novels gradually realize and openly declare that they prefer fictional life to real life. The storytelling transforms the site of exile to which they came in spite of themselves into the site of escape.

I suggest that that the frame narratives examined here are a variation, even the culminating point of agency-hiding excuses. We can view them as illustrating a stage in the establishment of literature as a legitimate practice. The excuses with which authors deny their agency in inventing a story are made to satisfy Augustine's imperative to *use* (uti) earthly things rather than *enjoying* (frui) them, as God alone can be enjoyed.

For to enjoy a thing is to rest with satisfaction in it for its own sake. To use, on the other hand, is to employ whatever means are at one's disposal to obtain what one desires, if it is a proper object of desire; for an unlawful use ought rather to be called an abuse. Suppose, then, we were wanderers in a strange country, and could not live happily away from our fatherland, and that we felt wretched in our wandering, and wishing to put an end to our misery, determined to return home. We find, however, that we must make use of some mode of conveyance, either by land or water, in order to reach that fatherland where our enjoyment is to commence. But the beauty of the country through which we pass, and the very pleasure of the motion, charm our hearts, and turning these things which we ought to use into objects of enjoyment, we become unwilling to hasten the end of our journey; and becoming engrossed in a factitious delight, our thoughts are diverted from that home whose delights would make us truly happy. Such is a picture of our condition in this life of mortality. (Augustine 1994: 523)

For centuries following Augustine, the delighting quality of letters was considered necessary solely to increase the efficiency of the moral teaching they purported to communicate. It is for this reason that the storytellers engage in composing fiction in spite of themselves. Yet Boccaccio and Margaret also hint at the possibility that these stories can also be enjoyed on their own right, without the cover-up of any instructional value. Marguerite spells it out indirectly, by means of her characters and of the monks who prefer fiction to the Scriptures. Boccaccio declares that people who are not looking for diversion should not read his tales: "for those who have something else to do it is folly to read the tales, even when they are short [...] To those who read for pastime, no tale can be too long if it succeeds in its object." (561)[24]

To conclude, I have examined two aspects of the frame narratives of the *Heptameron* and the *Decameron*. The first is the physical

---

[24]   "a chi per tempo passar legge, niuna cosa puote esser lunga, se ella quel fa per che egli l'adopera" (776).

                    Irina Dzero

change of location which must take place in order for fiction to be produced and enjoyed. I see it as a metaphor for the experience of writing and reading. Just as the storytellers forget their life and exchange it for the life of the character of the story, writer and reader forget about their real self and immerse themselves in the life of fictional characters. Secondly, I examined the force majeure condition that sets off both narratives. The storytellers are shown producing and enjoying fiction in spite of themselves, and gradually realize that they actually prefer it to real life. Margaret and Boccaccio hint at the possibility that the entertaining aspect of literature may be important in its own right. These works illustrate an important stage in the establishment of literature as a legitimate cultural practice.

Bibliography

Augustine, 1994. 'On Christian Doctrine' in *Nicene and Post-Nicene Fathers: Augustine's City of God and On Christian Doctrine* vol. 2 (trans. J. F. Shaw, ed. Philip Schaff). Peabody, Mass.: Hendrickson Publishers.

Boccaccio, Giovanni. 1949. *The Decameron* (trans. Richard Aldington). Garden City, New York: Doubleday & Company.

—. 1967. *Il Decameron*. Bari: Editori Laterza.

Cholakian, Patricia Francis. 1993. *Rape and Writing in the 'Heptaméron' of Marguerite de Navarre*. Carbondale, IL: Southern Illinois University Press.

Duval, Edwin. 1993. ''Et puis, quelles nouvelles?': The Project of Marguerite's Unfinished *Decameron*' in John Lyons and Mary McKinley (eds.). *Critical Tales: New Studies of the 'Heptameron'*. Philadelphia: University of Pennsylvania Press.

France, Marie de. 1932. *French Medieval Romances From the Lays of Marie de France*. London: J.M.Dent & Sons.

Gast, Luce de, and Hélie de Boron. [1230-40] 1994. *The Romance of Tristan* (trans. Renée L. Curtis). Oxford: Oxford University Press.

Kirkham, Victoria. 1985. 'An Allegorically Tempered *Decameron*' in *Italica*, vol. 62, no. 1.

Lipari, Angelo. 1945. 'On Meaning in the *Decameron*' in *Italica*, vol. 22, no.3.

Lorris, Guillaume de, and Jean de Meun. [1230, 1275] 1995. *The Romance of the Rose*, trans. Charles Duhlberg. Princeton: Princeton University Press.

Migiel, Marilyn. 2003. *A Rhetoric of the 'Decameron'*. Toronto: University of Toronto Press.

Navarre, Margaret of. [1558] 1984. *The Heptameron of Margaret, Queen of Navarre*, trans. P.A. Chilton. New York: Penguin Books.

Navarre, Marguerite de. [1558] 1999. *Heptaméron* (ed. Renja Salminen). Geneva: Droz.

Pizan, Christine de. [1403-5] 1966. *The Book of the Duke of True Lovers* (trans. Alice Kemp-Welch). New York: Cooper Square Publishers.

—. [1405] 1982. *The Book of the City of Ladies* (trans. Earl Jeffrey Richards). New York: Persea Books.

—. [1405] 2001. *Le Livre de l'advision Cristine*. Paris: Honoré Champion Editeur.

Sommers, Paula. 1984. 'Marguerite de Navarre's *Heptaméron*: The Case for the Cornice' in *The French Review*, vol. 57, no.6.

Troyes, Chrétien de. [1170-90] 1928. *Arthurian Romances by Chrétien de Troyes* (trans. Wilstar W. Comfort). London: J.M. Dent & Sons.

9. Pilgrimage, Transformation and Poetical Anthropology. Hubert Fichte's Journeys into the Afro-American Religions in Brazil

Andreas Stuhlmann

Our story begins in the summer of 1968. At such an iconic moment, what is a successful young German writer, author of the first German language beat-novel (and a bestseller to boot) – to do? The book in question, *Die Palette, (The Palette)* is his second novel: it sold 23,000 copies immediately, remained on the bestseller list for six months, made him a star for a short while and brought him 20,000 Marks he hadn't expected. So the precise question is: how to spend what amounts to a small fortune? The down-payment on an apartment? A Picasso drawing? Or burn it all? This is the dilemma confronting the writer Jäcki in Hubert Fichte's novel *Explosion*, with its subtitle, a "novel of anthropology". Should the windfall be spent on clothes? Stuff for the kitchen? Art books? Oysters? Presents for his friends, for Tante Hilde and Mum? Well, that's a given. A journey, maybe? A journey "we will never again be able to afford. Brazil. Three months in Brazil. An eternity in Brazil. With Touropa. … Rio de Janeiro, new for Germany, it said in the Touropa catalogue."[1]

So Jäcki and his partner, Irma, a photographer, leave behind what are turbulent political events in the old world in the aftermath of the so-called Prague Spring. The holiday in a five star hotel on Rio's Copacabana, with organized trips to Brasília and Bahia, is partly a

---

[1] "– Eine Wohnung anzahlen. / – Schließlich. Eine Eigentumswohnung. / – Eine Picassographik? / – Nebenher verplempern? Kleider? Küchengeräte? Kunstgeschichten? Austern? / – Das wäre unordentlich? / – Geschenke an Freunde, Tante Hilde, Mutti? / – Das sowieso. / – Eine Reise! / – Eine Reise, die wir uns nie wieder leisten können! / – Wohin? / – Nach Brasilien! / – Drei Monate Brasilien! / – Eine Ewigkeit Brasilien! / – Mit Touropa! … Rio de Janeiro, neu für Deutschland, stand im Touropa Prospekt." (Fichte 1993: 11ff.).

hippie-style break-away, planned as an escape from the unrelenting social and political turbulence at home. Yet little do they know it is actually going to be the beginning of a pilgrimage that will last fifteen years, fifteen years of travelling and writing, and researching. (Cf. Linck 1995)

In the story of Jäcki and Irma, Hubert Fichte (1935-1986) re-wrote events of his life and the life of his partner, the photographer, Leonore Mau (*1916), and the novel *Explosion* which he completed only weeks before his death of lymph gland cancer, was only posthumously published seven years later, in 1993.[2] It reconstructs the three journeys to Brazil they took together – in 1968, 1971, and in 1981. But the characters Jäcki and Irma are more than just alter egos or simply masked autobiographical references. "My books are no masquerades. They describe experiments: living a life so as to find a form of expression for it,"[3] Fichte said in an interview with the German weekly newspaper, *Die Zeit,* in 1972. Irma and Jäcki become doubles in Antonin Artaud's style of Fichte and Mau in this search for expression and they are participants in an experiment, which was to become Fichte's so-called "roman fleuve" *Die Geschichte der Empfindlichkeit* (History of Sensitivity). (Cf. Roscher 2002)

From the early 1970s to the mid-1980s, Fichte pursued this enormous 19-volume project, in itself actually a large-scale experiment with the contingencies of novel form. It combines three narrative strands to achieve a style of "thick description" (cf. Geertz 1973): (a) the autobiography of Jäcki with observations and reflections on art, literature, architecture and photography, on various incidents and groupings around the German "Gruppe 47", extending as far as New York's Pop Art scene; (b) research into milieus of urban subculture, from Hamburg's infamous red-light district along the Reeperbahn to Rio and Dakar, as part of travelogues of extensive journeys on four continents. His research into the diversity of Afro-American traditions, and especially into religious rituals in Africa, North and South America, the Caribbean and Europe, forms the third strand (c).

---

[2]   The actual cause of Fichte's death is still surrounded by rumor; cf. the roundtable discussion on the occasion of Fichte's 65th birthday, which has been documented by Herbert Jäger, Hermann Peter Piwitt and Josef Winkler 2000: 75, and Peter Braun 2005: 278ff.

[3]   "Meine Bücher sind keine Maskierungen. Sie beschreiben ein Experiment: zu leben um eine Form der Darstellung zu erreichen." (Zimmer 1985: 116).

He published extensively on his pilgrimages to the holy shrines at Bahia and the Casa das Minas in São Luiz Maranhão in Brazil, on the Dugu-rituals in Belize and the cult of the deity Xango in Haiti and Trinidad.[4] On numerous occasions, his texts were accompanied by Mau's photos.[5] Three similarly interwoven literary styles correspond to these three strands: the fictional framework to the novel, a politically-engaged journalistic approach and an ethnographical one.

An integral part of his personal literary technique and an ingredient of "thick description" are interviews. In German, French, English, Spanish and Portuguese, Fichte conducted and documented interviews with presidents and doctors, prostitutes and diplomats, callboys and artists, bus drivers, voodoo-priestesses, pimps and people living in slums and added them to the corpus of the *roman fleuve*.

This paper will focus solely on the three journeys to Brazil, which provide a framework for all of Fichte's studies of the Afro-American cultures.[6] After the decision for Brazil was made in the summer of 1968, Fichte and Mau came to experience Rio's carnival for the first time in 1969. The second time they managed to stay a full year from 1970 into 1971, renting an apartment in São Salvador da Bahia de Todos os Santos, 1,000 miles north of Rio on the coast. From Bahia they travelled to Chile, where Fichte conducted his famous interview with the newly-elected Salvador Allende in June and to Argentina, where he met with Jorge Louis Borges. In 1981 they again stayed for almost a year, mainly in Belém and São Luiz de Maranhão, where Fichte regularly visited the Candomblé temple Casa das Minas.[7] The sources documenting Fichte's own observations and memo-

---

[4] The project of the "Geschichte der Empfindlickeit" and his "poetical anthropology" have both attracted a wide range of critical responses: Cf. Torsten Teichert 1987, Hartmut Böhme, Nikolaus Tiling, eds. 1991, David Simo 1993, Manfred Weinberg 1993, Rekha Kamath-Vaidyarajan 1993, Herbert Uerlings 1997.

[5] Cf. Hubert Fichte 1972: 12-17; 1974: 34-46 and the travelogues (1976; 1980), each accompanied by a folio-sized volume of Leonore Mau's photos (Mau 1976; 1980); cf. also *Hälfte des Lebens* (Mau 1996).

[6] There are two major studies on *Explosion* and the journeys of Fichte and Mau in Brazil: Ulrich Carp 2002 and Miriam Seifert-Waibel 2005.

[7] The dates of the three journeys can be reconstructed in part from letters and from Fichte's passports kept in his estate at the Staats- und Universitätsbibliothek Carl von Ossietzky in Hamburg. An itinerary can be reconstructed from this catalogue: Winfried F. Schoeller 2005. Ulrich Carp has identified 2nd Jan-

ries of the journeys are, in fact, limited in that all we have is very few
letters, no diaries at all, and only a few dates can be reconstructed
from his essays in *Xango* (Fichte 1976). Accordingly, we will have to
have to rely on Jäcki's accounts of events to elucidate traces of his
journeying.

Pilgrimage

The notion of pilgrimage can characterize this story in the light of the
structure of the journey and of the essential role of rites and religious
exploration in Jäcki's and Irma's project.

The Finnish anthropologist René Gothóni sees the pilgrimage as
one of the central and universal rites of passage. Revising Victor
Turner's paradigmatic theoretical model of pilgrimage that has dominated religious studies for decades, Gothóni emphasizes the aspect of
transformation that he sees as essential to every pilgrimage: "a pilgrimage should be conceived and defined as a transformation journey." (Gothoni 1993: 101-113, 113)

As a good structuralist – and we will see in part three how
closely structuralist anthropology applies to the topic of this paper –,
Gothóni defines the form of the pilgrimage as an ellipse "with the sequence structure: departure-journey-return" (113), which also provides a metaphorical structure for the essentially "binary character" of
the pilgrimage, namely as transformation.

This transformation is also a qualitative issue. Every pilgrim's
experience progresses, according to Turner and Gothóni, from "worldliness" to "spirituality" during the pilgrimage. Jäcki's descriptions of
his own spiritual state indicate that he perceives this journey as a
transformation right from the start. As the plane leaves Dakar, the lay-

---

uary 1969 as the departure date and the novels states that the journey lasted
three months (cf. *Explosion*. 1993: 12). The first day in Brazil might have
been 4th January, according to a clipping in Fichte's estate from the title page
of the *Gazeta de Noticias* from that day (NHF 25.19.73.-802-), cf. Carp 2001:
37. The only points of reference for the second journey are a date given in
Hubert Fichte's *Xango* (1976: 49) and a date written on the case of a tape, also
to be found in Fichte's estate entitled "Anfang Nanã / Einweihung Nanã -
23.10.71" (NHF 34.29.17.-1-), cf. Carp 2001: 42. The third journey must have
lasted from early May 1981 (travelling onboard the Concorde from Paris to
Rio) to May 1982. Cf. Hubert Fichte 1985a: 241-246, and Carp 2001: 75.

over airport, and heads out over the Atlantic, he declares: "Flying into the new world, Jäcki thinks – / Do they all perceive this as being born?"[8] This question underlines another point Gothóni emphasizes: the important difference between the event of a pilgrimage as a mass spectacle and the individual nature of such a journey as: "private undertaking, [...] individual, spontaneous and voluntary" (113). Crucial to our context is Gothóni's observation that the transformation phase "provides a period of reflection, during which the pilgrim mirrors and reviews his life" (113). Gothóni's definition can be extended to follow the paradigm of pilgrimage as a setting of "identity in motion",[9] but the idea of identity has also to be taken with a grain of salt here, since we are dealing with the main character's identity as ever-changing, unstable over the course of the novel, and of course different in turn from the author's. (Cf. Bandel 2008)

Departure

Jäcki made excessive preparations for this New World: he bought the respective Guide Bleu and a map of Rio. He also held a discussion with playwright Affonso Grisoli,[10] which has left him with the impression that Brazilian theater, under the influence of both Bertolt Brecht and August Strindberg, is all about "Theories. Futurism. Estrange-

---

[8]   "In die neue Welt fliegen, denkt Jäcki – / Ob sie es alle als Geburt empfinden." (1993: 14)

[9]   The term apparently first appears in Anna Deavere Smith's play *Fires in the Mirror,* which deals with the Crown Heights clashes between Chassidic Jewish American and African American groups in New York in the fall of 1991 (Smith 1993). It has since travelled further into various sociological and anthropological contexts: e.g. cf. Chris Barker 2000. He relates it to the concept of "Diaspora", connecting travelling, Diaspora, and identity: "identities in terms of contingency, indeterminacy and conflict; of identities in motion rather than of absolutes of nature or culture. Routes rather than roots." (201) Rowe and Licona (2005: 11-14) use the term in relation to changing identities and localities in feminist theory. For our context here it could be utilized for the transformation of identities by the process of ritualized travel.

[10]   Grisoli had visited Hamburg amongst other German cities in 1968 as part of a tour sponsored by the Goethe Institute.

ment. Cruelty".[11] These four terms become leitmotifs in his perception of the country. Being raised in and around theatres, where his mother was a prompter, the formation of Jäcki's intellect is grounded in the theatre and its rituals; they are part of his "way of worldmaking" (Goodman 1978),[12] of his "identity in motion". From early on he was also playing a series of roles, changing them, trying on new personae to present to the world: the juvenile actor in Hamburg's existentialist theatre scene, later the shepherd in France, the farm hand, the poet *maudit*, the successful young writer. Not surprisingly, his pantheon of literary role-models includes Antonin Artaud, Jean Genet and Marcel Proust; each of them experimenting with role-playing and changing identities. The character of Jäcki can be read as a trickster-figure, in the tradition of the confidence tricksters like Thomas Mann's infamous Felix Krull, who challenges the conventions of inclusion and exclusion in society. (Cf. Hyde 1998; Hynes 1993) Sexuality, marginalization, cruelty and rebellion come together in his poetic quest. Being bisexual himself, the treatment of homosexual men becomes for Jäcki a litmus test for tolerance, openness and freedom in a truly modern society. He does initial research into torture and assaults on homosexuals, prostitutes and the poor by the military regime (1964-1985), issues also described by the journalist and politician Marcio Moreira Alves. (Alves 1966)

In Rio Jäcki, therefore, quickly replaces the tedious pleasures of a package holiday, the dinner parties with diplomats, politicians and other artists and even the conversation with the world famous architect of "Utopopolis",[13] with explorations into the street carnival and its forbidden subversive gatherings and into the gay subculture around the station Central do Brazil, the public restrooms, dirty cinemas and cheap hotels.

But it is the post-mortem examination of a political victim at the Instituto Médico Legal Nina Rodrigues, the Institute for Forensic Medicine at the Medical Faculty at the University of Bahia and the

---

[11]   "Theorien. Futurismus. Verfremdung. Grausamkeit." (Fichte 1993: 12). My translation of the Brechtian term "Verfremdung" follows Frederic Jameson (2000: 35-42).

[12]   Cf. also Fernando Peixoto 1997: 46, and Jochanan Trilse-Finkelstein 2005: 74-77.

[13]   The architect is a double of Oscar Niemeyer. On Niemeyer's legacy and his vision of Modernism, cf. Styliane Philippou 2008.

Macumba-ritual Irma and Jäcki witness in the favela of Vigario Geral in Rio, that become the turning points of their journey. They decide to return the next year, to study the syncretistic cults of Afro-American religions "more thoroughly", "to understand what's going on there".[14]

The religious traditions the African slaves, mainly Yorùbá and Ewe, brought to the New World have forged a variety of African-American identities, and these identities have developed through a new religious syncretism[15] shaped by the conditions of slavery and forced Christianization. In these religions – Candomblé, Vodou, and Santería – various gods of the Yorùbá and other African nations are rendered analogous to the Roman Catholic saints (Todos os Santos – All Saints). The evil ghosts and devils of Africa are given prominent and respectful treatment, and some ritual practices like trance and spiritual healings are incorporated. Some temples of Candomblé have also incorporated Native American gods, and Umbanda combined African deities with Kardecist spiritualism. Fichte apparently saw the syncretistic nature of these Afro-American religions as a cognate to his own poetic practice of bricolage and montage: "In the voodoo-temples, as in the poorest districts of a modern city, / every available object is put to use. / A religion of bricolage, a patchwork mythology." (Fichte 1996: 115)

The journey towards "poetical anthropology"

Travelling, writing, the interviews, the ethnographic research and the spiritual pursuit eventually become different dimensions of the same artistic strategy, and come together in the form of "ethno-poetics," or as Fichte later called it more correctly "poetical anthropology" (Fichte

---

[14]   "– Es ist das erste Mal, daß ich an einem afroamerikanischen Kult teil-genommen habe, denkt Jäcki / – Ich habe mir nie vorstellen können, daß man da rankommt. / – Und wenn man es gründlicher machte, sagt Jäcki. / – Warum nicht / – Ich meine ganz gründlich. / – Daß man weiß: was geht da vor. / – Würdest du ein Jahr drangeben? / – Mich interessieren mehr die Lichtbe-dingungen, wenn ich fotografieren kann." (Fichte 1993: 72).

[15]   The modern meaning of the term "syncretism" dates back to a letter by Erasmus to Melanchthon of April 22, 1519. He refers back to the traditional meaning in Plutarch, to the federation of previously disagreeing Cretans, and uses them as an example to designate the coherence of dissenters in spite of their differences in theological opinions; cf. Andre Droogers (1989).

1985) which he claims to have inherited from Herodotus' *Histories* (cf. Neumann 1991). In the above mentioned interview with *DIE ZEIT*, Fichte summarized the aim of his *roman fleuve*: apart from a few exceptions, there are two groups of people: "Those who travel the world with Touropa and those who raid military canteens because of starvation. It is my objective, to describe the development of the first group and its reaction to the second."[16] He called the encyclopedic texts of the *roman fleuve* "Reiseformen des Wissens" (passage forms of knowledge), a cultural mode of perception, of recording experiences of the heterogeneous, surprising, alien, scandalous, mysterious or frightening faces of the "other" and transforming them into Jäcki's and Irma's experiences.

It could be claimed that the most important impulse for this transformation of Fichte's life and work was the encounter with the African-American religions and their in-depth examination. "I want to begin to live for my writing and not, like I've done so far, live to have something to write about," Fichte said in another interview (Cf. Fuhse 2006).

But it has already become obvious, that the three roots, or strands, of the narrative, the search for individual transformation, the ethnographical fieldwork and the poetological transformation of Fichte's whole existence are not in balance, but in conflict, or rather in a complex dialectical relationship.

To illustrate this struggle, we can refer to a selection of the inherent problems. There is, for example, Jäcki's ambivalent position or suspicion towards all forms of ritual, based on his own experience in a Catholic orphanage during the war and his early career as a juvenile actor: "If he tried to summarize his ideals, his aims, his undertaking, it would have definitely been to disintegrate / to dissolve rituals."[17] Or

---

[16]   "Dieter E. Zimmer: Sie schreiben also an einem einzigen Buch, einem roman fleuve, von dem es bisher nur Bruchstücke gibt. / Hubert Fichte: Ja, roman fleuve? 'Fluß ohne Ufer'? Vielleicht 'Roman Delta'. / Z.: Und wie müßte der heißen? / F: 'Die touristische Entwicklung in der zweiten Hälfte des zwanzigsten Jahrhunderts'. / Z.: Wie bitte? / F: Von Ausnahmen abgesehen, gibt es zwei Gruppen von Leuten: Die mit Touropa reisen und die vor Hunger Militärkantinen plündern. Es geht mir darum, die Entwicklung der ersten Gruppe zu schildern und seine Reaktion auf die zweite." (Zimmer 1985: 88)

[17]   "Denn wenn er versuchte zusammenzufassen, was sein Ideal gewesen war, seine Idee, sein Unterfangen, dann doch wohl Riten aufzulösen." (Fichte 1993: 426)

as he phrased it ten years earlier in *Xango*: "My problem: / the natural (logic) of Enlightenment and the perverted logic of all things ritual." (Fichte 1976: 248) This is where the Cameroon Fichte-scholar David Simo sees a typical western problem exhibited in Fichte's writing, the problem how to mediate between two contradictory forms of knowledge: on the one hand the analytical, scientific way of shaping a world, which has dissolved the magical powers of religion in the course of the Enlightenment along with the magical power of ritual to create a world. While Jäcki is, on the one hand, excited and enchanted by the rites and rituals he observes and feels strangely attracted to them, he also tries to scrutinize ethnographically the litanies, the incantations, conjurations and chants of the "perverted" ("das 'Widernatürliche'"). He tries to bring the magical forces to a stand-still, not actually allowing them any power over him. (Simo 1991: 135) But, as Jean Genet put it in his interview with Fichte in 1975, the ritual is the "acknowledgement of the transcendental, it is the repetitive acknowledgement of the transcendental, day by day, week by week, the whole world is ritualized" (Fichte/Genet 1992: 4).

So when Jäcki and Irma are seeking to watch the secret bathing in blood, a ritual of spiritual healing in which the warm blood of freshly slaughtered animals is splattered across a "possessed" person, their position is still very much one of curiosity, they even hope to make money by selling the story and the photos of this forbidden practice at home. (Cf. Wafer 1991; van Wetering 1983) Not surprisingly, and this is a major theme of the "novel of anthropology", the sages and priestesses have been made aware of the value of true bathing in blood for anthropologists and tourists alike and tell them obviously fabricated stories and offer them staged events to watch for up to 2,000 dollars.

But Jäcki's true fascination begins when he learns from existing research and from his conversations about the point of true subjection to the trance, the "shattering of consciousness" (Obrigação da consciencia / Zerbrechen des Bewußtseins).[18] This is when he becomes interested in the "King of Condomble", Joãozinho da Gomeia (Fichte 1976: 26; 1993: 85; cf. Carp 2001: 125). The same interest also leads to his own collection of plants, a herbarium Humboldt-style, with

---

[18] The term "Obrigação" refers to various forms of ritual obligation, e.g. a gift, sacrifice or ceremony. Cf. Sérgio Figueiredo Feretti 1996: 302, and Carp 2001: 169.

hundreds of samples of sacred plants used for ritual potions and oint-
ments, for which he consults Pedro "The Leafshaker," Pedro de Bate-
folha, a sage from Belem and Jose Gabriel da Costa from the temple
Uniao do Vegetal.

But his skepticism makes it hard for him to ever subject himself
fully to the rites of passage the priestesses and sages have to offer,
even for the not-initiated. It helps, though, to provide the critical distance necessary for the anthropological work that goes into his writing.

Fichte, who had never attended university, was surprisingly serious about his anthropological fieldwork. The fact that he submitted
Xango (inevitably unsuccessfully) as a dissertation in Anthropology at
the University of Bremen, his collaboration with the young Brazilian
Anthropologist Sergio Ferretti on his book about the Casa das Minas
in Sao Luiz and his lecture "Heretic Remarks on a New Science of
Man" at the Leo-Frobenius-Institute in Frankfurt in 1977, are all evidence of his pursuit of an independent position in the field of anthropology. Since in his texts he dismissed not only the whole tradition of
structuralist anthropology from Levi-Strauss (cf. Fichte 1996) onwards – while praising the eccentric models of Herodotus, Leo Fro-
benius and others – but also most of the previous research on the Brazil's Afro-American cultures by authorities as Pierre Verger, who actually features as the character of "Pope Pierrie" in *Explosion*, Alfred
Metreaux, Gisèle Binon Cossard, or Roger Bastide, he attracted fierce
criticism of his own works as well.[19]

As the critic Herbert Uerlings has successfully shown, Fichte
did not get past the stage of merely collecting facts and describing the
obvious[20] and, therefore, he only compiles additional evidence for
theories already verified. His colleague Jeroen Dewulf goes even further, calling Fichte's texts "worthless" from an anthropological point
of view.[21] Fichte's attempt to read the Candomblé as a community

---

[19]   E.g. Roger Bastide 1969, Gisèle Binon Cossard 1970, Alfred Métreaux 1958,
        Pierre Verger 1968. Cf. Claudius Armbruster 2003: 234.

[20]   "Aus der Sicht der Ethnographie [bleibt Fichte] beim bloßen Sammeln von
        Informationen und Beschreiben von unmittelbar Beobachtbarem stehen, [so
        dass er] vor allem neue Belege für bereits Bekanntes [versammelt hat]" (Uer-
        lings: 299).

[21]   "Da kommt noch hinzu, dass Fichtes Schriften in rein anthropologischem
        Sinne fast wertlos sind." (Dewulf 2007: 45; 2007: 218-19, 227ff.). Cf. Fich-

based on accepted and incorporated homosexuality and androgyny, with the central icon of the double-edged axe of the deity Xango, blew the factual influence of "queered" identities in these cults out of proportion. (Conner/Sparks) This served, as Dewulf argues, exactly the purpose Fichte himself criticized strongly in others: he distorted the facts to fit his own interests, mainly to provoke a society still distinctly homophobe and to affront traditional Western Catholic beliefs.

Research foundered – the return

When finally, towards the end of their third journey, Jäcki is allowed to see the inside of the Condomblé-temple, the sanctum, he considers himself learned and yet he actually still seems to expect a spiritual transformation after fifteen years of travel and research – but "the sanctum is empty," (Fichte 1993: 708) all he sees is a void space.

When Jäcki realizes the temple remains empty for him, that he cannot experience anything transcendental, his quest to become part of a new culture and to become a 'bi-continental man' comes to an end. The novel ends with a melancholic tone, just like the ending of the earlier novel *Forschungsbericht* (Research Report), where Jäcki states laconically: "Research foundered".[22]

If, therefore, Jäcki's anthropological curiosity alone counts as the main motivation behind the pilgrimage, we probably would agree that it must have failed. If we look at the question of the poetological project of the transformation of Fichte's life and writing, we might find a different answer.

Eventually there have been three ellipses, as Gothóni described them: three departures, three extensive periods of travel, exposure, questioning and reflection, and three returns.

With each step of this journey, Fichte experiments with new literary styles and the narrative becomes more and more complex and polyglossial. The literary return from those fifteen years of engagement with the Afro-American religions is a whole string of books: the

---

te's use of the Gilette razor blade as a modern representation of this symbol of Xango as a concetto in "Die Rasierklinge und der Hermaphrodit" (Mau 1976: 53-61).

22   "Forschung gescheitert." (Fichte 1989: 127)

travelogues *Xango* (1976) and *Petersilie* (1980) in collaboration with Mau, the manual *Lazarus und die Waschmaschine* (1985), and at least four volumes of the *Geschichte der Empfindlichkeit*: *Das Haus der Mina in Sao Luiz de Maranhao* (vol. 14, Paralipomena vol. 4, 1989), *Forschungsbericht* (vol. 15, 1989), *Die Geschichte der Nanã* (vol. 12, 1990), *Explosion. Roman der Ethnologie* (vol. 7, 1993).

The various layers of texts, Jäcki's narrative, a first-person narrator, the many interviews, clippings from Brazilian newspapers (Fichte calls them "newsreels" as a reference to Dos Passos, cf. Suárez), the 5,000 index cards filled with observations, quotations from oral and written sources and the herbarium are combined, cut and pasted together as a multilingual patchwork in German, Portuguese, Spanish, English, Greek, Ewe etc.

In some passages, as Simo has observed, Fichte tries to stage a "mimetic repetition" (Simo: 173), so the text forms a fictitious imitation of the experience, for example an initiation, a possession, a healing, told in the perspective of one of the characters, and this mimesis makes it appear even more realistic. The interviews serve the same purpose, taking the focus away from Jäcki, or the interviewer, and letting the interviewee "authentically" tell their story with (at first glance at least) as little intervention as possible.

But the judgment of Brazilian Anthropologist Sérgio Figueiredo Ferretti, Fichte's collaborator on the Casa das Minas–project in São Luiz remains troubling. He claimed that Fichte did not only betray all anthropological ethics, but also his sources, whose personal confessions or clandestine parts of their life stories Fichte not only coaxed them to reveal, but then shamelessly exploited for his novels and so-called "glossaries" of his "History of Sensitivity"-project. In consequence, he acquired the reputation of a "sensationalist". (Cf. Carp 2001: 125)

There is a noticeable difference from the approach which Leonore Mau takes with her photos (Cf. Braun 1997). From all we know, and what we maybe can conclude from her double, Irma, it's fairly safe to say that Mau's own involvement in the spiritual quest was very limited. As a professional photo journalist who published with the finest magazines, Mau seems aware of the fine line between engagement and even enthusiasm, which a good photo-story needs, and the exploitation and sensationalism which Feretti sees in Fichte's work.

For Fichte, an escape from between the Scylla of anthropological truthfulness and the Charybdis of spiritual engagement, and the only way to stay on course, came by laying open as much as possible of the process of the travel, the search and research in his writing. And only the form of the novel offers enough scope to master the overwhelming complexity of the experiences on those three journeys.

How should this be described? / A Vaudou ceremony is everything at once. / Acute. History. Structure. / And everything all over again – deliberated upon, refracted in imagination; imaginations returning in a new structure, and floating back into the story.[23]

Instead of presenting final results, Fichte engages in what Simo calls an "exercise of approximation", in which he blends all of his material into the stream of one radically subjective and fictional *roman fleuve*. That gives him the scope to exhibit all the doubts, questions, failures, briberies and misinterpretations that render the text of each part of the project, here *Explosion,* meandering and fragmentary. Failure is in the same way an intrinsic part of the venture, analogous to the claim to totality that is associated with the project of Modernity and of the modernist novel, in particular in Proust, Joyce and others. It is up to us, his readers and investigators, to distil our own images and views from these texts and photos, but also to question these images and the way Fichte generates them in us. In this, his last narrative, Fichte pushes the dialectical impulse of the fieldwork and the faith, and of the literary and spiritual enhancement, a few inches further along the Sisyphean road seeking to "live so as to find a form of representation".

Bibliography

Armbruster, Claudius. 2003. 'Literatur und Ethnologie. Zur Repräsentation von Religionen und Ritualen in deutschen, brasilianischen und französischen Brasilienbildern – Hubert Fichte, Pierre Verger und Jorge Amado' in Orlando Grossegesse, Erwin Koller, Armando Malheiro, Mário Matos (eds.) *Portugal–*

---

[23]   "Wie soll man alles beschreiben? / Eine Vaudouzeremonie ist alles. / Akut. Geschichte. Struktur. / Und alles noch einmal reflektiert, gebrochen in Vorstellung; Vorstellungen, die wieder ablaufen, strukturiert und in die Geschichte zurückgenommen werden." (Fichte 1985: 263)

Alemanha–Brasil. Actas do VI Encontro Luso-Alemão vol. II. 6. Deutsch-Portugiesisches Arbeitsgespräch. Braga: Universidade do Minho Hespérides.

Bandel, Jan-Frederik. 2008. *Nachwörter. Zum poetischen Verfahren Hubert Fichtes* (Hubert Fichte Studien vol. 8). Aachen: Rimbaud.

Barker, Chris. 2000. *Cultural Studies: Theory and Practice*. Thousand Oaks, CA: Sage.

Bastide, Roger. 1969. *Les religions africaines au Brésil. Vers un sociologie des inter-pénétrations de civilisations*. Paris: Presses Universitaires de France.

Braun, Peter. 1997. *Die doppelte Dokumentation. Fotografie und Literatur im Werk von Leonore Mau und Hubert Fichte*. Stuttgart: M&P, Verl. für Wiss. und Forschung.

—. 2005. *Eine Reise durch das Werk von Hubert Fichte*. Frankfurt a.M.: S. Fischer.

Carp, Ulrich. 2001. *Rio Bahia Amazonas: Untersuchungen zu Hubert Fichtes Roman der Ethnologie mit einer lexikalischen Zusammenstellung zur Erforschung der Religionen Brasiliens*. Würzburg: Königshausen und Neumann.

Rowe, Carrillo, Aimee Marie and Adela C. Licona, 2005. 'Moving Locations: The Politics of Identities in Motion' in *NWSA Journal* 17.2.

Conner, Randy P. and David Hatfield Sparks. 2004. *Queering Creole Spiritual Traditions: Lesbian, Gay, Bisexual, and Transgender Participation in African-Inspired Traditions in the Americas*. New York: Harrington Park Press.

Cossard, Gisèle Binon. 1970. *Contribution a l'étude des candolmblés au Brasil. Le candomblè Angola*. Paris: Ph.D. dissertation, Faculté de Lettres et Sciences Humaines, Université de Paris.

Dewulf, Jeroen. 2007. 'Hubert Fichte vorweggenommen. Die afrobrasilianischen Religionen bei den Exilautoren Richard Katz und Ulrich Becher' in *Monatshefte* 99.1.

—. 2007. *Brasilien mit Brüchen. Schweizer unter dem Kreuz des Südens*. Zürich: Verlag NZZ.

Droogers, Andre. 1989. 'Syncretism: The Problem of Definition, the Definition of the Problem' in Jerald D. Gort, Hendrik M. Vroom, Rein Fernhout, Anton Wessels (eds.) *Dialogue and Syncretism: An Interdisciplinary Approach*. Grand Rapids, MI / Amsterdam: W.B. Eerdmans and Rodopi.

Feretti, Sérgio Figueiredo. 1996. *Querebentã de Zomadonu. Etnografia da Casa das Minas do Maranhão*, 2nd ed. São Luís: EDUFMA.

Fichte, Hubert. 1972. 'Die Bluttaufe' (Fotos Leonore Mau) in *ZEIT-Magazin* No. 23, 9 June.

—. 1974. 'Wudu. Rendezvous mit den Geistern' (Fotos Leonore Mau) in *Stern* 27, No. 6, 31. January.

—. 1976. *Xango. Die afroamerikanischen Religionen. Bahia, Haiti, Trinidad II*. Frankfurt a.M.: S. Fischer.

—. 1980. *Petersilie. Die afroamerikanischen Religionen. Santo Domingo, Venezuela, Miami, Grenada IV*. Frankfurt a.M.: S. Fischer.

—. 1985. *Lazarus und die Waschmaschine. Kleine Einführung in die afroamerikanische Kultur*. Frankfurt a.M.: S. Fischer.

—. 1985a. 'Die Pflanzen der Casa das Minas' in Ekkehard Schröder (ed.) *Ethnobotanik* (Beträge und Nachträge zur 5. Internationalen Fachkonferenz Ethnomedizin in Freiburg, 30.11.-3.12.1980) (= Ethnobotany). Braunschweig Wiesbaden: Vieweg.

—. 1989. *Forschungsbericht. Roman*. Frankfurt a.M.: S. Fischer.

—. 1993. *Explosion. Roman der Ethnologie*. Frankfurt a.M.: S. Fischer.

—. 1996. *The Gay Critic* (trans. Kevin Gavin with an introduction by James W. Jones). Ann Arbor/MI: University of Michigan Press.

Fichte, Hubert / Jean Genet. 1992. *Ein Interview*. Aachen: Rimbaud.

Fuhse, Mario. 2006. 'Ich will anfangen, fürs Schreiben zu leben, nicht wie bisher leben, um etwas zum Schreiben zu haben. Zu Leben und Werk von Hubert Fichte' *Forum Homosexualität und Literatur* 47.

Geertz, Clifford. 1973. 'Thick Description: Toward an Interpretive Theory of Culture' in *The Interpretation of Cultures: Selected Essays*. New York: Basic Books.

Goodman, Nelson. 1978. *Ways of Worldmaking*. Indianapolis: Hackett.

Gothóni, René. 1993. 'Pilgrimage = Transformation Journey' in Tore Ahlbäck (ed.) *The Problem of Ritual* (Based on papers read at the Symposium on Religious Rites held at Åbo, Finland, on the 13th-16th August 1991). Åbo: The Donner Institute for Research in Religious and Cultural History / Stockholm: Almqvist & Wiksell.

Hyde, Lewis. 1998. *Trickster Makes this World. Mischief, myth, and art*. New York: Farrar Straus Giroux.

Hynes, William J. 1993. 'Inconclusive Conclusions. Trickster – Metaplayers and Revealers' in William J. Hynes, William G. Doty (eds.) *Mythical trickster figures. Contours, contexts, and criticisms*. Tuscaloosa: University of Alabama Press.

Jäger, Herbert, Hermann Peter Piwitt, Josef Winkler. 2000. 'Verwörterung der Welt. Hubert Fichte zum 65. Geburtstag' in *Forum Homosexualität und Literatur*.

Jameson, Frederic. 2000. *Brecht and Method*. London New York: Verso.

Kamath-Vaidyarajan, Rekha. 1993. *Hubert Fichte: Schichten statt Geschichten. Selbst- und Fremderfahrung bei Hubert Fichte*. Bielefeld: Aisthesis.

Kay, Ronald (ed.) 1996. *Hälfte des Lebens. Leonore Mau: Hubert Fichte*. Hamburg: Dölling und Galitz.

Linck, Dierck. 1995. ''Nun ist alles anders' Über Hubert Fichtes Reise-Begehren' in Hartmut Böhme, Nikolaus Tilling (eds.) *Medium und Maske. Die Literatur Hubert Fichtes zwischen den Kulturen*. Stuttgart: Metzler.

Mau, Leonore. 1976. *Xango. Die afroamerikanischen Religionen. Bahia, Haiti, Trinidad I*, Bildband. Texte Hubert Fichte. Frankfurt a.M.: S. Fischer.

—. 1980. *Petersilie. Die afroamerikanischen Religionen. Santo Domingo, Venezuela, Miami, Grenanda III*. Bildband. Texte Hubert Fichte. Frankfurt a.M.: S. Fischer.

—. 1996. *Hälfte des Lebens. Leonore Mau: Hubert Fichte* (ed. Ronald Kay). Hamburg: Dölling und Galitz.

Métreaux, Alfred. 1958. *Le vaudou haitièn*. Paris: Gallimard.

Moreira Alves, Márcio. 1966. *Torturas e torturados. Pref. de Alceu Amoroso Lima*. Rio de Janeiro: Idade Nova.

Neumann, Klaus. 1991. 'Hubert Fichte as Ethnographer' in *Cultural Anthropology* vol. 6.3.

Peixoto, Fernando. 1997. 'Brecht heute in Brasilien' in Marc Silberman, et al. (eds.) *Drive b: Brecht 100, Theater der Zeit / Brecht Yearbook*.

Philippou, Styliane. 2008. *Oscar Niemeyer. Curves of Irreverence*. New Haven: Yale University Press.

Roscher, Gerd. 2002. *Konstruktion der Fremde. Antonin Artaud und Hubert Fichte.* In: Peter Braun, Manfred Weinberg (eds.) *Ethno/Graphie. Reiseformen des Wissens.* Tübingen: Narr.

Seifert-Waibel, Miriam. 2005. *Ein Bild aus tausend widersprüchlichen Fitzeln.* Bielefeld: Aisthesis.

Schoeller, Winfried F. 2005. *Hubert Fichte und Leonore Mau. Der Schriftsteller und die Fotografin.* Frankfurt a.M.: S. Fischer.

Simo, David. 1991. 'Interkulturalität und Intertextualität oder ethnographische Erfahrung und Polyglosie' in Hartmut Böhme and Nikolaus Tiling (eds.) *Leben, um eine Form der Darstellung zu erreichen. Studien zum Werk Hubert Fichtes.* Frankfurt a.M.: Fischer.

—. 1993. *Interkulturalität und ästhetische Erfahrung. Untersuchungen zum Werk Hubert Fichtes.* Stuttgart: Metzler.

Smith, Anna Deavere. 1993. *Fires in the Mirror.* New York: Anchor.

Suárez, Juan A. 1999. 'John Dos Passos's USA and Left Documentary Film in the 1930s: The Cultural Politics of 'Newsreel' and 'The Camera Eye'' in *American Studies in Scandinavia* 3.1.

Teichert, Torsten. 1987. *Herzschlag außen. Die poetische Konstruktion des Fremden und des Eigenen im Werk von Hubert Fichte.* Frankfurt a.M.: Fischer.

Trilse-Finkelstein, Jochanan. 2005. 'Theater und Revolution in Brasilien' in *Ossietzky* 14.21.

Uerlings, Herbert. 1997. *Poetiken der Interkulturalität. Haiti bei Kleist, Seghers, Müller, Buch und Fichte.* Tübingen: Niemeyer.

Verger, Pierre. 1968. *Flux et reflux de la traite des nègres entre le golfe de Benin et Bahia de Todos os Santos.* Paris: Mouton.

Wafer, Jim. 1991. *The Taste of Blood, Spirit Possession in Brazilian Candomblé.* Philadelphia: University of Pennsylvania Press.

Weinberg, Manfred. 1993. *Akut. Geschichte. Struktur. Hubert Fichtes Suche nach der verlorenen Sprache einer poetischen Welterfahrung.* Bielefeld: Aisthesis.

Wetering, W. van. 1983. 'The Effectiveness of Rite. Exorcism of Demons in an Afro-American Religion' in *Analysis and Interpretation of Rites* (= Nederlands Theologisch Tijdschrift) 37.3.

Zimmer, Dieter E. 1985. 'Genauigkeit, ein Versteck. Gespräch mit Hubert Fichte' in Thomas Beckermann (ed.) *Hubert Fichte. Materialien zu Leben und Werk.* Frankfurt a.M.: Fischer.

—. 1985. 'Leben, um einen Stil zu finden, Schreiben, um sich einzuholen. Ein Gespräch mit Hubert Fichte' in Thomas Beckermann (ed.) *Hubert Fichte. Materialien zu Leben und Werk.* Frankfurt a.M.: Fischer.

The one hundred year old priestess Nana[24]

---

[24]   Leonore Mau 1976: 33. Used here by permission.

In a shop for devotional items: heroizing the slave[25]

---

[25]   Leonore Mau 1976: 32. Used here by permission.

10. Magic of the City:
Travel Narratives of the Project "Año 0"

Ketevan Kupatadze

Y nosotros mismos. ¿Volveremos tal cual nos vamos? […] Un filósofo pesimista nos dice: "No; no volveréis así. No. El que se va, no vuelve nunca. Quien vuelve es otro, otro que es casi el mismo, pero que no es el mismo."
[And we ourselves, will we return just as we left? […] A pessimistic philosopher tells us: "No; you will not return so. No. He who leaves, never comes back. He who comes back is another, another who is almost, but not quite the same"]
Enrique Gómez Carrillo

Magic may be a major alternative to rejection of the city as a bad, unmanageable place.
Jonathan Raban

The idea for the project "Año 0" (Year 0) was conceived by the Spanish writer Gabi Martinez who asked a number of authors to travel to various metropolitan cities and based on their experience write a book that could incorporate any narrative genre, including novelistic, documentary, epistolary, or journalistic. Being fully conscious of the tradition from which the project was emerging, the authors set themselves up for a harsh critique. On the one hand, they blatantly performed all the clichés of travel narrative genre, bound to provoke general outrage for their political incorrectness. On the other hand, in the body of their texts they took an oppositional and analytical stance defying the very clichés put forward by their performance. Working within the stereotypical boundaries of reference, their works as meta-texts of travel narrative genre frequently expose and censure its premises.

Traditionally, travel writers have been seen as "enthusiastic amateurs" and "wondering subjects". (Holland, Huggan 1999: 6) Frequently typecast as cosmopolitans and reprehended for it, they were almost inevitably identified as privileged intellectuals traveling to the city of their choice for the satisfaction of their curious minds.[1] Holland and Huggan point out that the hybrid genre of travel narrative has predominantly been a "white, male, Euro-American, middle-class" medium, (Holland, Huggan 1999: XIII) frequent agent of imperial and later, post or neocolonialist discourses, and a mechanism of "western cultural domination" (Holland, Huggan 1999: X). The authors of the project highlight their performative stance as privileged subjects insisting on a part-time recreational nature of their literary activity. Being journalists by profession, some of them consider literature to be their hobby. Rodrigo Fresán's humoristic comments are emblematic in this case:

Intento ser periodista hasta el mediodía y, después, escritor. Es decir: me despierto non-fiction y me acuesto fiction. Pero, por supuesto, no me prohíbo momentos mix y momentos loop y momentos sampler. Ya sea Lado A o Lado B, en cualquier caso, lo que hago es escribir. [I try to be a journalist until noon and then, a writer. That is to say: I wake up 'non-fiction' and go to bed 'fiction'. But, of course, I don't forbid myself to have mix moments, loop moments and sampler moments. Whether it's side A or side B, in either case, what I do is write.] (Fresán 2002)

Short description of the project provided by Mondadori, the Spanish editorial that financed it, only reiterates the stereotypical, and neocolonialist, connotations of travel narrative. The text reads as follows:

En el Año 0 del Nuevo milenio una serie de escritores de habla hispana han viajado a conocer cómo son algunas de las ciudades más importantes del mundo: el Moscú actual, fuertemente corrupto, el México DF, magnético y disparatado, un Pekín de belleza oriental y miseria oriental, Nueva York, la ciudad de las ciudades, El Cairo, Madrás, Roma [...] Realidad y ficción se conjugan en novelas cortas y largas, crónicas caleidoscópicas o diarios de viaje. Los autores de Año 0 han abandonado el

---

[1]   Ulf Hannerz considers artists (writers and painters) traveling predominantly to Paris to be archetypes of cosmopolitans: they have 'independent means' for living; they do not travel to increase their income; they are neither tourists, nor anthropologists. (Hannerz 1990: 241-3)

In a specifically Latin American tradition the Guatemalan author, Gomez Carrillo comes to mind. He can be considered an interesting archetype of a peripheral author, who fully identifies with the European culture and especially France, considering it his "home". In his *Crónicas e impresiones de viaje*, Gómez Carrillo travels to different countries for the sake of satisfying his pure curiosity. The vocabulary he uses when his adventures are the following: "nómada ideal" (Gomez Carrillo 1994: 14), "Júbilo infantilem" (16). What he looks for is "algo [...] frívolo, [...] sensación" (7).

territorio de sus mentes para trasladarse a escenarios palpables. Y están de vuelta para contarlo. [In the year 0 of the new millennium a number of Spanish speaking writers travel to get to know some of the most important cities of the world: contemporary Moscow, highly corrupt, Mexico City, magnificent and crazy, Beijing of the oriental beauty and oriental misery, New York, the city of all cities, Cairo, Madras, Rome [...] Reality and fiction conjure in short and long novels, kaleidoscopic chronicles and travel diaries. The authors of Year 0 have left the territories of their minds in order to be transferred to palpable scenes. And they are back to tell their stories.]

Describing the places visited by these writers as magnetic, beautiful, or exotic,[2] the editorial note fails to question the trajectory of travel and its effect on travellers' identities; without scrutinizing the possibility of returning to the familiar territories, it talks about their assured return "home" after having gone "abroad", ignoring the "connection and contiguity" (Gupta, Ferguson 1996: 18) of cultures in today's global sphere.[3]

The project "Año 0" unavoidably participates in "sterling service to tourism" (Holland, Huggan 1999: 3). Holland and Huggan note that contemporary travel writing, disguised as an "adversary" of the tourist industry through its claims for "moral superiority", as well as "non-exploitative" nature, is often manipulated by the tourist, as well as publishing industry to serve their lucrative ambitions. (Holland, Huggan 1999: 2-3) The project "Año 0" is explicitly presented as a "business venture" between writers and the publishing industry; it is endorsed beforehand and its participants are selected based upon the privilege of friendship between the organizer and the contributors; its authors deliberately perform the part of "white-heterosexual-middle-class-males" traditionally writing travel literature.

One text that perhaps more than others exposes the underlying motives of the project, as well as cautions the readers against the lucrative and populist foundations of the travel narrative genre is Rodrigo Rey Rosa's *El tren a Travancore*. The text creates a chain of de-

---

[2]   The imperialistic, as well as post and neocolonialist connotations of travel writings are analyzed in great detail in several studies from the last few decades. Some of the most notable are: Pratt, Mary Louise 1992; Spurr, David 1993; Porter, Dennis 1991.

[3]   See Gupta, Akhil, Ferguson, James, 1996: 6-23. The authors consider the relationship between "we" and "other", "here" and "there", "home" and "abroad" obsolete in the time of globalization with an increased mobility and displacement of people, proposing instead to look at cultures as hybrid, interconnected and interdependent.

ceptions for its fictional and real readers. The addressees of the fictional author's letters – a girlfriend, an old friend, an editor, a godson, parents, and a XX – are all his victims, since it is evident that all his power and talent for writing are directed towards one aim: to extract money from them. He pretends to have suffered a tragic accident, which left him paralyzed, in order to demand money from his parents as well as from his editor, who had sent him on a mission to write a book about his travels to metropolitan India. He initiates a business venture with his old friend in order to later tell him that the merchandise never came to the port and that it was lost or stolen. He invites his godson to visit and then refuses to host him, retaining the money for the ticket that was sent by the boy. At the end he writes to a XX (an anonymous addressee? an implicit reader? 20th century?) the following:

Los astros no me han sido avaros en materia de dinero – no mediante las letras, como podrías creer – , pero ¿a qué engañarnos? Te dare detalles y tal vez te haga más confesiones en el tren a Travancore. [The stars have not been stingy with me when it comes to money – not through writing, as you might believe. But, why should we deceive ourselves? I'll give you details and maybe I'll come clean to you on the train to Travancore.] (Rey Rosa 2002: 137)

Travancore, the place that the title promised to visit, only appears in the text as the last word, a territory that is constantly mentioned but at which one never arrives, just as the novel is never written. Thus, deception and disillusionment of and by the literary author becomes the topic of the book. Though Rodrigo Rey Rosa agreed to take on the project, he puts the purpose and the value of the project under scrutiny. He questions the relationship between the literary author and the editor; the reasons for the novelist to accept the conditions of the offer; the validity of his experience in the urban space; as well as the sincerity and genuineness of his account. Rey Rosa does not offer a way out, but rather reflects upon the status of literature, viewing it in a corrupted state, defined as a business interaction. Here greed becomes a force that forfeits anything that stands in its way.

El tren a Travancore turns out to be a consciously paralyzed text: it reflects theoretically on the process of "making" fiction as parallel to making money; but at the end refuses to take part in this process. Telling the story of the fictional literary author's picaresque adventures, Rey Rosa himself never goes to Travancore; neither does he write a type of novel that is expected of him. By doing so, he assesses critically the place of a literary author and a literary text in contemporary society. The authors of the novels that follow could use Rey Rosa's text as a cautionary reminder of the place of literature at present and of their role in shaping its future.

In order to find their own place in literature, the authors of the collection "Año 0" need to scrutinize traditional and stereotypical figures associated with urban travel narrative. By way of bringing back the figure of the flâneur, as well as recuperating the specifically Latin American urban chronicle genre, these writers confront and encroach upon the tradition of the literary field. My intention here is not to give an overarching description of the traditional, and possibly "bygone", figure of the flâneur or the activity of "strolling" in the streets and experiencing the city, but rather to highlight those specific attributes of this figure that are revisited and challenged by these texts.[4] For the purposes of my analysis I will rely on Julio Ramos' discussion of the activity of "flanear" in the nineteenth century Latin American tradition. I believe that it is predominantly the specificities of this very tradition that the project "Año 0" authors use as their starting point.

The modern traveler has conventionally been viewed as having a "god-like" and "panoptic" gaze, a "solar eye", as someone ascending to the highest point of the city (or some symbolic center representing the cultural identity of the country) in order to "look down upon the intricate landscape of streets and buildings and the restless flow of human activity" (Harvey 1989: 1). Speaking about the artist's gaze, Julio Ramos underlines how in the activity of "flanear" the space becomes hierarchized. Ramos uses Rubén Darío's example to note that the poet speaks from this height in order to "demarcate urban hetero-

---

[4]   In the Introduction to the volume titled *The Flâneur*, Keith Tester notes that the flâneur, and particularly Walter Benjamin's reading of the figure centered on Baudelaire, is frequently identified with a specific place and time, namely turn-of-the-century Paris. (Tester 1994: 1-21) Undoubtedly, Baudelaire's *The Painter of Modern Life* and Benjamin's reflections on it have turned the flâneur into an emblematic figure for the experience of modernity in urban space, as well as have become the most important references for those who wish to use this figure in their writings. Stefan Morawski in the same volume speaks of a flâneur as a useless and out-of-date figure due to the emergence of the mass and of the postmodern cultures, since in their presence there is no need in an artist (intellectual) who is seen as a voice of authority in different spheres of our life. (Morawski 1994: 181-97)

geneity, condensing its multiplicity into the frame of a magnificent spectacle" (Ramos 2001: 127). Hence, the height gives him an opportunity to experience the "wholeness" of the space and, consequently, to speak and be heard as an ultimate authority.

Ramos writes about the rhetoric of strolling in the Latin American fin-de-siècle tradition as a "cultural institution" and a "distinct form of entertainment" (Ramos 2001: 127). Speaking about the cities such as Buenos Aires and Mexico, he notes that strolling symbolized the passage to modernization, and became an expression of a "class character". "Flanear" was an entertainment characteristic of a specific social class, who looked at the city as if it were an object on exhibition. The city, through the gaze of a flâneur, was a "contained object behind the store display window" transformed into an "object of consumption" (Ramos 2001: 128). For Ramos, the chronicler-stroller is a "curious" individual who sets to "incorporate" and, later to "showcase" the private lives of the city dwellers. As such, s/he is "a voyeur, an urban onlooker" (Ramos 2001: 131). Being himself a voyeur, the city stroller is an almost anonymous, invisible figure, trying to experience the community that would alleviate his solitude.

The traditional flâneur shares certain characteristics with the tourist, particularly his "incognito status" and "intense curiosity". "The flâneur is a kind of tourist at home," notes Morawski, "a native who feels partly homeless," because unlike tourists, his task is to internalize the city, to reach deep into its soul. (Morawski 1994: 184)

Constant questioning and parodying of their status as travelers and writers is a way for the authors of the Project "Año 0" to redeem their chosen genre and gear it towards a new direction. They parody their own activity by constantly questioning writers' position in urban territories and creating the image of a traveler who is unable to transcend his status as a tourist. These authors insist on their presence in these cities as tourists and outsiders. Expressing an ironic desire to not be seen as tourists nor be read as tour guides, they show the inevitability of such states. "No estoy haciendo turismo. Investigo" [I am not doing tourism, I am doing research], says the fictional author of Rey Rosa's diaries (Rey Rosa 2002: 59). In fact, most of the texts of the Project "Año 0" ironically perform the role of the witness accounts of the cities. In order to prove to the reader the "historic" and "documentary" value of their accounts, some of the authors use their real names in the texts, presenting them in a documentary and autobiographical frame; some include excerpts from historical and sociological research of various epochs and even offer a bibliography of authors cited within their texts. Rey Rosa's text warns the reader: "Si te sueno a guía turística es que he estado leyendo las que hay acerca de esta parte de la India, y el estilo se me habrá contagiado." [If I sound to you like a tourist guidebook it's because I have been reading the ones they have about this part of India, and their style must have rubbed off on me.] (Rey Rosa 2002: 21) Héctor Abad Faciolince's fictional narrator is in search of a Hamed Abu Ahmed, an Egyptian man who could let him experience the city not as a tourist or an outsider, but as a native. But, unable to get in touch with the man, he opens tourist guides, which he immediately labels as "anticuadas".

These authors' insistence on their inability to go beyond the tourist's gaze should be viewed not as a nostalgic lament for an inexistent authenticity or origin, but rather as a positive state – one that is lowbrow, unprivileged and, most importantly, de-authorized. These travelers further emphasize their conscious refusal to speak from an authoritative and "panoptic" perspective by speaking about their physical deficiencies that would only allow them to look at the fragments of the city. One such example is the fictional author of Gamboa's *Octubre en Pekín*, who speaks distinctively about his illness, his "pies planos" [flat feet], which do not let him walk up the hill. Elsewhere, Gamboa also notes that "no [le] alcanzan los ojos para ver" [his eyes can't see far enough] (Gamboa 2001: 75).

José Manuel Prieto defies the perception of a flâneur as an anonymous figure and a voyeur, on a mission to experience the urban space, by complicating the relationship between the artist and the city. At the beginning his behavior seems to replicate that of a typical leisurely traveler: he finds a café where he chooses to sit and observe the passers by in order to write his book. But this association with the traditional image of the traveler/voyeur is soon destabilized, when he is turned into an object observed by a passer by. Suddenly, the authorial voice turns into an object behind the store window, inverting the relationship between the flâneur and his product. Suddenly, he becomes this very product. It is not the writer who tells the story of the streets, but his object of consumption. It is she – a muscovite Daria Savina – who lives attuned to the pulse of the city and thus, can give an accurate account of it. The writer instead speaks of himself as "el puntito más insignificante tras el cristal de la ventana" [the most insignificant drop behind the window glass] (Prieto 2001: 18). How can one interpret this destabilization and inversion of the traditional image of an artist in the city? What does it mean for the subject observing the scene to turn into an object in the window, being observed by the city dwellers? This scene provokes an existential moment in the mind of the narrator: "¿Quién soy y de dónde sale todo ese tejido nuevo que sale de mí, pero que ni yo mismo sé para qué sirve?" [Who am I and where does all this new tissue that is coming out of me come from, and which even I don't know what it's good for?]. (Prieto 2001: 44-45)

This insistence on the fragmentariness of the traveler's view, as well as his inability to turn the city into an object that can be coherently organized, is directed, of course, against the traditional flâneur who, as viewed by Baudelaire and consequently, Benjamin, was an emblematic modern figure in the city, in constant search for an order. In contrast to the uniformity and order of modern cities, the contemporary metropolises are characterized as places where multiplicity and difference thrive (Sassen 2000) and where disorder and incoherence are celebrated (Robins 2001). Prieto speaks about his eyes, as if they were a camera and his account of the city promises to be fragmentary, incomplete, which once again points not at the impossibility of transmitting a whole message but, rather at the deceptive nature of such an account. The order in these texts is an inseparable part of the oppressive rule engendered by the process of nation building and is in a complete opposition with their image of the city.

Another distinctive characteristic of the Project, one that undoubtedly goes back to nineteenth century tradition, is its authors' deliberate inversion of the trajectory of travel and the traditional image of a traveler. Traveling from the periphery towards the center was a necessary progression from "barbarous" to "civilized" space. One text that scrutinizes and relentlessly ridicules the traditional, nineteenth century, figure of a traveler is Héctor Abad Faciolince's *Oriente empieza en El Cairo*. Making use of an authorial voice that is saturated with the western tradition of travel in general and travel to the Orient in particular, Abad Faciolince's text exhibits the difficulty involved in the contemporary author's overcoming this very tradition and, as a result, his inability to experience the life of the "cairotas". The writer is a figure who by his very profession is unable to experience unmediated life: "mientras navegaba por las aguas del Nilo," he says, "leía sobre el Nilo, en vez de mirar al Nilo" [while navigating in the Waters of Niles, I was reading about Niles, instead of looking at Niles]. (Abad Faciolince 2002: 169) In this case, the travel writings that he has in mind, those texts that he has to rely upon belong to nineteenth century tradition: the narratives of Flaubert, Kipling, Thackeray, Twain, etc. They are "anticuadas", produced out of the wish to "dream" about the Orient as an exotic place; the wish to "digest" the Orient; as well as from the still strong-standing perspective of the world as a dichotomous place, divided between East and West.[5] Hence, when it comes to experiencing the city, these readings are "puro humo" [pure smoke]. (Abad Faciolince 2002: 32).

The texts of the "Año 0" collection either refuse to participate in the propagation of the dichotomy or put it explicitly in the center of their narrative, scrutinizing it, exacerbating the opposition to the extent of its total depreciation. The authors who participate in the project travel to cities such as Mexico, Peking, Hong Kong, Moscow, Cairo, Madras (or Chennai), etc. They choose to go to those territories that have conventionally been considered colonial and/or subaltern, as well as peripheral in relation to Europe, the west, and its *cosmopolitan* centers.[6] In some cases they go to the cities that for a long time had been at the center of civilization, but now have become marginalized. It is the decentralized and dethroned status of these cities that attracts these authors.

Speaking about the inevitably ironical and self-parodying voice of the contemporary travel narratives, Holland and Huggan rightly acknowledge that the majority of these texts are aware of the tradition in which they are automatically placed and appear deliberately anachronistic. The question they pose is: can the travel writing go beyond

---

[5]   Abad Faciolince here is in dialogue with Edward Said's *Orientalism*, making use of the very vocabulary of the critic. Explaining Orientalism Said writes: "[it] is the discipline by which the Orient was (and is) approached systematically as a topic of learning, discovery, and practice. But in addition I have been using the word to designate that collection of dreams, images, and vocabularies available to anyone who has tried to talk about what lies east of the dividing line." (Said 1979: 73)

[6]   Saskia Sassen talks about the new kind of socio-special order in the contemporary global cities that creates "a new politics of traditionally disadvantaged actors operating in this new transnational economic geography" (Sassen 2000: 80).

this deliberate imitation, which is constantly returning to its own obsoleteness? Can the use of an outmoded genre help the writers say something new and even, transgressive? The "belatedness" of these writers, according to Holland and Huggan, points at the idea that even today they are inevitable heirs of post or neo colonial tradition. Speaking about today's transnational cities, Sassen describes them as "post colonial spaces" arguing that "[t]oday's global cities [...] contain conditions for the formation of a postcolonial discourse" (Sassen 2000: 89). It is worth asking whether travel narratives of the project "Año 0" authors can also be counted as a perpetuation of colonial attitude. What is the status of these authors in such places as Beijing, Cairo, or Moscow? Perhaps, the fact that the writers themselves represent the other of the western tradition and travel to non-western territories could liberate their narrative from the stigma of colonialism. These authors' texts confront the centuries old tradition of travel trajectory which pointed from the colony to the center, in order to absorb the civilized and modern discourse, as well as from the center to the periphery, in order to colonize, incorporate or satisfy the thirst for the exotic. They certainly put forward the possibility of reassessing the colonial premises of the ritual of travel and travel narrative.

One text that finds a way to renew the travel narrative discourse is perhaps Rodrigo Fresán's *Mantra*. As a text driven by the stream of consciousness and the ritualistic power of the word, it theorizes on the subject of spiritual evocation and functions as a symbolic image of a city and a travel narrative. The architecture of the novel – its formal construction, its body – defies the premises of rationality and structure. In contrast to the organized and coherent figure of modern urban space and an authoritative figure of traditional traveler, what the reader gets is a labyrinthine body of text (and the city) that is impossible to catalogue or contain.[7]

---

[7]   In this respect, Fresán's text enters in dialogue with current debate over globalization and its effects. Speaking about the cultural aspect of globalization, Arjun Appadurai highlights the fragmentary and disorderly nature of new imagined communities that is brought about by an increased migration and consequent transculturation. He talks about the global world as chaotic and uncertain. The author considers global culture(s) to be in constant fluctuation, "making the search for steady points of reference exceedingly difficult" (Appadurai 1996: 44).

Beginning with the title, the novel *Mantra* enacts a continuous chain of ritualistic repetitions: the abundance of the letter "m" in the text is not only a formal exercise, but rather all the words that start with this letter construct a sequence of topics, such as "memoria", "muerte", "mascara", that are central to the novel and to the history of Mexico, especially as constructed by the literary as well as the popular cultural traditions. Evoking chaotically and indiscriminately images, individuals, and cultural icons, the text creates a web of references that inhabit or co-habit the Mexican territory. The text, as an emblematic image of the city, builds a "labyrinth" of (in)coherent associations that intersect continuously and are impossible to be ordered rationally.

The city in this case acquires multiple identities, impossible to contain in one single name, thus turning into a stream of names, such as "Tenochtitlan (a.k.a.) México D.F. (a.k.a.) Ciudad de México (a.k.a.) Distrito Federal (a.k.a.) D.F. (a.k.a.)". It is precisely this magical power of the city to be hospitable to different and even dichotomous discourses, to be able to change and adapt to numerous and diverse ways of life that is underscored by Fresán.[8]

The flow of consciousness is alphabetically categorized in the second part of the novel to create an illusion of order in a text where the proliferation, or as Edmundo Paz Soldan calls it, the "saturation" of information and cultural references achieves chaos, where it becomes impossible to enclose one's consciousness. Alphabetical organization of the text makes one reflect on the futile urge of containing the totality of knowledge. In the case of this novel, there is no illusion

---

[8] One should recall Jonathan Raban's critical study of the city, which confronted a conventionalized image of the metropolis as a space for rationalized and organized systems generated by modernity. Raban argued for the city's unique sense of hospitality, because it was capable of change and able to adapt to each individual's personal and private needs; to be susceptible to "remak[ing]" and acquire a character that was shaped around an individual citizen. (Raban 1974: 1) The city was of an encyclopedic nature, an "emporium of styles," "random," and "plastic" too heterogeneous to be classified and organized rationally. (Raban 1974: 86)

Kevin Robins's discussion of the metropolis in contemporary reality as an alternative to nation is also very pertinent. Robins highlights the "multitudinous qualities" of the cities (London, in his case) that undermine the imagined unity and coherence of the nation. These contemporary metropolises are "profoundly complicating our established models of cultural coherence and order", says the author. (Robins 2001: 486)

of such possibility, only its relentless criticism.[9] The second and largest part of the novel constructed alphabetically "como un diccionario
de DF" [like a dictionary of DF] (Bolaño 2001) has been compared to
Borges' story "Aleph", and alludes to the magic character "aum" – the
source of all mantras and the most sacred syllable in Hinduism, symbolizing the infinite and the entire universe. Creating characters that
function as alter egos of the author, Fresán condemns their constant
search for an origin. Fresán's narrator goes to Mexico in search of his
father. Only, instead of mythology his symbolic imagery is that of the
mass media and technology (his mother is "mi computadora madre-
cita", his father is called "Mantrax, Capitan Godzilla", and his name is
P.P.Mac@rio). The narrator is in a fruitless search for (his?) childhood, "la única patria possible" [the only homeland possible] (Fresán
2001: 18), for the (his) name, which "se [le] escapa como un pez entre
las manos" [escapes from him like a fish from one's hands] (Fresán
2001: 28), and the (his) lost identity, the (his) country of origin, or the
(his) birthplace. Behind the shadow of Marcel Proust, who appears as
a constant reference in Fresán's novels, his characters search in vain
for the memory of the past as the key to understanding their present.

Fresán's ritualistic epilogue functions as counterpoint to his
character's quest for origins and as an alternative to his searching. Instead of a total text/city what one has is a "mega-mix". In the final
part of the novel, Fresán expresses gratitude to those who "contributed" to the process of writing the book. The author pays his dues indiscriminately to a constellation of writers, artists, scientists, popular and
mass culture heroes, and so on. Not only people, but also cities become part of the constellation, as they too participate in the creation of
a book about Mexico, DF. The author thanks these places where it was
made possible to envision and write the book.

---

[9]   Also it is very reminiscent of Julio Cortázar's *Hopscotch*, because of the pos-
        sibility to read it lineally or jump from one chapter to another without any par-
        ticular order. Speaking about Fresán's debt towards Cortázar and particularly
        his novel *Hopscotch*, Edmundo Paz Soldan notes that "[e]n Cortázar, la con-
        ciencia es capaz de abarcar la información; En Fresán, la información excede
        la capacidad de la conciencia de abarcarla." [In Cortazar conciousness is ca-
        pable of embracing the information. In Fresán, the information exceeds the
        ability of consciousness to embrace it.] (Paz Soldan 2003)

Si bien *Mantra* fue escrita para ocupar el casillero del Distrito Federal en una colección de libros sobre metrópolis, su escritura se extendió a lo largo y ancho de muchas otras partes donde esta novela fue creciendo con la ayuda de nuevos aires. Avignon & París &Illiers-Combray (el viaje de las primeras anotaciones), Guanajuato &Jatitzio& Guadalajara (momias y altares de nuestros y luchadores enmascarados y computadora nueva), New York [...], Praga & Budapest (donde todo terminó de encajar en su sitio, al fin y por fin) fueron y son, también, parte de Tenochtitlan (a.k.a) México D.F. (a.k.a.) Ciudad de México (a.k.a.) Distrito Federal (a.k.a.) D.F. (a.k.a.) Nueva Tenochtitlan del Temblor. Y por supuesto, Barcelona, donde ahora escribo todo esto y donde escribí casi todo aquello. [If *Mantra* was written to occupy Mexico City's place in the collection of books written about metropoli, its writing has reached across many other places where the novel was germinating with the help of new airs. Avignon& Paris &Illiers-Combray (the trip of the first notes), Guanajuato &Jatitzio& Guadalajara (mummies and altars of our people and of the masked wrestlers and a new computer), New York […], Prague& Budapest (where everything finally fell into place) were and still are also, part of Tenochtitlan (a.k.a.) México D. F. (a.k.a.) Mexico City (a.k.a.) Distrito Federal (a.k.a.) D.F. (a.k.a.) New Tenochtitlan of the Earthquake. And of course, Barcelona, where I am writing all of this now and where I wrote almost all of that.] (Fresán 2001: 534)

The ritualistic repetitions, or mantras performed throughout Fresán's novel evoke hope, as the city, with its mixed identities that coexist in it, becomes a potential space imagined outside of modernity.

My intention was to look at the collection "Año 0" as a project that theorized urban space, the contemporary megalopolis and the role of literature and particularly that of travel narrative in it. The authors of the Project "Año 0" convey the experience of traveling and writing about unknown places from a fragmentary, sometimes "kaleidoscopic" perspective, without an intention to create a projection of a whole, but rather celebrating the shortsightedness of a writer, his/her de-authorized standpoint, as well as the impurity of the literary space of travel narrative genre. This, however, does not mean that their intervention is minor. On the contrary, from their decentralized angle, they defy the principles of the society they encounter in these urban territories, as well as the premises of the literary tradition preceding theirs.

Bibliography

Abad Faciolince, Héctor. 2002. *Oriente empieza en El Cairo*. Barcelona: Mondadori.

Appadurai, Arjun. 1996. *Modernity at Large: Cultural Dimensions of Globalization*. Minneapolis: University of Minnesota Press.

Bolaño, Roberto. 2001. *Un paseo por el abismo*. Solo literatura: Literatura Hispano-americana.com.
http://www.sololiteratura.com/bol/bolfresan.html (on 13/06/2011).

Fresán, Rodrigo. 2001. *Mantra*. Barcelona: Mondadori.

—. 2002. *Mantra es un libro muy mío*. Terra. Argentina.
http://www.terra.com.ar/canales/libros/46/46604.html (on 13/06/2011).

Gamboa, Santiago. 2001. *Octubre en Pekín*. Barcelona: Mondadori.

Gómez Carrillo, Enrique. 1994. *Crónicas e impresiones de viaje*. Guatemala: Artemis-Edinter.

Gupta, Akhil, Ferguson, James. 1992. 'Beyond Culture: Space, Identity, and the Politics of Difference' in *Cultural Anthropology* 7,1.

Hannerz, Ulf. 1990. 'Cosmopolitans and Locals in World Culture' in Featherstone, Mike (ed.) *Global Culture: Nationalism, Globalization and Modernity*. London: Sage Publications.

Harvey, David. 1989. *The Urban Experience*. Baltimore and London: The Johns Hopkins University Press.

Holland, Patrick, Huggan, Graham. 1999. *Tourists with Typewriters: Critical Reflections on Contemporary Travel Writing*. Ann Arbor: University of Michigan Press.

Morawski, Stefan. 1994. 'The Hopeless Game of Flânerie' in Tester, Keith (ed.) *The Flâneur*. London New York: Routledge.

Paz Soldan, Edmundo. 2003. *En la era de la saturación mediática*. La Paz, Bolivia: La Prensa.
http://www.sololiteratura.com/edm/edmenlaera.htm (on 13/06/2011)

Prieto, José Manuel. 2001. *Treinta días en Moscú*. Barcelona: Mondadori.

Raban, Jonathan. 1974. *Soft City*. London: Hamish Hamilton.

Ramos, Julio. 2001. *Divergent Modernities: Culture and Politics in Nineteenth-Century Latin America* (trans. John D. Blanco). Durham: Duke University Press.

Rey Rosa, Rodrigo. 2002. *El tren a Travancore: cartas indias*. Barcelona: Mondadori.

Robins, Kevin. 2001. 'To London: The City Beyond the Nation' in Morley, David and Robins, Kevin (eds.) *British Cultural Studies: Geography, Nationality, and Identity*. New York: Oxford University Press.

Said, Edward W. 1979. *Orientalism*. New York: Vintage Books.

Sassen, Saskia. 2000. 'The Global City: Strategic Site/New Frontier' in *American Studies* 41 (2/3).

Tester, Keith. 1994. 'Introduction' in Tester, Keith (ed.) *The Flâneur*. London New York: Routledge.

11. Topographies Real and Imagined in Sarah Orne Jewett's *A White Heron*

Adrienne Bernhard

In *Moby Dick*, Melville describes Queequeg as "a native of Koko-voko, an island far away to the West and South. It is not down in any map", he says (chapter 12). "True places never are." Topographies of arrival and departure are not limited solely to the real in literature. While a cartographer reads the surface of the earth to map its arrangement and relations, the preservationist writer might describe a topography whose features are both reassuringly real and phantasmagorically shifting. Topography in literature allows readers a better understanding of the physical traits that make up a textual space and the more essential qualities that give space meaning.

In this paper, I want to suggest that Sarah Orne Jewett takes a preservationist stance toward changes in American life, changes that are reflected in the topographical landscape – both real and imagined – of her short story, *A White Heron*.[1] Much as the wilderness-conservation advocates of the late 19th century sought to maintain historically sedimented sites, Jewett captures and protects the sacred spaces of nature through her fiction. *A White Heron* does not merely attempt to preserve a forgotten or disintegrating terrain. In fact, Jewett posits an environmentalism that protects the space of the imagination – building a kind of metaphorical conservation park for places that never quite existed. My discussion will move beyond a Regionalist interpretation (which has historically dominated Jewett criticism) and argue for a more nuanced, "eco-critical" look at the production of space in *A White Heron*. I'd like to redirect the reader's attention to several environmental themes in the story: natural preservation, de-

---

[1] Unless otherwise indicated, quotations are from "A White Heron" in Andrew Delbanc (ed.) 2001. *Writing New England: an anthology from the Puritans to the present*. Harvard: Harvard University Press.

scription of place, the treatment (and anthropomorphism) of animals in the story, the figure of the hunter as outside the private space of Nature, Sylvia's ascent up the tree – and suggest that these locodescriptive spaces hover between the fictive and the real. If you accept this invitation, you may be more likely to view Regionalism's convincing epistemology as due, in part, to the production of regions as spaces of fantasy.

A number of critics have successfully read Jewett's short story as a rite of passage, as a feminist stance against patriarchy, as an appeal for country values or an archetype of "local color" fiction with nostalgic or ambivalent reactions to historical transition. Even some of the most valuable of this work, however, seems to me to ignore the preservationist protocols of environmental theory that are clearly present in Jewett's story. Judith Fetterly and Marjorie Pryse, for example, run the risk of fencing in regionalism when they suggest, in *Writing out of Place*, "the etymology of the word 'region' does not suggest any connection to 'natural' or geographical boundaries [...] the territory of the realm is the *real*" (Fetterley and Pryse 2005: 5). Ecocriticism has a special, if delicate, purchase on space as a problem in literature: eco-critics share with regionalists the burden of identifying the environment as a meaningful trope in texts, one that offers new contributions to a reader's understanding of spatial production. While regionalist literature has often given voice to the dislocated, the uprooted, and the wandering, eco-critical literature encompasses nonhuman as well as human contexts and considerations. Human accountability for the environment becomes part of the text's ethical orientation: readers are asked to consider what is at stake for the climate, not just what is at stake for the characters (Love 2003: 166).

These charged references to space and environment, increasingly posited in contemporary literary discourse, bring us to *A White Heron* (1886). Set in turn-of-the-century coastal Maine, Jewett's story holds up for inspection local patterns of life that have vanished. The story centers on nine-year-old Sylvia, who is searching one night for her stray milk cow in the woods of New England. She is startled by the sudden appearance of a young man with a gun, who proclaims that he is an ornithologist and has come to this rural region to hunt and stuff birds for pleasure. When he entreats Sylvia's aid, she leads him to her grandmother's farm. The young stranger enlists their help by offering much needed cash, in locating the nest of a rare white heron.

Less than ten pages, *A White Heron* remains one of the most widely anthologized of Jewett's nearly 150 short stories, as well as one of the most frequently cited in Regionalist criticism. Jewett's strategically resistant mapping of geography as an expression of memory, or re-remembering. And, until the 1970s, many of these critics relegated the intersection of literature and environment to ideological positions (scientific/political) or pastoral criticism (cultural/literary). It is precisely the eclectic field of geography, with its critical postures and questions, which unites these two approaches; geography "has done most to bring place and nature-centered insights of writers and thinkers into the purview of scholarly investigation" (Love 2003: 91). Landmark criticism by Lawrence Buell, Cheryll Glotfelty and Glen Love, for example, inaugurated a preoccupation with eco-poetics, nature writing, environmental justice, the revaluation of place, and eco-theory – all of which are now grouped under the umbrella subject-heading of eco-criticism. (Cf. Burgess 1996) But what, exactly, is eco-criticism? And how does it significantly revise current critical approaches to Jewett's story?

Prior to the emergence of environmental literary studies as an academic field in the late 1980s, "there was no discourse of eco-criticism per se" (Mazel 2001: 3). In *The Eco-criticism Reader*, a group of articles considered seminal texts in this emerging field, Glotfelty defines eco-criticism as "the study of the relationship between literature and the physical environment". Buell is more formulaic: his idea of environmentally oriented work conforms to standards such as "the nonhuman environment is present not merely as a framing device but as a presence that begins to suggest that human history is implicated in natural history" or "the human interest is not understood to be the only legitimate interest" (Buell 1996: 7). Although *A White Heron* functions as a cultural and regional archive, it does not serve to simply read the story as a model eco-critical text; one must additionally consider the text as it lends authenticity to the field of eco-criticism, that is, its capacity to bring eco-criticism into conversation with other theoretical approaches. Because of space limitations, I give only the briefest explanation of eco-criticism; but I stress the importance of an eco-critical perspective which allows geography and ecology to re-imagine region's spatial and formal constraints.

Jewett's narrative both emphasizes and de-emphasizes geographical landscape, thereby capturing a region's "fly-in-amber quality", its region-specific physical, economic and local characteristics. The story's descriptive opening lines, for example, situate readers in a world not quite corporeal, yet distinctly graphic:

> The woods were already filled with shadows one June evening, just before eight o'clock, though a bright sunset still glimmered faintly among the trunks of the trees. A little girl was driving home her cow…they were going away from the western light, and striking deep into the dark woods, but their feet were familiar with the path, and it was no matter whether their eyes could see it or not. (436)

Here, Jewett provides relational and temporal information ("just before eight o'clock"; "away from the western light"; "driving home her cow"), typically "regional" details in their quotidian diminutiveness. But Jewett also includes the forms of a more vague, indeterminate territory: "the woods were filled with shadows"; "light glimmered faintly among the trunks of the trees". Sylvia and the cow have traversed the path before, known somewhat indiscriminately by its contours and shapes; they don't need to perceive it in order to feel assured of its existence. Nor must readers explicitly "see" the minute details of Jewett's topography, as a map would distinguish, but only "sense" the privileged space these two figures occupy – privileged because they are initiated members.

Jewett situates her protagonist between the natural world and the magical world of an idealized Nature; this orientation challenges readers to see Sylvia as guardian (or conservationist) of a bygone *terra infirma*, and to consider how the text of *A White Heron* communicates both regional and global (ecological) concerns. Sylvia is originally an outsider, who acquires regional identity partly through her empathy for nature:

> Everybody said that it was a good change for a little maid who had tried to grow for eight years in a crowded manufacturing town, but, as for Sylvia herself, it seemed as if she never had been alive at all before she came to live at the farm. (437)

Nature's restorative effect on humans is a salient theme in *A White Heron,* and one that Jewett would continue to explore years later in her famous novella, *The Country of the Pointed Firs* (1896), giving rise to an important question: did Jewett intend us to experience her characters as "particularized instances of a geographically and historically specific type, as subjects encompassed by their environment" (Breitwieser 2007: 201)? Sylvia is absolutely a product of her environment – hers is "an existence heart to heart with nature and the dumb life of the forest," almost holographic in its reflection of the outside world. Sylvia understands her personal connection to these Maine woods, though she remains, as befits a child, unable to articulate it: "She was not often in the woods so late as this, and it made her feel as if she were a part of the gray shadows and the moving leaves." Oftentimes Sylvia is indistinguishable from her natural backdrop, as when, up in the great white oak tree, "she was almost lost among the dark branches and the green leaves."

Jewett's girl protagonist might resemble a modern incarnation of Hawthorne's Pearl, who is described as "an airy sprite" invested "with a strange remoteness and intangibility [...] as if she were hovering in the air and might vanish" (Hawthorne 1850), and who is typically pictured gathering wildflowers and wading in brooks. Like Pearl, Sylvia blends ethereally with the landscape, but ecology also informs her ethics. We see this time and again, in Sylvia's fixed study of a toad outside the farmhouse, for example, or her careful effort not to disturb a singing bird; in her treatment of the cow as a loyal "companion" and her deep confusion over the hunter's brutal treatment of "unsuspecting singing creatures". Sylvia's heart gives "a wild beat" when the hunter mentions his quest for the elusive heron. Mrs. Tilley points out her granddaughter's sympathy with the small creatures of the forest, explaining, "Last winter she got the jay-birds to banging here, and I believe she'd 'a scanted herself of her own meals to have plenty to throw out amongst 'em, if I hadn't kep' watch." At a certain level of abstraction, Jewett projects a conservationist slant through Sylvia's experiences. I would argue that Sylvia's wildness manifests a more fraught and complicated "eco-centricity" than many critics have recognized, because her love for the heron is a love of scenery from which man is excluded: an identification of space not intended for human tenure or utility.

If Sylvia safeguards the space of the heron, the hunter disrupts it as a "determined and somewhat aggressive" force antithetical to an environmental ethic. The figure of the hunter recalls John Audubon, the popular ornithologist who painted, catalogued, and described birds he discovered. Of course, Audubon published *Birds of America* in 1830; so, strictly speaking, he is anachronistic as an analog for Jewett's hunter. But the connection is still important. One of Audubon's biographers reveals, "The rarer the bird, the more eagerly he pursued it, never apparently worrying that by killing it he might hasten the extinction of its kind" (Hart-Davis 2004: 41). Though Jewett's story does not express open anxiety about the poaching or extinction of the species white heron, the story obliquely objects to this outsider and "the sharp report of his gun".

In the 19th century, so-called nature writers ushered in a fascination with rusticity and wilderness through their representations of America as a wild, unsettled continent. Wildlife conservation at the turn of the century stood at the forefront of American consciousness, and writers began to advance a stewardship or "sustainable development" model of environmental protection (Howarth 1999: 509). In fact, the *Atlantic Monthly*, in which *A White Heron* was first published in 1886, featured a number of articles urging man's return to nature, with ads promoting wilderness camping and conservationism. This same era saw passage of the 1902 Reclamation Act, hailed by Theodore Roosevelt because it sold public lands "for the purpose of reclaiming the waste areas of the arid West by irrigating lands otherwise worthless, and thus creating new homes upon the land". Activist Frederick Jackson Turner's historical speech, "The Significance of the Frontier in American History", argued that writers needed to "take imaginative possession of the land" in order to counteract harmful systems of land-tenure. Warnings like Turner's helped create the United States Forestry Commission and the Wildlife Conservation Society (1895) and inspired the conservation efforts of John Muir and John Burroughs, which helped to protect wilderness areas and advance wildlife conservation efforts. (Bowler 1992: 318-22)

Perhaps more significant to Jewett's story was the advent of recreational hunting, which contributed to the modern environmental conservation efforts just surveyed. John Muir, and Teddy Roosevelt were themselves hunters, who, moved by a loss of land, became the founding fathers of the modern Conservation movement. Hunting preserves, and the figure of the hunter in *A White Heron* necessarily complicate environmentalism both in and outside of the story. Hunting preserves were meant to allow the trapping and killing of wild animals in private. There is something inherently paradoxical about this idea — setting aside land in order to kill the creatures that inhabit it. Ironically, though hunters were rarely motivated by a desire to protect wilderness, the sport's enthusiasts often claimed environmental motives when lobbying for hunting preserves. In some sense, the space of the hunting preserve is at once real and constructed. The hunter's role as an intruder in Jewett's story is equally ambiguous: though he represents the "cosmopolitan" outsider who invades the heron's (and Sylvia's) exclusive space, the hunter will ultimately find his prey elusive and its territory impenetrable.

In his philosophical essay, "Of Other Spaces", Foucault explores this binary between real and fabricated spaces, reflecting, "Spaces of illusion that expose every real space, all the sites inside of which human life is partitioned, are still more illusory" (Foucault 1984: 25). The figure of the tree embodies this idea. The tree's natural architecture produces hierarchies of space that articulate strong ligatures between the "real" spaces of human life and "relations to imaginative production" (Blair 1998: 551). The great pine might be understood as a site of "human life partitioned", a meridian between an ancient past and a fading present. Jewett's narrator describes it thus:

Half a mile from home, at the farther edge of the woods, where the land was highest, a great pine tree stood, the last of its generation. Whether it was left for a boundary mark, or for what reason, no one could say [...] but the stately head of this old pine towered above them all and made a landmark for sea and shore miles and miles away. (442)

A White Heron's environmental ethic is made clearer through her representation of the tree's geographical placement. As "the last of its generation", the lone pine reminds readers of the deforestation that was, at the time, physically changing the topography of New England's coastal regions. Maine once trafficked in firs and pines, which were cut to build masts for shipping; Jewett implies the industry's decay by mentioning, "The woodchoppers who had felled its mates were dead and gone long ago." Still, "a whole forest of sturdy trees, pines and oaks and maples, had grown again," as if to suggest Nature's own regenerative autonomy has triumphed over man's destructive forces. Whether Jewett meant to exercise preference for a Conservationist or Preservationist ethic in this description remains unclear. The former focused on the proper use of nature, whereas the later sought the protection of nature from use; that is, conservation sought to regulate human use, while preservation sought to eliminate human impact altogether. An author's personal beliefs and those stated or implied in her works are not necessarily consistent, and I am wary of extrapolating Jewett's environmental principles from *A White Heron* alone. One cannot deny, however, the extent to which Jewett celebrates unbounded, uncultivated terrain, which held for her the promise of "gave a sudden sense of space, for nothing stopped the eye or hedged one in — that sense of liberty in space and time which great prospects always give" (Jewett 1896: 58).

Fixated on the heron's secret hiding place, Sylvia steals from her bed in the early hours of the morning and sets out to find the heron. She spies the tree, "asleep yet in the paling moonlight". Consider Sylvia's ascent:

The tree seemed to lengthen itself out as she went up and to reach farther and farther upward. It was like a great mainmast to the voyaging earth; it must have truly been amazed that morning through all its ponderous frame as it felt this determined spark of human spirit creeping and climbing from higher branch to branch. Who knows how steadily the least twigs held themselves to advantage this light, weak creature on her way! (443)

The tree's mythical proportions resemble a kind of fantastical lighthouse, which shines its supernaturally powerful beacon of light and guides sailors in "sea and shore miles away", obscuring any sense of regional enclosure. Jewett seems to humanize or, at the very least, anthropomorphize this non-human referent, as the tree occupies a position of grandfatherly "stateliness". But the personification of the tree suggests that Jewett, "even while writing with such apparent faith in the capacity of objects to disclose meaning, raises considerable doubt about their legibility" (Brown 2003: 118). The tree is difficult to read or imagine, except for Sylvia.

What does it mean that the tree serves as an alternate protagonist of *A White Heron*? Jewett's use of the word "love" suggests that the tree is content to assist in the little girl's project, and this symbiotic dependency allows Jewett to animate a natural structure with conscious life and sentience. Sentimentalism puts these kinds of personifications under certain constraints, however. Even if "[the tree] too", has a "spark of human spirit", one cannot draw with surety the conclusion that Jewett's aim is to impose guilt on society for deforestation. Instead, one might argue that the tree's purpose is an imaginative one: as a "ponderous" elevator that buoys Sylvia higher and higher into the sky and promotes her "voyage of discovery". This "country child's" pilgrimage is, of course, a metaphor for the passage from innocence to experience, but also a self-identification with the neglected ideals (and they are idyllic) of beauty and sanctity found in primordial Nature. Regionalist writers often used rhetorical and fictional strategies to evoke feelings of nostalgia, but Jewett is more concerned here with signaling the decomposition, or, at the very least, the change of the region's ecology. And the ecological "status" of second growth forests like this also poses some very interesting questions, beyond the scope of Jewett's story.

Up in the tree, Sylvia surveys the world around her, and wonders: "Where was the white heron's nest in the sea of green branches, and was this wonderful sight and pageant of the world the only reward for having climbed to such a giddy height?" (442) Frequently, in the critical literature on Regionalism, the botanical metaphor of rootedness is used to suggest "that this body of literature has a virtually organic connection to place" (Howarth 1999: 525). But the metaphor here is of mythic flight, of pilgrimage and "giddy height", not of grounded solidity. At some halfway point between the tree and the earth below, solid rootedness gives way to the clouds above, and "all that is solid has indeed melted into air" (Blair 1998: 547). The anatomy of the treetop Sylvia reaches is almost an impossibility, since Jewett distorts the space's objective reality, "at first creating and then dissolving the landscape" (Sundquist 1982: 181). Yet this shifting shadow world appears real and substantial to Sylvia, whose perceiving eye retains its integrity through childlike fancy. The narrator even concedes, "It was almost too real and too great for the childish heart to bear." For readers, the scene isn't real enough: A White Heron's narrative gaze, that which creates Sylvia's human figure and the topographical landscape, can no longer suspend disbelief or sustain the illusion of this space. Sylvia's great enterprise is to "reclaim a tree symbolic of the American pastoral vision itself", a vision which restores the fading imaginative territory of the American Frontier (Sundquist 1982: 118). As if viewing nature for the first time, Sylvia celebrates an agrarian space, a psychologically recessive space, a privileged space. She may, as critics have argued, signify a bridge between the civilized and the natural world, between childhood and adolescence. More importantly, Sylvia straddles fictive and factual topoi.

In this way, Sylvia's preservation of the heron's secret situates her story in a kind of fairytale nature preserve, since it is the animal in the story who redefines human estate by pressing nature's claims upon

it. Sylvia has spied the heron, but she will not give its secret away to
the hunter:

No, she must keep silence! What is it that suddenly forbids her and makes her dumb?
Has she been nine years growing, and now, when the great world for the first time
puts out a hand to her, must she thrust it aside for a bird's sake? The murmur of the
pine's green branches is in her ears, she remembers how the white heron came flying
through the golden air and how they watched the sea and the morning together, and
Sylvia cannot speak; she cannot tell the heron's secret and give its life away. (447)

What silences Sylvia is the "the murmur of the pine's green branches"
whispering in her ears, as if to remind her of the bird's stake in the
fragile ecosystem of her cognitive experience. When she makes a
moral decision not to tell the hunter where the mysterious bird nests,
she is "protecting her alter ego, the heron, against the collector not
because the heron is a symbolic extension of her but because she feels
herself to be an extension of it" (Buell 1996: 198). The heron and Sylvia both are elusive, even reflexive; Jewett's narrative shifts, for example, show how the "solitary gray-eyed child", like the heron, occupies a space of secrecy and rarity. The mark of Sylvia's belonging to a
sacred space of nature is her allegiance to maintaining the integrity
and privacy of her environment; her understanding of this geographical particularity, and the dear cost of giving it up, is withheld from
the uninitiated (the hunter). Sylvia moves from an antipathetic environment to an empathic one; her pilgrimage allows an opportunity for
the reader to empathize with nature – hence, the heron as a symbol of
Sylvia's preservationist ethics. (Fetterley and Pryse 2005: 356)

The Realist assumption that one can see – and describe – with
increasing precision the closer one gets to the center of Jewett's pastoral world is subjected to scrutiny in *A White Heron*. It is useful to
think of the story as a subjective map of spaces, for above all, *A White
Heron* stresses the notion that maintaining a liaison between the lost
world and the world at hand still requires a rendering of the world at
hand. In order to illustrate this idea more clearly, I have divided
Jewett's relational information into four types: position, direction,
landscape and imaginary space [See Fig. 1]. Cartography rests on the
premise that the world is measurable and that we can make reliable
representations or models of that reality. Jewett's reality, however,
relies less on the vocabulary and procedures of a geographer than the
intimate practices of emplacement, embodiment and location through

which subjects are bound together. In spite of her casual disregard for faithful realism, her simultaneously material and abstract sketches of place, Jewett's map is altogether convincing for its imaginative power.

Looking at my figure, readers can visualize Jewett's conceptual atlas, a map predicated on a diffuse distinction between real and imagined territory. It is not difficult to imagine similarities between the landscape composition of *A White Heron* and the grainy, textured depictions of harsh wilderness in a Winslow Homer painting or the brilliantly lit landscapes of realist artist John Singer Sargent. Jewett is both a regional writer and a cultural-geographer who records impressions artistically, a maker of views through language. Her story is a dioramic, miniaturized ecosystem constructed with magisterial comprehensiveness and drafted onto an imaginary grid, with fewer historical coordinates than a regionalist critic might detect.

From microscopic bacteria to vast galaxies, nature has given us spaces that only the human imagination can make visible – or believable. Buell eloquently explains how the legitimation of environmental fiction need not depend on a realistic rendering of topography: "By demanding that imaginary gardens have real toads in them, it makes discourse accountable to the object-world." (Buell 1996: 91) I might add that the claims of eco-criticism do not always negate a Regionalist's interpretation, but rather, hold it in counterpoise. Jewett's geographical representations have a dual accountability to matter and to imagination, and the boundary is, as I have attempted to show, significantly porous. A White Heron represents isolated vestiges of a past expressed in nostalgic and romantic tones, but the story also emphasizes the way in which these sites converge around the thesis of an environmental-imaginary axis. The ambiguity of loving wild birds and shooting them, the paradox of cultivated wilderness, and the mystical tree tell us something about how to approach the geography and ornithology of the imagination; A White Heron makes an endlessly interesting focus for the meditations of eco-criticism, because it suggests that the human claim of spatial or material possession in Nature is precarious. As with Queequeg's Kokovoko, the terrain itself is ephemeral – or perhaps an imagined construct – but this only makes it all the more true.

Figure I

<table>
<tr><td>

I. Position: Latitude/Elevation

-Swamp-side
-Great boughs overhead
-High in the treetop
-Higher and higher upward
-Over at the other side of the woods
-Half a mile from home at the farther edge of the woods, where the land was highest, a great pine-tree stood
-The white heron's nest in a sea of green branches
-Not far beyond were the salt marshes and beyond those was the sea
-To his home in the green world beneath
-The dead hemlock-tree by the green marsh

</td><td>

II. Direction/Movement

-Into the dark woods
-In some bright green swamp grass
-The white oak tree that grew alongside
-Round the tree's great stem
-Dawn grew bright in the east
-Hastening toward the open ground beyond
-Westward, the woodlands and farms reached miles and miles into the distance
-Away from the western light
-Grows larger and rises
-Sylvia makes her perilous way down

</td></tr>
<tr><td>

III. Imaginary Space

-She might sink in the soft black mud underneath and never be heard of more
-Among the clouds
-And the tree stood still and held away the winds that June morning
-Stately head
-Flying through the golden air
-It was almost too real and too great for the childish heart to bear
-The old pine must have loved his new dependent
-The murmur of the pine's green branches is in her ears
-[the sea's] great voice could often be heard above the noise of the woods on stormy nights.

</td><td>

IV. Landscape

-Lonely house
-Shady wood-road
-Pasture as half a swamp
-Shoal water
-Brook
-Narrow footpath
-Where tall, nodding rushes grew
-An open place
-A whole forest of sturdy trees, pines and oaks and maples, had grown again
-Out of the house and followed the pasture path through the woods
-Westward, the woodlands and farms reached miles and miles into the distance

</td></tr>
</table>

Bibliography

Bader, Julia. 1982. 'The Dissolving Vision: Realism in Jewett, Freeman and Gilman' in Eric J. Sundquist, ed. *American Realism: New Essays*. Baltimore: Johns Hopkins University Press.

Bishop, Ferman. 1959. 'The Sense of the Past in Sarah Orne Jewett' in *University Studies* 32 no. 41.

Blair, Sara. 1998. 'Cultural Geography and the Place of the Literary' in *American Literary History* 10, no. 3.

Bowler, Peter J. (ed.) 1992. *The Norton History of the Environmental Sciences*. New York: W.W. Norton & Company.

Breitwieser, Mitchell. 2007. *National Melancholy: Mourning and Opportunity in Classic American Literature.* Stanford: Stanford University Press.

Brodhead, Richard. 1993. *Cultures of Letters.* Chicago: University of Chicago Press.

Brown, Bill. 2003. *A Sense of Things: The Object Matter of American Literature.* Chicago: Chicago University Press.

Buell, Lawrence. 1995. *The Environmental Imagination.* Cambridge: Harvard University Press.

Burgess, Cheryll. 1996. 'Toward an Ecological Literary Criticism' in H. Fromm and Glotfelty, C. (eds.) *The Ecocriticism Reader: Landmarks in Literary Ecology* (based on paper read at the annual meeting of the Western American Literature Association held at Coeur d'Alene, Idaho, on the 13th October 1989). Athens: University of Georgia Press.

Dainotto, Roberto Maria. 1996. 'All the Regions Do Smilingly Revolt: The Literature of Place and Region' in *Critical Inquiry* 22, no. 3.

Dudden, Arthur P. 1961. 'Nostalgia and the American' in *Journal of the History of Ideas* 22, no. 4.

Fetterley, Judith and Pryse, Marjorie. 2005. *Writing Out of Place: Regionalism, Women, and American Literary Culture.* Chicago: University of Illinois Press.

Foucault, Michel. 1984. 'Of Other Spaces' in *Architecture, Mouvement, Continuité.*

Fromm, Harold and Cheryll, Glotfelty (eds.) 1996. *The Ecocriticism Reader: Landmarks in Literary Ecology.* Athens: University of Georgia Press.

Hart-Davis, Duff. 2004. *Audobon's Elephant: America's Greatest Naturalist and the Making of the Birds of America.* New York: Henry Holt & Company.

Hawthorne, Nathaniel. 1850. *The Scarlet Letter.* Boston: Ticknor, Reed and Fields.

Howard, June. 1996. 'Unraveling Regions, Unsettling Periods: Sarah Orne Jewett and American Literary History' in *American Literature* 68, no. 2.

Howarth, William. 1999. 'Imagined Territory: the Writing of Wetlands' in *New Literary History* 30, no. 3.

Hsu, Hsuan. 2005. 'Literature and Regional Production' in *American Literary History* 1,7 no. 1.

Jewett, Sarah Orne. 1886. 'A White Heron' in *A White Heron & Other Stories.* Boston: Houghton, Mifflin & Company.

—. 2001. 'A White Heron' in Andrew Delbanco (ed.) *Writing New England: an anthology from the Puritans to the present.* Harvard: Harvard University Press.

—. 1896. *Country of the Pointed Firs.* Boston: Houghton, Mifflin & Company.

Kilcup, Karen L. 2003. ''I Like These Plants That You Call Weeds': Historicizing American Women's Nature Writing' in *Nineteenth-Century Literature* 58, 1.

Love, Glen. 2003. *Practical Ecocriticism: Literature, Biology and the Environment.* Virginia: University of Virginia Press.

Mazel, David (ed.) 2001. *A Century of Early Eco-criticism.* Georgia: University of Georgia Press.

Mobley, Marilyn Sanders. 1991. *Folk Roots and Mythic Wings in Sarah Orne Jewett and Toni Morrison.* Louisiana: Louisiana State Press.

Renza, Louis A. 1984. *A White Heron and the Question of Minor Literature.* Madison: University of Wisconsin Press.

Sundquist, Eric (ed.) 1982. *American Realism: New Essays.* Baltimore: Johns Hopkins University Press.

List of Contributors

Bernhard, Adrienne, MA:
Postgraduate Studies at Yale University and Columbia University. Freelance editor and writer for numerous publishing houses, including Random House, *The New York Times*, Farrar Straus & Giroux, Encounter Books, *The New Criterion*, *The Jewish Review of Books*, and *Abroad Magazine*; assistant to the Deputy Editor at *The New Yorker Magazine*.
Research on global orientalism and on "Paganism in the Novels of Thomas Hardy" (Yale Research Thesis 2005); 2007-08 editor of Volume XI of the Yale Human Rights and Development Law Journal (YHRDLJ).

Buchanan, David:
PhD Candidate in the Comparative Literature Program of the University of Alberta.
Founding editor of *Inquire: Journal of Comparative Literature*, project coordinator for the research websites *Popular Romanticism* and *Streetprint Bratislava*, and author of scholarship on nineteenth-century print history in *New Word Order: Transnational Themes in Book History* (2011); *Romanticism and Victorianism on the Net* and *European Romantic Review*.

Dzero, Irina, PhD:
PhD in French literature at Yale University, 2010; currently lecturer in French at Kent State University.
Research interests include: European Renaissance literature and philosophy, Francophone and Hispanic postcolonial literature. Published in *Bibliothèque de l'humanisme et la Renaissance* ("Step Upward, Step Down: The Ladder of Perfection in Marguerite de Navarre's 'Prisons'"), *Humanism and Reformation* ("The Quill Pen in a Funeral Oration: Clément Marot Innovates the Ancient Genre"), *The French*

Review ("The Meanings of Hybridity: Rabelaisian Laughter in Aimé Césaire's Discourse on Colonialism").

Hofmann, Gert, Dr. habil., PD:
National University of Ireland Cork (UCC) and University of Rostock. Co-director of Comparative and World Literature at UCC.
Teaching German and Comparative Literature. Research on literary theory, law and literature, border areas between literature, arts, and religion. Selected publications: *Dionysos Archemythos. Hölderlins transzendentale Poiesis* (1996); *Schweigende Tropen. Studien zu einer Ästhetik der Ohnmacht* (2003); *Figures of Law. Studies in the Interference of Law and Literature* (2007); *German and European Poetics after the Holocaust: Crisis and Creativity* (co-ed.) (2011).

Antonija Zaradija Kiš, Dr. Sc., Prof:
Philologist and palaeo-Slavist by education; Senior Research Consultant at the Institute of Ethnology and Folklore Research in Zagreb. Head of the Croatian national research project on *Cultural Animalistics: literary, folkloristic, ethnological and culturo-anthropological contributions* and Associate of the project on *Issues of Oral and Folk Poetic*.
Particular interests include the Croatian Middle Ages and early traditional literature in the context of European hagiography and narrative literature. She has written 3 books: *The Book of Job in Croatian Glagolitic Literature*; *Saint Martin: the Saint's Cult and its Tradition in Croatia*; *Šimun Greblo and His Interpretation of the Passion of Christ*. She also teaches Literature and Language in the Croatian Middle Ages and Animal Studies at the Department of Croatian Studies of the University of Zagreb.

Kupatadze, Ketevan:
Lecturer of Spanish at Elon University.
Research interests: Contemporary Spanish-American narrative with particular focus on the themes of hospitality and cosmopolitanism; Postmodern trends in Western and Latin-American literatures; language pedagogy. Publication: "The Theme of Hospitality in Manuel Puig's Eternal Curse on the Reader of These Pages" in *Dissidences. Hispanic Journal of Theory and Criticism* (2008). She also published numerous literary translations.

Outhwaite, John C., MA:
University of Southampton, Dept of Modern Languages.
Interested in the social, cultural and political role of the practice of pilgrimage in Western Europe. In particular, tracing the influence of ideas, images and motifs of pilgrimage in canonical works of European Literature inspired by periods of critical social and philosophical transformation.

Potter, Martin Gabriel, PhD:
Teaching at University of Pitesti and University of Bucharest.
Research on Catholic literature and aesthetics. Selected publications: *Three Great Artists Reflecting on the Spiritual Purpose of Art: A Study of Goethe's* Wilhelm Meisters Lehrjahre, *Keller's* Der Grüne Heinrich *and Thomas Mann's* Doktor Faustus. Lewiston (2009); with Monica Oancă, *Visions of Salvation in Medieval English Literature* (2009).

Shields, Michael:
Lecturer in German at National University of Ireland Galway (NUIG). His recent research interests have focused on musical and literary approaches to medieval and early modern German and European lyric, scientific and lyrical poetology in 14th and 15th-century lyric; lyrical and graphic deconstructions of seeing and being, post 1945. Recent publications deal with 13th-century political song (*Sirventes, Sangspruch*); a new case of polyphony in a *Rei* (dance song) by Oswald von Wolkenstein; portrayals of humanists in the "Letters of Obscure Men"; possible reception of French poetics in Central Germany ca.1400; deconstructions of the portrait genre in the graphic work of Caspar Walter Rauh.

Stuhlmann, Andreas H., Dr., PD:
University of Hamburg.
Research on German literature of the 19th and 20th Century, travel literature, German exiles 1933-1945, questions of intermediality and media convergence. Recent work about the concept of the dispositif, contemporary documentary practices, mashup videos and transmedia iconography. Selected publications: *"Die Literatur, das sind wir und unsre Feinde." Literarische Polemik bei Heinrich Heine und Karl Kraus* (2010); "Dank! Dank! Dank! Dank! Dank! Vier Postkarten und

ein Brief Else Lasker-Schülers an Monty Jacobs und Arthur Michel" in *Text. Kritische Beiträge* (2011); "'Father, I don't like America!' – Das Preisausschreiben der American Guild for German Cultural Freedom 1937-1940" in *The Many Faces of Germany. Transformations in the Study of German Culture und History* (2004).

Zorić, Snježana, Dr., Ass. Prof.
University of Zadar. Head of the Department of Ethnology and Cultural Anthropology.
Teaching and researching anthropological theory and methodology, Asian studies, ritual studies and interculturality; field research in Korea, Japan, Taiwan, Indonesia (Java and Bali), Malaysia (Sabah), Sri Lanka and India.
Book publications: *Yŏngsan Taejae. Buddhistički ritual kao zrcalna slika korejske kulture.* (*Yongsan taejae. Buddhist Ritual as a Mirror-image of Korean Culture*) Zagreb: Institut za etnologiju i folkloristiku (2004); *Obred i običaj (Ritual and Custom).* Zagreb: Institut za etnologiju i folkloristiku (1991).

Index

CPSIA information can be obtained at www.ICGtesting.com
Printed in the USA
BVOW021045081012

301998BV00003B/2/P